DOMESTIC BUDGETS IN A UNITED EUROPE

Domestic Budgets in a United Europe

Fiscal Governance
from the End of Bretton Woods to EMU

MARK HALLERBERG

Cornell University Press   ITHACA AND LONDON

First published 2004 by Cornell University Press

Printed in the United States of America

Library of Congress Cataloging-in-Publication Data

Hallerberg, Mark.
  Domestic budgets in a United Europe : fiscal governance from the end of Bretton Woods to EMU / Mark Hallerberg.
    p. cm.
  Includes bibliographical references and index.
    ISBN 0-8014-4271-0 (cloth : alk. paper)
  1. Fiscal policy—European Union countries. 2. Finance, Public—European Union countries. 3. Budget—European Union countries. 4. Fiscal policy—Europe—Case studies. 5. Finance, Public—Europe—Case studies. 6. Budget—Europe—Case studies. 7. Europe—Economic integration. I. Title.
  HJ1000.H35   2004
    336.4—dc22   2004005010

Cloth printing   10 9 8 7 6 5 4 3 2 1

To my wife, Sabine Junginger

Contents

Acknowledgments ix

1 Introduction: The Political Economy of Fiscal Policy in Europe 1

2 Forms of Fiscal Governance 20

3 European Union Fiscal Policy Coordination and Domestic
Budget Making 44

4 The Delegation Form of Fiscal Governance 63

5 The Commitment Form of Fiscal Governance 115

6 Why Minority Governments Are Different: The Mixed Systems
of Fiscal Governance in Sweden and Denmark 151

7 Italy: Change in Party System, Change in Fiscal Governance 182

8 Party System Instability and Incomplete Forms of Fiscal Governance 196

9 Conclusion: Applications of the Fiscal Governance Approach
in Europe and Beyond 218

Bibliography 227

Index 239

Acknowledgments

Books are major undertakings. I cannot imagine producing this work without the help and support of many people.

When Jürgen von Hagen hired me as a postdoctoral scholar at the University of Mannheim in fall 1995, he encouraged me to theorize about why European countries adopt the sets of fiscal rules that they do. This book reflects the many discussions we have had. It also builds on joint work on fiscal institutions. Rolf Strauch has provided support for my work since I first met him in Mannheim. He has read almost everything I have written and has been a terrific commentator. Discussions and debates with William Roberts Clark have sharpened this work and my thinking on political economy.

Several people have read one or more chapters in this book. I am grateful for their comments. They include Thomas Bräuninger, James Cameron, John FitzGerald, Jeffry Frieden, Steffen Ganghof, Miriam Golden, Patrick Honohan, William Keech, Bertholt Leeftink, Ivo Maes, Ingvar Mattson, Helen Milner, Per Molander, Sandro Momigliano, Gianfranco Pasquino, Nils Ringe, Alberta Sbragia, Georges Steinlet, Francesco Stolfi, George Tsebelis, Salvatore Vassallo, Katja Weber, and Sami Yläoutinen. I have given talks based on the book manuscript at several universities, and I thank the seminar participants from the following universities for their comments as well: the Center for European Integration Studies at the University of Bonn, Claremont Graduate School, Harvard, the Max Planck Institute, New York University, Notre Dame, University of Washington, UCSD, and UCLA. Four anonymous reviewers provided constructive comments on how to make the book better. I could not incorporate all the suggestions, but I appreciate the time they took in reading the manuscript's first draft.

The University of Pittsburgh has been a good place to do this type of book. Two colleagues in particular deserve special mention. Alberta Sbragia has provided commentary and ideas throughout the project, and B. Guy Peters often has had an idea about where to get information that I thought was not available. Readers of the manuscript may wonder how many languages I speak after checking the bibliography. Pitt attracts students from all over the world, and students who worked for me covered every European

Union national language except Finnish and Greek. Students who assisted me with particular countries include Maria Pia Scalfo (France, Italy, Portugal, Spain), Patrik Marier (Denmark, Sweden), June Park (Ireland, United Kingdom), Nils Ringe (Austria, Germany, United Kingdom), and Paul Mullen (Greece). Simon Reich has been a gracious supporter in the preparation of the manuscript. The University Center for International Studies as well as the Center for West European Studies/European Union Center provided me with generous funding for necessary travel to Europe.

The German Marshall Fund of the United States awarded me a grant for spring 2001 to write much of this book. The German Marshall Fund provides an important source of funding for work on Europe, and I am grateful for their support. Part of chapter 3 is reprinted by permission of Sage Publications Ltd. from Mark Hallerberg, "Introduction: Fiscal Policy in the European Union," *European Union Politics* 3, no. 2 (2002): 139–150. Copyright © 2002 by Sage Publications.

Roger Haydon at Cornell University Press has been a welcome supporter of the project. I appreciate his willingness to answer my many questions during the process.

Two people have helped with the manuscript: my father, James W. Hallerberg, has been a stickler for grammar since I could speak; he naturally had comments on the manuscript. And Joan McColly has read every word; her attention to detail is greatly appreciated.

My mother, Virginia Hallerberg, has been a constant source of support, and I thank her as well for her patience. It must have become tiring for her to ask routinely how the book was going and to offer regular words of encouragement.

Many people helped me with contacts in European capitals. Two persons I thank for their help in navigating Rome and Athens, respectively, are Claudio Radaelli and George Tsebelis. Others need to remain anonymous, but I am also grateful to them.

With one or two exceptions, I interviewed at least one person from the central bank, the finance ministry, and the staff from the finance committee from every member state. In many cases, I interviewed multiple people from each institution. In fourteen of fifteen capitals, those interviews took place in person. I also interviewed several former government officials who had held cabinet rank in their governments. The ground rules for those interviews were that I would not reveal their names in any published work, but I do thank them for their willingness to talk with me and for their frank comments.

This leads me to the biggest thank you of all. I spent literally months on the road to do interviews for this book. Even when I was in Pittsburgh, I quaffed countless cups of coffee in various cafés sitting in front of my laptop. My wife, Sabine Junginger, has been a terrific supporter through it all. She also challenged me to keep at this manuscript until it was finished, and to be sure to "scope" on occasion so that the project remained manageable.

DOMESTIC BUDGETS IN A UNITED EUROPE

1

Introduction: The Political Economy of Fiscal Policy in Europe

On May 2, 1998, the Council of Ministers of the European Union decided that fourteen of fifteen countries could join a new common currency, the euro, upon its introduction seven months later. The council based its decision largely on the budget performance of the individual states. Almost seven years earlier, the Treaty of Maastricht had established a set of economic criteria that countries would have to fulfill if they wanted to circulate the euro. These criteria included an expectation that budget deficits be below 3% of their Gross Domestic Product (GDP). Why did countries in the European Union (EU) succeed in getting their budget deficits below this threshold? A look at the fiscal performance of member states before 1997 indicates why this question is important. During the period 1973–91, European Union countries had had varying levels of success in maintaining the fiscal discipline most had enjoyed prior to the breakup of the Bretton Woods system. The United Kingdom and France had relatively low deficit and debt levels, whereas others, such as Belgium, Italy, and Greece, suffered chronic deficits. The convergence in budget performance that occurred in the mid-1990s was remarkable—all the member states but Greece had brought their annual deficits below 3% of GDP by 1997, and the following year Greece succeeded in doing so as well.

Domestic Budgets in a United Europe examines why this convergence occurred. The obvious answer is that countries wanted to participate in Economic and Monetary Union (EMU), and the Treaty of Maastricht required deficits below 3% of GDP in order for states to qualify. Yet this answer by itself is unsatisfactory. It does not explain why states that previously had run chronic deficits even in good economic times were suddenly able to develop a fiscal backbone. It also does not indicate *how* states made the transition to fiscal austerity or, if they had maintained relatively tight fiscal policy in the past, whether the Maastricht treaty had any impact on their practice. Important questions

1

remain. What role did forces external to the country, such as world markets, the European Commission, and pressure from other European Union states, play? Did states initiate fundamental reforms in their budget-making process, or did they reach the targets without reforms to domestic institutions? Were the cuts in deficits real, or, as some commentators suggest, did states rely mostly on accounting tricks to qualify?

Answers to these questions are crucial for several reasons. Twelve of fifteen member states currently participate in what is known technically as "Stage Three of Economic and Monetary Union." They have adopted a common currency, the euro, and they have delegated the setting of their monetary policies to a newly established central bank in Frankfurt. The European Central Bank has a mandate to maintain price stability in the euro-zone. This delegation, therefore, removes one of the two main macroeconomic tools available to national policy makers. An understanding of how member states made fiscal policy in the run-up to the common currency allows one to evaluate how they use the only policy tool remaining at their disposal today. One can also consider whether the European cases provide lessons for other countries that experience deficit and debt problems. Finally, and more broadly, budgets lie at the very heart of politics. The most important decisions governments make in most years concern the budget. Budgets set the government's priorities into law. They determine what groups in society will receive public funding and what groups in society will pay for them. If Maastricht indeed changed the way that European countries make budgets, it also changed domestic politics. An understanding of the budget process is crucial to an understanding of politics. A book about the seemingly mundane topic of "fiscal policy" is by definition political to its core.

In this book I develop and apply an institutional approach to explain the convergence of budget policy within the European Union. Although changes in deficits are most obvious in the 1990s, beginning the analysis in the year of the Maastricht treaty, 1991, is too late to capture the changes that occurred in budget institutions in some EU states. Therefore, I focus the study on the period from 1973 to 2000. I argue that budget performance converged because states either introduced or maintained certain fiscal institutions to keep deficits in check. In some countries the Maastricht framework encouraged these reforms, but without institutional reforms there would have been no convergence. *Domestic Budgets* addresses *what* reforms states made and *why* they made them.

Political Economy of Europe

Domestic Budgets in a United Europe is firmly in the political economy tradition. It seeks to explain fiscal policy formation in the fifteen countries that composed the European Union in 1999, the year that the euro was introduced. Although political economy per se has existed at least since Adam Smith and Karl Marx, political economy done explicitly by political scientists with a focus on Europe has developed relatively recently. Before the 1990s, much of the work on the political economy of Western Europe focused on the development of the welfare state. The neocorporatist literature considered the interplay among unions, employer groups, and government in shaping the policy packages that defined the welfare state (Schmitter 1977; Lehmbruch and Schmitter 1982). Katzenstein (1985) and Cameron (1978) identified the important role economic openness played in structuring the strategies that small states pursued in order to survive in a world where they had heavy exposure to the vagaries of world markets. Esping-Andersen (1990) wrote about the distinctions among different welfare states. There were exceptions in the literature that focused more broadly on economic policy (Hall 1986 and Scharpf 1991 are representative), but the welfare state was often the critical variable.

The welfare state literature remains important, but the political economy of Europe literature has, since the 1980s, become more varied.[1] Institutions such as central banks and policy areas such as monetary policy are increasingly objects of study (Cukierman 1992; Goodman 1992; Bernhard 1998, 2002; Iversen 1999). One of the latest waves of scholarship focuses on macropolicy, more broadly defined (Boix 2000, 2001; Franzese 2002; Clark 2003).[2]

In the area of research on the European Union, there is a growing, and increasingly sophisticated, literature that examines the political economy of European integration. By far the most-covered topic is the Economic and Monetary Union. The focus is often on explaining why European Union countries agreed to EMU in the form it was written into the Treaty of Maastricht in December 1991.[3] The varied explanations include the role of monetarist ideas (McNamara 1998), epistemic communities (Verdun 1999), interest groups that care about potential trade and investment benefits (Frieden 2002), the member states (Moravcsik 1998; Garrett 2001; Kaelberer 2001), the member states plus additional actors such as the European Commission (Dyson and Featherstone 1999; Ross 1995), and American intransigence on exchange rate policy (Henning 1998).

---

1. The welfare state literature is quite developed. Representative works are Garrett and Lange 1991, Scharpf 1991, Garrett 1998, and Huber and Stephens 2001.

2. A book that was ahead of its time was *Crisis and Choice in European Social Democracy* (Scharpf 1991), which was published originally in German in 1987. In it Scharpf examines why four states chose a given set of macroeconomic policies in response to the economic crisis Europe faced after the collapse of the Bretton Woods system and the first oil shock.

3. The twelve countries that signed the Treaty of Maastricht were all members of the European Community rather than the European Union, which became the official name only in 1993; but to avoid confusion and following convention in other works I call this organization the "European Union" throughout.

In comparison to this literature on the origins of EMU, there is very little work on why countries met the macroeconomic goals they set for themselves at Maastricht. The work that does exist usually considers individual countries or does not consider explicitly the effects of Maastricht on the making of budgets. Moreover, with few exceptions, the work concentrates on the performance of the large countries.[4] There has been no book-length treatment of how, and most importantly why, all countries but Greece qualified for Economic and Monetary Union.[5] There are, however, several partial explanations that I will now discuss in turn. In each case I explain why the given argument is not a satisfactory explanation for the changes in fiscal policy in EU countries.

Political Economy of Fiscal Policy under EMU

One common argument is that EU member states qualified for EMU by relying on a series of accounting maneuvers. States did not really make changes to their budgets, so there is nothing to explain. Dafflon and Rossi (1999), for example, discuss different "tricks" employed in four countries during 1995–97. Melloan (1997, 17, as cited in Dafflon and Rossi 1999, 63) generalizes the argument to the entire Union when he states that "it is uncertain that any country will qualify with honest accounting." If states simply relied on accounting tricks, then they made few, or no, changes to the way they made budgets. As Willett (1999b, 61) notes in his discussion of the EU's fiscal policy framework, "The problem is not that the Maastricht and Stability Pact [the Stability and Growth Pact, which set deficit targets of no more than 3% of GDP] criteria were wrongheaded, but rather that the opportunity to piggyback domestic budgetary reforms on the EMU project has borne so little fruit."

The case studies in this book will provide ample evidence that states did make changes to their budget processes. The point is not that *all* states made changes in the mid-1990s but rather that the states that needed to make changes mostly did so. (Portugal is the most glaring exception.) Technically speaking, "tricks" do explain why some countries just managed to get their deficits under 3%; some states, and in particular the four states that Dafflon and Rossi (1999) identify, did use several one-off measures that assured that they were able to get their deficits below the critical deficit reference point.

Yet these measures cannot explain the general change in budgetary policy. If the tricks were the main story, one would expect that deficit levels would

4. For Italy, see Sbragia 2001 and Chiorazzo and Spaventa 1999; for the United Kingdom, Thain and Wright 1995; for Germany, Strauch and von Hagen 2001 and Sturm 1998. The exception for the smaller countries is Mattson's (1996) comparison of the budget processes in Denmark and Sweden.

5. There have, however, been some excellent works on the macroeconomics of EMU written by economists that consider fiscal policy. See especially DeGrauwe 2000 and Eijffinger and De Haan 2000.

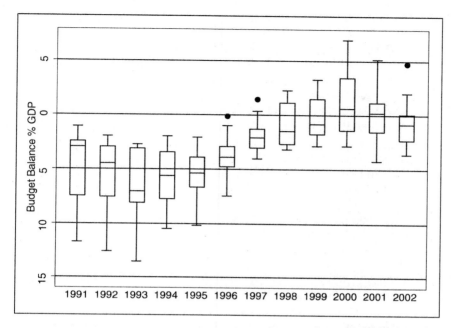

Fig. 1.1. Budget performance of EU member states, 1991–2002. The "box" indicates the center half of the data, that is, the data between the 25% and 75% points; the "whiskers" indicate the 95% confidence intervals; and the solid line is the median. Black dots are outliers. Figures for Greece 1991–94, Spain 1991–94, and Sweden 1991–92 are according to the ESA 79 accounting standards, while all remaining figures are calculated according to ESA 95. Luxembourg is not included. Source: European Commission 2003.

rise again after 1997, once countries had qualified for EMU. There should be little convergence in budget performance. States should have had fairly high budget deficits in the early 1990s and moved to low deficits in 1997, and then deficits should have gone back up after 1997. Budget performance of EU member states during 1991–2002, in fact, varied from country to country; some had high deficits in the early 1990s and some had low deficits (fig. 1.1). There is indeed a convergence toward 1997, but that convergence continues after 1997, while the median moves to budget balance. Although the accounting tricks argument can explain some movement in 1996–97, it cannot explain why there was divergence in the early 1990s nor why the convergence continued after Stage Three of EMU began.

A more political argument concerns the role of partisanship. The political left is traditionally identified with a preference for employment over inflation, while the reverse is true for the political right (Hibbs 1977). One could argue that left-wing governments are more tolerant of budget deficits than right-wing governments. Oatley (1999, 1005) combines this argument with the Mundell-Fleming model to argue that left governments run budget deficits when they have fixed exchange rates and open capital. In his study of Organisation for Economic Cooperation and Development (OECD) countries (generally those that are industrialized) during the period 1968–94, he notes that "throughout the period analyzed, leftist governments offered lower real interest rates and ran larger deficits than rightist governments" (1005). Empirical evidence for the partisanship thesis is nevertheless weak. Clark and Hallerberg (2000) reexamined the Oatley hypothesis for both OECD and EU countries during the period 1981–92 and could find no partisan effects. Clark (2003) also found no evidence for partisan effects on fiscal policy. Using regression techniques, I examined the argument for the fifteen members of the European Union (the EU-15) over the period 1980–97 and again found no evidence of a partisan effect (chapter 2). There may be noticeable differences across parties in how money is spent, but there is no clear difference in outcomes relating to the size of deficits.[6]

Another explanation of the convergence centers on the adoption of a fixed exchange rate. In 1979, a subset of member states formed the European Monetary System (EMS), which required that states maintain their exchange rates within a band. Although there were regular devaluations in the 1980s, the EMS was generally considered a success, and the member countries agreed to narrow the bands in 1988. The United Kingdom, the principal large state that had not joined in 1979, became a member in 1990. The EMS crisis in 1992, which pushed the British pound, the Italian lira, and the Spanish peseta out of EMS, and the pressure on the French franc a year later that led to a widening of the band for France, together left Denmark, the Benelux countries, and Germany as the only remaining "hard" currencies in the system. Maastricht required countries to return to the EMS fold at least two years before joining the common currency. Did the adoption of fixed exchange rates under EMS lead to increased fiscal discipline? There is both empirical evidence for this argument and a more general theoretical rationale. In a study of OECD countries during the period 1973–93, Garrett (2000) found that states with fixed exchange rates and open capital mobility maintained lower budget deficits than states with floating rates. In summarizing the conventional wisdom on why this result is expected, Garrett (2000, 163) notes that "the reasoning is straightforward. Capital mobility impels countries to fix their exchange rates to ward off financial speculation. But in so doing, national governments are also forced to give in to the markets and significantly reduce their fiscal activism. They must cut budget deficits."[7]

---

6. However, Bräuninger and Hallerberg (2003) could not find partisan effects even when looking at the composition of spending.

7. It should be noted that Garrett (2000) attacks the thrust of this conventional wisdom and adds that the effects of fiscal policy on trade competitiveness also should be added to explain his empirical result.

There are two general problems with this argument. The first is empirical. There is no empirical evidence of a fixed exchange rate effect for the EU countries. Anecdotal evidence from the case studies in this volume explains this finding. While the Netherlands got its fiscal house in order during its EMS membership in the 1980s, its southern fellow EMS member, Belgium, did not. Another EMS member further to the south, Italy, experienced a doubling of its gross debt burden to more than 120% of GDP during its EMS membership.

The second problem with the fixed exchange rate argument is more theoretical. The basic Mundell-Fleming model from macroeconomics provides a reason to be suspicious about the fiscal benefits of fixing an exchange rate (Mundell 1963; Fleming 1962). In the presence of capital mobility, which was likely high in Europe by the mid-1980s at the latest (Hallerberg and Clark 1997), a fixed exchange rate makes fiscal policy a more effective tool to influence the macroeconomy. A series of works on countries in the OECD, the EU, Eastern Europe, and Latin America indicates that countries with fixed exchange rates and open capital mobility tend to use deficit spending before elections as a way to influence the outcome, while countries with flexible exchange rates do not (Clark and Hallerberg 2000; Hallerberg, Vinhas de Souza, and Clark 2002; Clark 2003; Clark, Hallerberg, and Hiroi 2003). Willett (2001) emphasizes the time inconsistency that develops when countries use a fixed exchange rate. The benefits for more effective fiscal policy accrue immediately, while the possible costs are only felt later. Moreover, when a fixed exchange rate requires adjustment, the government feels the costs immediately while the benefits of the change in policy accrue over time. Taking this research all together, it is clear that a fixed exchange rate is not a fiscal panacea. Willett (2001) concludes (as I do) that the sources of fiscal discipline need to be internal to be effective.

Yet, in order to know for sure that external pressure does not explain the change in budget policy, we must evaluate two further arguments. The first is that markets made states adjust. Some authors argue that, in a world of greater capital mobility, it is more difficult for states to run budget deficits because markets will punish lax states (Garrett and Lange 1991; Simmons 1999; Oatley 1999 provides contrary evidence). Countries with large debt burdens may have been particularly sensitive to market sentiment. Capital might have dried up in states such as Belgium and Italy if they had remained outside EMU and outside the new "core" of the EU. The financial penalty for missing the euro boat could have been severe in both counties. As an analyst for ABM AMRO Bank told the *Independent* (U.K.) in 1997 when commenting on Italy, "There is no middle ground here. Either Italy makes it and Italian bonds converge towards German bonds, or Italy doesn't and bonds go stratospheric. It's a binary game."[8]

8. "Italy's Turn to Make Waves," *Independent* (U.K.), March 29, 1997. The analyst is Philip Chitty. For a contrary view see Mosley 2000.

Each case study chapter of *Domestic Budgets* evaluates the extent to which market pressure led to changes in budget policy. Yet, even without the case studies, there is reason to believe that, while market pressure can increase the costs of certain budget policies, these costs are not prohibitive. Mosley (2000) examined the determinants of interest rates on government bonds in fifteen developed democracies during the period 1981–95. She found that every 1% of GDP decrease in the budget deficit reduces the interest rate on ten-year government bonds by 0.05%. A move from 6% of GDP to the Maastricht level of 3%, for example, would lower the interest rate 0.15%, or fifteen basis points. When she restricted her analysis to the 1990s, the period where there could be market effects that complemented "Maastricht" effects, the results did not change substantively. The direct evidence that market pressure forced states to get their budgets in order during the post-Maastricht period is also unconvincing. The clear outlier in the size of the debt burden was Italy. Italy had a debt level more than double the Maastricht treaty's reference value of 60% of GDP in 1995–97, and it provides a nice upper bound for the influence of markets. Favero et al. (2000) calculated that of the 214 basis point reduction between German and Italian forward rates from March 1996 to 1997, only 65 basis points can be attributed to changing perceptions of Italy's likelihood of EMU participation. Similarly, one can evaluate the interest rate premia that EU member states that have not adopted the euro must pay. Some argue that Denmark may pay up to a 0.5% interest rate premium because it has maintained its own currency (Financial Times, November 27, 1995). The conclusion from these different cases is the same—there is some cost to staying out of the euro, but the cost is relatively low, and, as Denmark has shown, it is one that states can bear.

Another source of possible external pressure is the European Union itself. One blunt version of this argument is that the EU somehow "made" states get their budgets in order. This is implausible; four of fifteen states did not introduce the common currency in 1999, and through 1997 there was genuine uncertainty about how many states would qualify. If the EU simply forced states to join there would have been no uncertainty. A somewhat more subtle, and more common, explanation is that there was some sort of Maastricht effect. Deficits came down because of Maastricht; moreover, if there were domestic fiscal reforms, the EU framework encouraged these changes. To address the role of the European Union, in chapter 3 I introduce the overall fiscal setting at the European level. Every case study will also evaluate the extent to which changes in fiscal policy, and in fiscal institutions, can be traced to Maastricht. To summarize findings later in the book, the case studies do indicate that there is a Maastricht effect, but it is uneven. The treaty largely explains policy change in Portugal; and it explains the timing of the accounting tricks discussed earlier for four additional countries. The treaty may account for change in some fiscal rules in Greece and Italy. In a majority of countries, however, I cannot find a clear Maastricht effect.

Domestic Budgets pays particular attention to the link between institutions and fiscal policy, and there is an important literature that deserves consideration, namely one that considers the role of institutions. This literature can be divided essentially into two types, one that looks at the relationship between political institutions and fiscal outcomes and one that analyzes the effects of fiscal rules on fiscal behavior. (Because all the countries in the European Union are parliamentary democracies, I cover material on presidential systems only if I present a general model.)

Political institutionalists identify a series of attributes of the political system that affect fiscal policy. Coalition governments are particularly guilty of fiscal irresponsibility, although the reason why coalition governments are poor fiscal stewards varies. One argument contends that coalition governments are poor managers during economic downturns. After a negative economic shock, governments need to make some sort of adjustment, but none of the coalition partners want to bear the costs of the new policy. A "war of attrition" develops in which coalition partners cannot agree on a solution, and deficits, as well as the overall debt burden, increase (Alesina and Drazen 1991; Padovano and Venturi 2001). Extending this logic, recent work contends that increasing the number of cabinet ministers, as well as the number of political parties in government, increases deficits (Kontopolous and Perotti 1999; Volkerink and de Haan 2001). A second reason why coalition governments perform poorly is that they have higher turnover rates. Cabinet ministers who do not expect to remain in power will not care about the future implications of their irresponsible behavior (Roubini and Sachs 1989; Alesina and Tabellini 1990; Alesina and Perotti 1995; Alesina, Roubini, and Cohen 1997). Because these attributes of coalition governments are usually found in countries with proportional representation systems, Persson and Tabellini (2003) generalize to argue that governments with majoritarian electoral systems maintain tighter fiscal discipline than governments formed under plurality electoral systems.

A related, and relevant, literature is the veto-player literature. Conceptually, the number of party actors, or coalition partners, in government can be treated as "veto players." The number of veto players is equal to the number of actors (usually parties) whose consent is needed for any bill to become law (Tsebelis 1995, 2002). Tsebelis (1995) demonstrates that governments with fewer veto players are able to engender change faster, and with greater depth, than governments with more veto players. The higher the number of veto players, the harder it is for the players to reach agreement to pass laws, and the greater the chance that the status quo will be maintained. Citing empirical evidence provided by Schick (1993), Tsebelis (1995) argues explicitly that increasing the number of veto players increases the size of budget deficits. In his more recent work, Tsebelis (2002) has changed the focus. Relying on the regression analysis of OECD countries over a thirty-five year period provided by Franzese (2002), he argues that increases in the number of veto players "lock in" certain policies. Countries with more veto players have consistently low, or consistently high, deficits. Tsebelis (1999, 2002) also emphasizes that it is the ideological distance between veto players, rather than the absolute number, that is most critical. The writings of Franzese and Tsebelis are important in that they break from the argument that coalition governments consistently perform less successfully than one-party governments.[9]

Still others contend that the most important cleavage is not between one-party and multiparty governments but between majority and minority governments. The original article that began much of the debate on the relationship between explicitly political variables and budget discipline, Roubini and Sachs 1989, states that minority governments are the most fiscally irresponsible of all. Edin and Ohlsson (1991), in a reanalysis of the findings of Roubini and Sachs, argue that the coalition effects go away once the regression equation is properly modeled but that the minority effects remain.[10] The reasoning is that governments must "buy" votes from opposition parties to get anything passed.

To summarize, the political institutionalists are concerned with how certain institutions in the political system affect fiscal policy. One problem with untangling the effects of each institution individually is that they are often found in distinct packages. Both Lijphart and Powell, in their classifications of majoritarian and consensual (Lijphart 1999) or majoritarian and proportional (Powell 2000) systems, note that proportional representation systems lead to more political parties in parliament, probably more parties in government, and, consequently, more veto players. In contrast, countries with plurality electoral laws or proportional representation with low district magnitudes *usually* have fewer (or, following Duverger 1954, two) political parties, one-party majority governments, and one-party veto players. This is one reason, in fact, that Persson and Tabellini focus their attention on electoral systems.

Yet the qualification "usually" is not a trivial one. There are countries with a proportional representation system but few parties in parliament. Austria has been one such case during much of its postwar history; and Ireland, with a single transferable vote electoral system that is proportional in practice, is another. Neto and Cox (1997) showed persuasively that there is

9. See Treisman 2000 for a similar argument about the "locking in" of inflation rates.

10. In De Haan and Sturm's (1994, 1997) reanalysis of Roubini and Sachs 1989, where they recoded several observations that Roubini and Sachs seem to have gotten wrong the first time, even these minority effects go away and there is no statistically significant relationship between government form and fiscal policy outcome.

an interaction effect between the electoral system and the number of salient cleavages. With plurality, one simply gets something approximating a two-party system. With proportional representation, the number of salient cleavages in society becomes important. A country with only one relevant cleavage that divides votes—which in practice is usually a right-left dimension on economic issues—is likely to have a one-party system even under proportional representation. A country with proportional representation and five relevant cleavages will have more parties. Both Austria and Ireland are European Union countries, and government-type effects can be separated from electoral system effects. This point becomes important when I argue that it is the party system, and not the type of electoral system or government system per se, that is the crucial explanatory variable.

To understand what it is that the party system determines requires an understanding of the institutional literature that examines the fiscal norms and rules that define how governments make their budgets. The "fiscal institutionalists" generally argue that a decentralized policy process leads to weaker fiscal discipline than a centralized one. The cause is what the literature refers to as a *common pool resource problem,* which arises when policy makers consider the full benefits of additional spending but do not consider the full tax implications.[11] In the European parliamentary democracies, the most important decision-making arena is the cabinet, and the common pool resource problem arises in this setting when individual ministers set the budgets for their ministries. The agriculture minister cares most about farmers, for example, while the defense minister worries about the size of the military's budget.

Centralization is therefore necessary to address this problem, if fiscal discipline is to be maintained; in practice this can take different forms. One of the classic texts on budgeting, Wildavsky's *Budgeting: A Comparative Theory of the Budget Process* (1975), portrays the finance minister as the "guardian" of the treasury who keeps the spending of "advocates" (or spending ministers) in check. Building on this premise, some argue that the stronger the finance minister in the budget process the more fiscal discipline there will be (von Hagen 1992; von Hagen and Harden 1994; Hahm et al. 1996). In making its recommendations on policy reforms, the Inter-American Development Bank (1997) took this literature to heart. While noting that most Latin American countries have strong finance ministers already, the bank argued that in countries where the finance ministers were not already strong, strengthening them would lead to greater budget discipline.

Although this emphasis on the role of the finance minister is a common one, some argue that there is an alternative approach that can centralize the budget process when the finance minister is weak. The players in the game can negotiate clear spending targets for each ministry at the beginning of

---

11. I rely on this literature on the common pool resource problem. Chapter 2 provides a formal model of the problem as well as a detailed discussion.

the term of a government. This approach seems to yield the same level of fiscal discipline as that seen in countries with strong finance ministers (von Hagen and Harden 1994; Hallerberg and von Hagen 1999; Hallerberg, Strauch, and von Hagen 2001). Under this construct, the parties are forced to consider the entire tax burden on the potential coalition when they negotiate budgets.

Although the discussion so far has concentrated on decision making in cabinets, fiscal institutionalists also consider the structure of other parts of the budget process. In a classic article, Weingast, Shepsle, and Johnsen (1981) identified the dynamics of a common pool resource problem in a legislature where each legislator worries only about the tax burden on her district but all spending comes from a common pool of funds. Legislators form "log rolls" where they support one another's spending requests. The way legislators vote on spending determines whether the log rolls happen. Note that if bills for spending in districts were voted on sequentially and separately, Congress members should vote for no bills but their own. Other bills simply increase the tax burden on one's voters without providing any tangible benefits. Some sort of institutional rule is needed to maintain log rolls in legislatures with many members. Other writers, such as Shepsle and Weingast (1994) and Baron (1991), argue that "closed rules" (simple up or down votes on bills with no possibility of amendment), as well as votes on packages of bills in the form of omnibus bills, allow for log rolls.

Hallerberg and von Hagen (1999) brought the two institutionalist literatures together, relating fiscal rule outcomes to the electoral system in place. Countries with plurality electoral systems, or with proportional representation systems where the district magnitude is low, are more likely to adopt a strong finance minister model, which we call "delegation." We argue that one-party majority governments, or governments where the parties present themselves to the public as electoral blocs, are most appropriate for a strong finance minister model. In contrast, countries with proportional representation systems with high district magnitudes are most amenable to negotiated fiscal contracts, which we call "commitment." In our empirical work, we showed that countries either have decentralized budget systems, which we refer to as "fiefdom" governments, because spending ministers run their ministries as their own fiefdoms, or they adopt a form of centralization that is consistent with the prediction. Those countries that have either delegation or commitment systems have better fiscal discipline than countries with a fiefdom system.

I believe our work nicely integrates the two literatures, but it also leaves some important questions unanswered. First, it does not attempt to explain *why* states move from fiefdom, or the decentralized case, to one of the two institutional solutions to the common pool resource problem. Second, it does not consider explicitly how minority governments may differ from majority governments.

The Making of Domestic Budgets

I build on the Hallerberg and von Hagen (1999) framework in the pages that follow. Consistent with our previous work, I argue that political institutions are highly relevant because they determine the types of fiscal institutions that may centralize the budget process. I take it a step further with the argument that political institutions can also explain why sound fiscal institutions fail to take root. Once this theoretical framework is in place, I then ask how, and whether, Maastricht may have changed the way budgets are made in Europe.

In chapter 2 I present the model that structures the remainder of the book. There are two crucial institutional variables that determine the type of fiscal framework a government can put in place: the party system and the minority/majority dichotomy. The significant aspect of the party system is whether governments that emerge from it are generally unified ideologically or whether there are real ideological differences among coalition partners. There are two situations in which the party system will produce unified governments. The first exists when there are only two effective parties in the system. In the European Union, the United Kingdom is the principal case. The Conservative and Labour Parties are the main political parties, and a government that emerges will have either the Conservatives in power alone or Labour in power alone. Another system that is functionally almost the same is one where parties cluster along the ideological spectrum. The French party system is a good example of such clumping. There have been right governments that brought together the Union pour la Démocratie Française (UDF) and the Rassemblement pour la République (RPR) and left governments that brought together the Socialist Party (SP) and the French Communist Party. The key point is that any government that forms has little or no internal discord based on ideological differences. If there is a one-party government, or if the parties in government are close to one another ideologically, the ministers can delegate the centralization of the budget process to a strong finance minister who can help maintain fiscal discipline. I refer to this type of budget centralization as a *delegation* form of fiscal governance. The budget process maintains tighter fiscal discipline when the finance minister has a lot of discretion.

The other extreme is a party system where there are several distinct ideologies. The various parties are generally not close to one another ideologically. Coalitions represent a broader ideological spectrum. Finland and the Netherlands are representative cases. When parties diverge ideologically, they are not willing to delegate power to one person—who can come from only one party—to centralize the budget process. An alternative way to centralize the budget process is for the parties to negotiate, and then to commit themselves to detailed fiscal targets for the life of the coalition. These targets, and the rules to enforce them, compose a fiscal contract. I refer to this form of fiscal governance as *commitment*. Unlike delegation, which relies on the finance minister's discretion, commitment functions best when there are clear rules. The rules will include certain types of fiscal targets, which can be by ministry or even by agency within ministry. These specific targets reinforce general targets such as deficit and expenditure targets. There are also rules for what to do when unanticipated economic shocks put pressure on the fiscal contract. A contract may mandate a cut in spending in certain ministries if economic growth is lower than forecast, for example, or mandate tax cuts if revenue collections are higher than forecast.

This brings us to our second relevant variable. With a majority government, either delegation or commitment is applicable. Note that both forms of centralization involve decisions at the cabinet level on both the formation and the execution of the budget. Although the legislature formally passes the annual budget, party discipline is high in the parliamentary systems found in Europe, and, if centralization exists, there is little that parliament can do to alter the budget.[12] However, with a minority government, the government needs one or more opposition parties on its side in order to pass the budget. The key again is whether or not the budget process is centralized. If the government must every year "buy" legislators and/or parties in the opposition, the result is then consistent with what Roubini and Sachs (1989) and Edin and Ohlsson (1991) predict, that is, that fiscal discipline will be undermined. An institutional solution is one that mixes both delegation and commitment. At the budget formation stage, a strong finance minister can centralize the process within the government. At the parliamentary stage, the government can then negotiate a fiscal contract with the opposition that includes every dimension of the budget. In this way, the parties consider the full tax implications of their decisions. I call this system a *mixed* form of fiscal governance.

If these options exist for governments to centralize their budget processes, and if the party system and the majority/minority government dichotomies predict specific packages of fiscal rules, why don't all countries adopt the relevant rules and be done with it? Once again, the key explanatory variable is the party system. Countries need *stable, competitive* party systems. Stability is needed so that the relevant fiscal rules can be institutionalized. Note that the predictions about what types of fiscal institutions are effective differ across the ideal types. Detailed rules on the many dimensions of the budget would needlessly limit the power of the finance minister in a country with a one-party government. Similarly, giving discretion to one central figure is not likely to work under multiparty coalition governments. If the shape of the party system changes greatly from election to election, the relevant packages of fiscal rules will change as well, and will not become institutionalized.

12. The one exception to this rule is Italy prior to the mid-1990s.

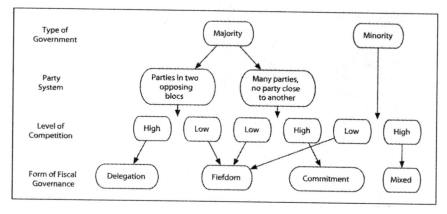

Fig. 1.2. The influence of political factors on forms of fiscal governance.

Changing the shape of the party system is not the same thing as changing the government, and indeed the second question concerns party competition. The very heart of the common pool resource problem is that there is a temptation to draw from the common pool to pay for specific goods. If there is no punishment for ignoring the full tax burden, then parties will spend and spend. The punishment ultimately comes from voters who punish irresponsible governments. Voters cannot punish governments if there is not a credible opposition. Fiscal reforms, therefore, will fail when there are uncompetitive party systems. An illustrative case is Italy before the early 1990s. It was impossible to conceive of an Italian government that did not include the Christian Democrats.

Domestic Budgets and the European Union

The arguments of *Domestic Budgets* can be traced in schematic fashion (fig. 1.2). Once this theoretical framework is in place, one can reexamine the meaning and the importance of the Maastricht process. In chapter 3 I explain the fiscal policy framework at the European level. Maastricht represents a package of rules and a series of mechanisms to enforce those rules. The process helped the production of budgets in all countries to some extent by increasing budgetary transparency. Eurostat, the European Union's collector of statistics, now produces harmonized figures for all countries, and it investigates and, on occasion, revises the figures that member states report. Yet, as the case study chapters demonstrate, the Maastricht framework (and later the Stability and Growth Pact) had, and has, an asymmetric effect on member states.

An important issue concerns the adoption of a set of fiscal rules. Maastricht created incentives for countries to reform their fiscal rules. Yet one finds surprisingly little support for the thesis that Maastricht is *the* reason why EU member states succeeded in reining in their budgets. Maastricht had the greatest impact in the southern European countries. They were countries where the European Union enjoyed strong popular support and where their elites worried about the possibility of becoming a "second-class Europe" if an inner French-German core formed an Economic and Monetary Union on its own. Other countries, however, such as the Scandinavian countries of Finland and Sweden, made reforms in the mid-1990s for reasons that had little to do with Maastricht. Still others revised their fiscal systems before Maastricht was signed. For this reason, one cannot start with the signing of the Treaty of Maastricht in December 1991 to make an argument about the development of fiscal institutions. Indeed, explaining why some states revised their fiscal systems during the economic difficulties of the early 1980s while others did not tells us something about the conditions under which countries reform themselves.

Each of the case study chapters, therefore, covers the period from the two oil crises of the 1970s through the introduction of the euro. During this time several European states confronted growing budget deficits. Some states, such as Denmark and the Netherlands, introduced new fiscal rules that became institutionalized over time. Other states, such as Sweden, suffered similar economic difficulties but did not initially revise their budget institutions. In each chapter, I trace the development of the party system and fiscal rules. I also examine the fiscal performance of each country in terms of the cyclically adjusted budget balance and the overall debt level. The cyclically adjusted budget balance allows the reader to see changes in discretionary policy that are not picked up when the simple budget balance is used. These figures are in general government terms and are based on Maastricht definitions of deficits and debt. For each country, I then determine the relevant participants in the budget process; trace the development of fiscal rules and the development of fiscal policy; and consider the explanations for the changes in policy.

In every case I consider two explicit hypotheses, in addition to the argument about the importance of fiscal rules. First, I try to determine what Maastricht effect, if any, existed as an explanation for fiscal performance. Second, I examine whether market pressures forced states to adopt tighter fiscal policies. In terms of sources, I rely on secondary sources where possible. Materials for the large countries are more readily available than for the small countries. Yet I found during the research process that there was no work that asked the same questions asked here for the same time period. I therefore conducted on-site interviews in the capitals of fourteen of the fifteen member states.[13] The people interviewed were public servants in finance

---

13. I was not able to conduct interviews in Vienna. I did, however, make phone calls and correspond via fax and e-mail with individuals in the Austrian National Bank and in the finance ministry.

ministries, economics ministries, regional governments, and parliaments. I also checked with academics and journalists who follow fiscal policy. As the reader will soon discover, these interviews were especially helpful in explaining events in countries for which a secondary literature was lacking.

To explain what happened when and why, *Domestic Budgets* looks at European Union member states according to the shape of their party systems. In chapter 4 I discuss countries that have consistent one-party majority governments, such as the United Kingdom and Greece. They are ideal settings for delegation to a strong finance minister. The United Kingdom adopted the appropriate fiscal institutions, and it serves as the model case for delegation. Greece does not have such a framework in place; it did, however, revise its institutions along delegation lines around 1997. Maastricht played a critical role in encouraging change in Greece. Two other countries, France and Germany, have party systems that pit blocs of parties against each other in elections. Delegation also functions in these cases, although, as the German case will illustrate, the somewhat larger ideological distance between coalition partners as well as the need to get some legislation through an upper chamber of parliament complicates matters and makes delegation less effective than in the United Kingdom.

In chapter 5 I consider countries that have party systems in which parties are not close to one another ideologically. The Netherlands is the ideal case. During the 1970s, it tried to move toward a delegation mode with centralization under Finance Minister Wim Duisenberg. This attempt failed when the parties in government refused to support the finance minister's austerity measures. In 1982, the liberals (VVD) and the Christian Democrats (CDA) signed the first true "fiscal contract." In 1994, after the Christian Democrats lost office, the new coalition tightened the contract. It included detailed spending targets at the subministry level as well as rules for how to adjust the contract if the budget did not perform as expected.

Belgium also had a party system with many opposing parties. All governments had to include parties from the two largest regions in the country, Flanders and Wallonia. Voters, or other parties, could not punish a regional party that overspent. Steps to federalize the country in 1989 and 1993 largely broke this log jam.

Finland illustrates the usefulness of explicit contracts with explicit rules. The country maintained fiscal discipline in the 1980s through essentially informal contracts. When it experienced a sharp economic downturn at the beginning of the 1990s, it introduced several changes to the way it makes budgets that moved the process closer to the commitment ideal.

In chapter 6 I examine two Scandinavian countries, Denmark and Sweden, that traditionally have one large party, the Social Democrats, that forms a minority government. In Sweden, centralization of the budget process behind the finance minister worked as long as the Communist Party granted the Social Democrats unconditional support from the opposition benches. In the late 1980s, the Communists changed tactics and the Social Democrats had to "buy" votes from moderate parties. Denmark similarly had been dominated by Social Democratic minority governments. It also had fiscal problems in the early 1980s. A minority center-right coalition introduced a series of fiscal reforms in 1982 that institutionalized regular negotiated "fiscal contracts" between the government and one or more opposition parties that covered all dimensions of the budget.

In chapter 7 I focus on Italy. This country experienced a fundamental reorganization of its party system in the early 1990s because of the "Clean Hands" trials that addressed political corruption, the collapse of Communism, and the change of the electoral system from proportional representation to a mixed system. Indeed, Italy moved from an uncompetitive party system, under which the Christian Democrats could not be unelected, to a competitive system composed of two rival blocs of parties. As the theory predicts, the form of fiscal governance changed at almost the same time from a fiefdom form of fiscal governance to a delegation form under a strong treasury minister. Maastricht probably was a sufficient reason for the timing of the tightening of fiscal policy in 1996 and 1997, but the necessary change in political institutions was at the party system level.

In chapter 8 I discuss four countries that have not maintained stable party systems. Austria and Ireland have bounced between systems that supported one-party governments, minority governments, and coalition governments. The reason was the rise of third parties that made it difficult to institutionalize a specific form of fiscal governance. In Ireland, the party system through the late 1980s made one of two forms of government possible—either a multiparty majority party (including Fine Gael, or FG, as one partner) or a minority one-party government (Fianna Fáil, or FF). It was not possible to institutionalize firm fiscal rules because the form of government changed repeatedly. In the early 1990s, however, the party system changed, and only multiparty coalition governments have been likely since then. Fiscal institutions consistent with a commitment form of fiscal governance have recently been introduced and strengthened.

Portugal and Spain have experienced difficulties somewhat similar to those in Ireland. Small parties have been strong enough to block one-party majority governments over significant periods of time. Instead of opting for coalition governments, as is common in Austria, however, the parties chose to form minority governments. There was some centralization of the budget process around the finance minister in Spain, but there was less change in Portugal. In the Iberian countries Maastricht affected the timing of the improvement in fiscal discipline. Spain, where fiscal institutional reforms were put in place, has, since 1997, performed better than Portugal, where significant reforms were not introduced.

In the conclusion I discuss the implications of the argument for the future of the fiscal framework in Europe. I suggest that the "one size fits all" approach at the European level is flawed. Detailed fiscal rules work well for commitment countries, but they may be counterproductive in delegation countries. It is consistent with this theory that two delegation countries, France and Germany, had difficulties in 2002 in keeping their budget deficits below 3% of GDP. The conclusion also discusses whether the model developed here can be extended to non–European Union countries and its general relevance to the study of comparative political economy. There are some outstanding political science books that consider the design of party systems, electoral systems, and the like as interconnected packages (Lijphart 1999; Powell 2000). The dependent variable in such work is usually an explicitly "political" one, namely effective representation. *Domestic Budgets* illustrates how such institutional packages extend to fiscal institutions and fiscal outcomes as well. Political stability and party competition are not only values to be preserved in their own right, they also contribute to the institutionalization of fiscal rules that lead to better fiscal performance.

2

Forms of Fiscal Governance

To understand budgetary outcomes one must understand how budgets are made. There are four ideal types of decision making, which I term "forms of fiscal governance." To illustrate these ideal forms, I begin with a simple formal model of the budget-making process in parliamentary democracies where the principal decisions on the budget are made in the cabinet. The key premise is that every government faces a common pool resource problem. In practice, the problem permeates decision making. Policy makers, for sound political reasons, do not have an incentive in most cases to consider the implications of their spending decisions on the full tax burden. If policy makers do little to address this problem, then a fiefdom form of governance predominates. Policy makers consider their domains their "fiefdoms," and they decide spending levels more or less in isolation from one another. There are, however, two "ideal" forms of governance conducive to solving the common pool resource problem, the modes of delegation and commitment. Delegation involves vesting the finance minister with significant decision-making powers over public monies. Under commitment a group of agents with similar decision-making rights enter an agreement, or a "fiscal contract," to commit themselves strictly to budgetary norms, that is, targets for budget aggregates set for one or more years. A third form of governance that solves the common pool resource problem, which is found in minority governments only and combines elements of both ideal forms, is the mixed form.

Each of these ways of solving the common pool resource problem has distinct implications for the adoption, and for the effectiveness, of fiscal institutions. In delegation states, the emphasis is on improving the *discretion* of the finance minister in the budgetary process. One expects formal or informal rules that enhance the position of the finance minister. Moreover, it is likely that there will be spending targets such as caps on personnel costs and explicit mechanisms to deal with open-ended expenditures and the like to make the budget more manageable for the finance minister. In contrast, in commitment states one expects a range of formal rules to maintain the fiscal contract among the political parties that make the initial agreements. This mode of governance is more *rule*-based, and one should expect a range of multiannual targets and subtargets, as well as rules to deal with unexpected shocks, so that the initial agreement is not broken. The mixed form of governance has elements of delegation in the budget deliberations that take place within the cabinet and elements of commitment in the "contracts" the government signs with one or more opposition parties in parliament.

To understand why states adopt the form of fiscal governance that they do one must first determine the *potential* form of fiscal governance. Delegation is unlikely to function when the ideological distance among cabinet members is great, while commitment does function in such a situation. A mixed form of governance exists under minority governments. The underlying party system can allow one to predict which of these forms of fiscal governance is most appropriate for a given country. Delegation can arise where there are two main parties that face each other in elections, or where there are two blocs of parties where the parties in each bloc are close to one another ideologically. Commitment, conversely, arises in countries where political parties are not bunched together and where they traditionally run against one another in elections even if they are in a coalition government. Finally, a mixed form develops in countries where the party system makes majority governments unlikely.

We can then predict the *actual* form of fiscal governance. Once again, the party system is crucial. An uncompetitive party system does not encourage parties to address the common pool resource problem. Fiefdom is the likely outcome, as cabinet ministers take care of their respective clienteles. An unstable party system also makes it difficult to institutionalize a given form of fiscal governance. A shift from one-party majority governments to multiparty coalition governments and back again does not allow the institutional structure to gel.

The Budget Process

There are three principal stages of the budget process: planning, decision making, and implementation. In reality the stages of the process may overlap, but in an ideal sense we can consider how these stages may differ in different systems. In the planning stage, governments make forecasts about revenues, spending needs, economic growth, and the like. The planning can be detailed and look forward several years. It can also bind the government to certain levels of spending and/or certain levels of revenue unless new legislation is passed to change the budget plan, as the multiannual plan does in Sweden today. The plan may also be vague, restricted to the upcoming budget year, and have little or no practical impact on the formation of the budget. This has been the case in Greece from redemocratization in 1974 until quite recently.

In the decision-making stage, the government formulates its annual budget and then the legislature passes a budget. In theory, the legislature ultimately possesses the power of the purse in all democracies. In practice, however, the legislature's input in the annual budget process varies widely. In some cases, the legislature makes significant changes to the executive's budget proposal. Members of Congress in the United States are fond of calling the president's budget "dead on arrival," implying that the president will get little of what he wants once Congress is through with the budget. In other cases, the legislature serves as little more than a rubber stamp of the government's original budget proposal.

The third stage is the implementation of the budget. In some countries, the government is legally required to execute the budget exactly as the legislature has passed it. In other countries, government ministers have either implicit or explicit permission to spend less or to spend more than the budget. For example, the Italian treasury minister in the mid-1990s, Carlo Ciampi, blocked the spending of money the Italian Chamber of Deputies had already approved. On the other side of the coin, a Francophone education minister in mid-1980s Belgium spent millions of francs more than his ministry was allotted with no more justification than a vague claim that there were more Francophone students than he expected. An important institutional question concerns how much the government knows about what it is spending and what revenues it collects as well as when it knows these figures. If the government (or the legislature) has little ability to monitor its spending and its revenue collection there may be fairly wide disparities between the budget that passes the legislature and the budget the government ultimately implements.[1]

A Model of Budget Making in Parliamentary Cabinets

Ministry and Party Ideal Budgets

There are three relevant groups in the model of decision making within the cabinet.[2] Spending ministers ($S_{1,2,\ldots,n}$) make bids for the level of spending

1. Some authors treat the monitoring of the budget as a separate stage; see, for example, von Hagen 1992 and Hallerberg, Strauch, and von Hagen 2001.

2. The model is based on similar models presented in von Hagen and Harden 1994, Hallerberg and von Hagen 1999, and Hallerberg 2000. Von Hagen and Harden (1994) write about the common pool problem in cabinets. This model does not have parties as actors; it assumes that ministers worry about ministry constituencies only, and it is a one-period game. The Hallerberg and von Hagen (1999) model is multiperiod and considers the effects of the common pool resource problem on the size of deficits. The focus remains on the cabinet, not the party. It also links the type of electoral system with the institutional choice of a solution to the

to be allocated to their ministries. They also spend the budgets allocated to them once they are approved. All spending ministers together form the government (G). A subset of the members of government belong to political parties ($P_{1,2,\ldots,1}$).

Spending ministers seek full funding for those programs they consider important for reaching their policy goals, and their proposals affect the spending side of the budget. I assume that members of the same political party share the same ideal budgets for each ministry.[3] The variable x_{ip}^* represents the ideal spending level of party p for ministry i. Ministers also seek to minimize the taxes that their constituencies must pay, and m_i is the amount of the total tax burden that the minister expects her constituency to bear. This amount can be equal to or less than the level of taxation on the minister's party constituency, so that $m_i \leq m_p$. Finally, the minister may benefit simply from having larger budgets, and as a consequence she will request funds that are greater than the minimum needed to reach her policy goals (Niskanen 1971). The degree to which she values additional spending is represented by λ. Assuming that the excess burden of taxation is quadratic, the ith minister will possess the utility function

$$U_i = \lambda x_i - \frac{\alpha}{2}(x_i - x_{ip}^*)^2 - \frac{m_i}{2}T^2 \tag{1}$$

where x_i is the amount of funding the ministry ultimately receives and α the relative weight that the minister places on spending concerns. If one assumes that there is a hard budget constraint[4] so that $T = \sum_{i=1}^{n} x_i$, then the spending minister j chooses a budget for his ministry that takes the form

$$b_{sj} = \frac{\lambda + \alpha x_{jp}^* - m_j \sum_{i=1, i \neq j}^{n} x_i}{\alpha + m_j} \tag{2}.$$

Now consider an alternative situation in which the spending ministers reflect fully the preferences of their political parties. In this case the ministers consider the effects of total spending and total taxation for party p, and they do not value higher spending for their ministry in its own right. The joint utility equation for the party is

---

common pool resource problem. Hallerberg 2000 develops an extensive form game that stresses the monitoring and punishment aspects of the different ideal types of government. This book explicitly considers parties as actors. Although the substantive conclusions do not differ significantly from the earlier models, the consideration of parties allows a more explicit comparison with coalition theorists.

3. This assumption can be relaxed by treating party factions as separate parties in the formal model.

4. Note that this hard budget constraint will be relaxed later in this chapter.

$$U_p = -\sum_{i=1}^{n} \frac{\alpha}{2}(x_i - x_{ip}^*)^2 - \frac{m_p}{2}T^2 \qquad (3)$$

and the budget for minister j would be

$$b_{pj} = \frac{\alpha x_{jp}^* - m_p \sum_{i=1, i \ne j}^{n} x_i}{\alpha + m_p} \qquad (4).$$

Note that the size of the budget in both equation 2 and equation 4 is dependent on what other ministers choose as their ideal budgets. To determine whether $b_{sj} > b_{pj}$ in practice requires one further step. So that the argument is easy to follow, I assume that the ideal budgets for the political party are the same across ministries so that $x_p^* = x_{1p}^* = x_{2p}^* = ... = x_{np}^*$. I also assume for any ministries i and j that the budgets the ministers ultimately select are the same, such that $b_j^* = b_i^*$. Finally, I assume that ministry constituencies do not overlap such that $m_p = \sum_{i=1}^{n} m_i$ and $m_i = \frac{m_p}{n}$. The solution that is ideal for the party is

$$b_{pj}^* = \frac{\alpha x_p^*}{\alpha + nm_p} \qquad (5)$$

while the ideal budget for the individual is

$$b_{sj}^* = \frac{\lambda + \alpha x^*}{\alpha + nm_j} = \frac{\lambda + \alpha x^*}{\alpha + m_p} \qquad (6).$$

Clearly, $b_{sj} > b_{pj}$ when the minister does not consider the entire tax burden on the party's constituency and/or so long as $\lambda > 0$, and this inequality indicates that the budget a given spending minister would like to propose is larger than the party's optimal budget.

Given the importance of the tax burden to the outcome, how likely is it that ministers will not consider the party's full budget? Partial consideration of the tax burden is generally the rule for the following reasons: First, ministers are often judged by how well they protect the interests of the constituents of their particular ministry. An agriculture minister may care most about the effects of spending and taxation on farmers, while a labor minister has similar worries about the effects of spending and taxation on workers. In Germany, for example, in the cabinet of Helmut Schmidt, Defense Minister Hans Apel, a working-class Social Democrat from the docks of Hamburg, became such a vociferous advocate for his ministry that he was the only Bundestag member within his party besides his chancellor to support the stationing of American short-range missiles on German territory in the early

1980s. The general point is that where one stands on budget issues within one's party depends on where one sits at the cabinet table. If cabinet members cared only about the tax burdens on their ministry's constituencies, then all m_i would sum to the total tax burden on the cabinet.[5]

There is some empirical evidence that ministers care only about spending and taxation for their particular ministries. Kontopoulos and Perotti (1999) have found that in a panel of OECD countries for the period 1970–95 the more ministers there were in a given cabinet the higher the level of spending and the higher the budget deficit. This is only one study, of course, but more empirical evidence will be presented in the case study chapters.

A second reason why ministers likely do not consider the full tax burden is that their parties are coalitions of different interests. Leaders within the party generally represent the spectrum of party supporters. In the March 2000 cabinet reshuffle in France, for example, Laurent Fabius as minister of finance represented the more monetarist wing of the Socialist Party, while Martine Aubry remained as a more left-leaning minister of employment. In Germany, Norbert Blüm came from a Christian Democratic Union (CDU) post, yet he was a steady advocate of prolabor policies as labor minister within Helmut Kohl's cabinet.

The ideological distance between different factions within a political party is not a random phenomenon across countries. This variable is, to some degree, a function of the underlying electoral system. Under proportional representation systems with high district magnitudes, one would expect many political parties with potentially narrow constituencies. In contrast, under a plurality system one expects a two-party system with "big tent" parties that bring together more diverse interests under one party label (Duverger 1954; Katz 1980). Moreover, plurality systems lead members of parties to care about geographically specific interests. As a consequence, Lancaster (1986) has argued that legislators in plurality systems provide more pork barrel projects than legislators in proportional representation systems. Weingast, Shepsle, and Johnsen (1981) similarly have contended that in the American system legislators care only about the spending and the tax burden in their districts. Assuming that the tax burden is distributed equally across a given country, they assume that the amount of the tax burden a legislator considers in a legislature with m members is simply $1/m$. Because in Europe cabinet members generally come from the legislature, there is reason to believe that they consider only part of the total tax burden.[6]

In sum, if ministers are left alone there are good reasons to believe that they commonly do not consider the full tax burden when they decide the

5. This logic is the basis for the model in Hallerberg and von Hagen 1999.
6. For a discussion of the relationship among electoral systems, party discipline, and the choice of open or closed rules in European parliaments see Hallerberg 2004; for Latin America, see Hallerberg and Marier 2004.

ideal spending level for their ministries. The shape the budget takes depends on the decision-making process.

Fiefdom Governance

How are individual budget bids translated into the total budget? In the fiefdom approach, ministers decide the spending levels for their respective ministries, and the budget process involves simply aggregating the individual budget bids into a total budget. In practice, this model applies when the general cabinet sets the budget and spending ministers can coordinate log rolls with one another that allow them to get actual spending levels that correspond to their spending bids.[7] What the budget ultimately looks like depends crucially upon the number of, and the ideological distance among, parties in government, because of the differences in ideal budgets across parties.

I begin with a one-party government. For simplicity and without loss of generality, I again assume that the ideal budgets for the political party are the same across ministries so that $x_p^* = x_{1p}^* = x_{2p}^* = ... = x_{np}^*$. I also assume that the budgets that the ministers ultimately select are the same, such that $b_j^* = b_i^*$. The aggregate level of spending if the ministers receive their ideal budgets is then

$$B_l = \frac{n\lambda + n\alpha x_p^*}{\alpha + m_p} \qquad (7),$$

which is larger than the collectively optimal budget of

$$B_p = \frac{n\alpha x_p^*}{\alpha + nm_p} \qquad (8).$$

The situation under a multiparty government is somewhat more complicated but nevertheless tractable. The model assumes that parties hold different ideal spending preferences for each ministry, which in the model means that the parties have different x_i^*. Many coalition theorists assume, in fact, that negotiations concern the distribution of portfolios among parties with different policy preferences (Laver and Shepsle 1996).

To simplify the discussion, consider the case with only two parties in government, party A and party B. Assume as well that party constituencies do not overlap so that $m_p = \sum_{i=1}^n m_i$ and $m_i = \frac{m}{n}$, where m is the total tax burden

---

7. The model developed by Baron and Ferejohn (1989) remains the most succinct one. In their terminology the cabinets discussed here are merely small legislatures where the number of legislators is equal to the number of cabinet ministers. Their formal model indicates that votes with open rules in small legislatures and a costly delay can lead to universalistic solutions. The "legislators" unanimously agree on the outcome with each legislator receiving her preferred budget.

on the coalition. If one simply adds up the spending requests of the different ministries under the two parties the total budget is

$$B_D = \frac{n\lambda + \alpha\sum_{i=1}^{n_A} x_{iA}^{*} + \alpha\sum_{i=1}^{n_B} x_{iB}^{*}}{\alpha + m} \qquad (9).$$

and $n_A + n_B = n$.

If the parties consider the full tax burden on the coalition instead, and if they set the spending levels that maximize their joint utilities (that is, they set the budget figures and not individual ministers so that $\lambda = 0$), then the budget takes the form

$$B_d = \frac{\alpha\sum_{i=1}^{n_A} x_{iA}^{*} + \alpha\sum_{i=1}^{n_B} x_{iB}^{*}}{\alpha + nm} \qquad (10).$$

Once again, spending under the fiefdom approach is higher than if the parties had jointly set the budgets.

The general problem is, therefore, the same under both one-party and multiparty coalition governments. When decision making is decentralized, the players suffer from a common pool resource problem. The greater the fragmentation of the cabinet, the smaller the tax burden a given minister considers and the larger the common pool resource problem. All of the ministries suffer from the additional spending by other ministers that comes from the same tax revenue pot. The utility equations for both individual ministers (equation 1) and political parties (equation 3) indicate that both types of actors suffer utility losses because of higher spending by ministers who do not consider the full tax burden. This common pool resource problem is, therefore, also a collective action problem. All actors would be better off if they considered the entire tax burden rather than considering only the tax burden on their ministry.[8]

One should note that, unlike in the forms of governance that follow, there is no internal logic that connects the institutions present at the three stages of the budget process to the fiefdom model. Instead, it is a matter of identifying whether fiefdom is present at one or more stages of the process. Concerning the decision-making stage, one looks for situations in which the party that receives a given portfolio determines the policies of the ministry without interference from other coalition partners. If the minister does exactly what the party wants, then the budget decision reflects consideration of the tax burden

8. This model is potentially applicable to parliaments, as well, if parliaments can change the budget and parliamentarians can set the budget figures for areas of their expertise as they choose. The question here concerns the relevant actors. Even in fiefdom states there is usually some party discipline, and majority governments usually pass their cabinet's budget proposals. Parliament does play a more crucial role in minority governments, and the fiefdom model appears in cases in which the minority government must buy votes from opposition parties.

on the minister's party only, not on the entire coalition. If the ministers determine their budgets more or less autonomously, then the budget outcome for a particular ministry matches that given in equation 9. One way to facilitate this outcome is to have the full cabinet make decisions on the budget. This allows the ministers to log roll their preferred ministerial budgets. One also expects little or no centralization of the budget process in the cabinet. The budget outcome is simply an aggregation of individual budget bids. The finance minister serves as a glorified accountant who may audit books and keep track of the budget figures. She has no say on the final budget outcome.

A likely symptom of fiefdom is that budget planning into the future has little or no practical importance, and indeed may be totally absent. There is no functional need for fiscal planning, because ministers are likely to ignore whatever planning does occur.

This form of fiscal governance can exist at the implementation stage if ministers can easily adjust their spending levels without regard to the effects of their decisions on the total tax burden. For example, it was routine in Italy under the five parties in government, known as the *pentapartito,* for parliament simply to approve any spending that went above a minister's original budget in midyear supplemental budgets.

States can avoid a fiefdom outcome at one stage of the process but not at others. In Belgium in the mid-1980s, for example, the prime minister often negotiated "fiscal contracts" with his ministers that led to budgets that, on paper, might have approximated the budget in equation 8, which was the solution the parties themselves favored. Yet, in practice, ministers could spend pretty much what they wanted during the implementation stage, which led to a serious common pool resource problem and budgets that approximated equation 7.

Delegation Governance

A significant body of literature concerns the question of how to solve collective action problems (Olson 1965; Ostrom 1990; Ostrom, Gardner, and Walker 1994). One possible solution is to appoint a central person to serve as an "entrepreneur," whose function is to assure that all actors choose to cooperate. To be effective, the entrepreneur must have the ability to monitor the other players and must possess selective incentives that he can use to punish defectors and/or reward those who cooperate; and he must have some motivation to bear the costs of monitoring himself (Olson 1965). The spending ministers have reason to delegate power to such a fiscal entrepreneur. Although most players have an individual incentive to "defect" or overspend, they usually prefer the solution where all cooperate rather than where all defect.[9]

9. It is true that if a spending minister were to ignore the tax effects of spending, he would always want more spending and would not support delegation to a strong finance minister; but such ministers should be rare.

Among the cabinet members, the minister of finance (or minister of economy or treasury in some political systems) is most likely to play the role of a "fiscal" entrepreneur. He usually has the responsibility to coordinate the formation of the budget, and, fair or not, the overall conduct of fiscal policy, including the size of budget deficits, is the principal indicator that others use to judge his effectiveness. He may also have a trivial budget when compared with other ministers so that he cannot defect in the "prisoner's dilemma game" being played in the cabinet. His interests, therefore, generally coincide with the general interests. Indeed, as former Swiss Finance Minister Otto Stich noted after his resignation in 1995, "every federal ministry has its lobby—I have only the taxpayers. They are the real majority, but their interests are unfortunately not well represented in parliament."[10]

A second reason why the minister of finance (or economy) is the most likely entrepreneur is that he may have the institutional capability to monitor the other ministries. The finance minister usually has an extensive staff trained in budgeting and accounting, and he is most likely to discover tricks spending ministers may use to justify additional spending. Because his prestige, and hence his personal benefits, depend on the effectiveness of his ministry, he has a private incentive to guarantee that the monitoring occurs. The only question is whether the finance minister has a privileged position in the budget process so that he can address the common pool resource problem.

As the case study chapters will show, the power a minister of finance has varies from country to country. Yet it is important at this stage to explain what rules (formal as well as informal) strengthen the hand of the finance minister vis-à-vis other ministers. There are generally two stages of the budget process when the common pool resource problem is relevant, and when, as a consequence, the power of the minister of finance matters: when the budget is being formulated (*ex ante*) and when the budget is implemented (*ex post*). *Ex ante* ministers submit budget bids that correspond to equation 2. Importantly, ministers would still like to receive budgets that correspond to equation 2, even if they do not receive this budget allocation in the budget law. This means that *ex post* ministers benefit from spending over their initial budget allocations. An effective finance minister must, therefore, hold a privileged position at both stages of the budget process to be effective.

There are a series of rules at the budget formation stage that strengthen the position of the finance minister. In the first stage, the minister of finance can serve as an agenda setter in the formulation of the budget by possessing the right to make the first proposal for the budget. This power is undermined if spending ministers can ignore the finance minister's budget and get cabinet votes on their budget bids, allowing them to ignore the finance minister's proposal. This procedure is the one commonly found in France. The

10. *Financial Times*, September 1, 1995.

minister of finance, together with the prime minister, issues a framework letter for every spending ministry that indicates the level of spending that ministry should expect to receive in the next budget year.

Another method *ex ante* is to have the minister of finance negotiate individually with the spending ministers, as is done in the United Kingdom. The
chancellor of the exchequer is generally regarded as second in power only
to the prime minister, and she usually negotiates with spending ministers
individually about their budget allocations. Disputes between the finance
minister and spending ministers go to a committee of senior ministers without portfolio for consideration and not to the full cabinet for resolution.
These ministers do not have budgets of their own, and a log-rolling situation
in favor of the spending minister is not possible. Because the senior ministers are appointed to consider the general interests of the cabinet as well,
they usually support the chancellor. Further rules that strengthen the power
of the finance minister include a right to veto any spending proposal, as in
Germany. One can strengthen this rule with a requirement that the cabinet cannot overrule the decision of the finance minister, which is the case
in Austria but not the case in Germany, where the chancellor plus a majority of the cabinet can overrule a finance minister's veto. A final rule can
require that the finance minister approve any changes to multiannual spending allocations.

An effective delegation to a fiscal entrepreneur also requires that the actors
ex post do not defect from their initial budget allocations. The minister of
finance, therefore, needs to have adequate monitoring power and a way to
punish intransigent spending ministers. As long as he has the ability to mod-
ify a spending minister's budget proposal, he can punish defectors in future
years. If immediate action is required, he can appeal to the prime minister
to take action, and, in the most extreme case, he can insist that the prime
minister relieve the spending minister of his position. For her part, the prime
minister generally enjoys a privileged position in any such battles. She can
call a vote of confidence on an issue that puts the very existence of the government in question if a given minister does not support her position (Huber
1996). Other powers that the finance minister may have, in practice, include
the power to block spending during the budget year, to approve all cash disbursements and to limit disbursements when the ministry thinks appropriate, and to approve all transfers across budget chapters.

This discussion also has implications for the parliamentary stage of the
budget. Parliaments that can easily change the government's budget proposal
undermine the effectiveness of the finance minister. Disgruntled spending
ministers can go around the backs of finance ministers and request that parliament pass their ideal budgets. An effective form of delegation, therefore,
requires that parliament also delegate its power in the budget process to the
finance minister. The expectation is that parliaments cannot significantly

change the government's budget without the government's approval, which, in practice, means the finance minister's approval.

If delegation were equally effective across all forms of government, one could stop here and suggest that all countries strengthen their finance ministers appreciably and weaken the role of parliaments in the budget process.[11] Yet the effectiveness of this form of governance depends on the party structure of the government. To see this, return to the model presented in the previous section and consider two parties in government, with party A controlling the finance ministry and some spending ministries and party B controlling some spending ministries. The ideal budget for party A remains the budget in equation 6, a budget that reflects the ideal spending preferences of party A only. The ideal budget for the coalition, however, is equation 8, which includes the ideal budgets of party B for those ministries that party B controls.[12] What this suggests is that the greater the ideological distance between party A and party B the less likely it is that party B will be willing to delegate budgetary power to a finance minister; in game-theoretic parlance, the "principal-agent" problem becomes more severe. Coalition members simply will not trust a central player who must inevitably come from only one party to monitor and punish spending ministers in a manner that does not benefit the minister of finance's own party. In coalitions where the parties will run against one another in future elections, there may also be a zero-sum game played between the parties. Any excessive spending by one party potentially helps that party in the next election and hurts its coalition partners. In contrast, in one-party governments, or in coalition governments in which ideological differences are minor, conflicts of interest among cabinet members arise primarily because of the common pool resource problem. The various ministers can be fairly sure that the finance minister holds more or less the same spending preferences as they do, and delegation of power to the finance minister is not problematic.

There is a second reason why delegation is most effective in governments with one-party governments. The punishment mechanism depends on the power of the prime minister, and by extension the finance minister, to reprimand or dismiss intransigent spending ministers. In one-party governments the dismissal of one minister from the same political party as the prime minister can be a heavy blow for the minister but have few consequences for the government. If the minister comes from a coalition partner, however, the

11. In its 1997 annual report, the Inter-American Development Bank suggested as much: "More hierarchical budget institutions that grant more power and responsibility to the finance minister (vis-à-vis other ministers) . . . can contain deficit bias and lead to permanent and meaningful improvements in fiscal discipline" (143).

12. Laver and Shepsle (1994, 9–10), for instance, in summarizing the findings of the case studies in their edited volume, note that the distribution of portfolios among members of the same political party has little effect on the policies that a government adopts; much more important is the distribution of portfolios among different parties.

partner may rally around the minister and force a showdown that can lead to a collapse of the government.

Delegation is, therefore, an option in one-party majority governments, such as the United Kingdom, where ideal budgets of the various ministries are close to one another and where all cabinet members will be on the same side in the next election. Delegation is also possible in countries where political parties are close to each other ideologically and where they usually run together as blocs in elections. In France, for example, the rightist RPR and UDF parties usually coordinate their electoral strategies. In Germany for the last twenty years the Free Democratic Party (FDP), Christian Democratic Union, and Christian Social Union (CSU) have in one bloc opposed the Social Democratic Party of Germany (SPD) and the Green Party. In such countries differences in ideal budgets among bloc partners are not large. Parties that expect to run together in the future do not have the worry that their partners will intentionally defect to increase their chances of winning the next election. Excessive spending hurts the coalition more generally.

Commitment Governance

The alternative to delegation that is available to coalition governments is committing to fiscal contracts. Parties that negotiate the budgets for every ministry consider the total tax burden on their coalition rather than merely the tax burden on their own parties, or, potentially even more damaging, individual ministries. They internalize the tax externality. Because the parties negotiate the budgets among themselves and set the contract, the benefit that individual ministers get simply from larger budgets for their ministries is also not included in the utility equation.

The natural place to negotiate such contracts is during the coalition negotiations. There are therefore two alternative ideal types of coalition agreements. The first type is the fiefdom model, where the parties simply negotiate the distribution of portfolios. The second type is commitment to fiscal contracts, and it involves detailed negotiations for every ministry. The prototypical example comes from the Netherlands. Future coalition partners negotiate detailed budgets for every ministry before the coalition negotiations are concluded.[13] This suggests that the *planning* stage of the budget is important to commitment states. Coalition partners negotiate multiannual plans, and they expect annual budgets to remain consistent with these plans.

In practice, the plans amount to "fiscal contracts." Questions that must be addressed by those making fiscal contracts include: What provisions exist to make sure that the parties stick by the contract? What happens if one or

13. This case, as well as the development of fiscal contracts in Belgium and in Finland, is discussed in detail in chapter 5.

more parties break the contract? and Under what conditions are contracts renegotiable?

First, negotiations among parties that result in commitment to a fiscal contract do not solve the common pool resource problem if the parties and/or ministers can easily violate the agreement *ex post*. Such violations could take place during either the decision-making phase, in which one or more parties might decide to break the agreement and demand more spending in one or more important areas, or during the implementation phase, in which one or more parties might choose to spend more than it was awarded in both the coalition agreement and in the annual budget.

In both situations, coalition members need to be able to detect possible defections. One issue concerns the contract design itself. Detailed provisions make it easier to determine whether an action violates the letter of the contract. Wide circulation of the provisions of the contract also makes it more likely that people outside government can identify defections. Within the government, the minister of finance can again play a role, but that role is necessarily more limited. Unlike the situation in delegation states, she will not have agenda-setting power and other strategic powers *ex ante,* because the common pool resource problem is addressed through the fiscal contract. Coalition parties have reason to suspect that the minister is biased toward her own party. While the finance minister can still assist in monitoring ministers *ex post,* the other parties will still want to monitor one another.

The obvious institution with enough staff and expertise to monitor cabinet members is the parliament. One would expect parliamentary committees to have the ability to monitor government ministries in commitment states. Committees may be designed so that they are responsible for keeping watch over one government ministry. The committee chair may be expected to come from a different party than the minister, which occurs in practice most of the time in countries such as the Netherlands. The committees may have other rights that reinforce their ability to collect information on the ministry under their jurisdiction, such as the right to call a minister before the committee for testimony and to subpoena ministerial documents.

What happens if a party defects? The punishment mechanism clearly differentiates commitment from delegation. A prime minister in a multiparty coalition cannot easily dismiss individual ministers who violate the contract if they come from a different party. Moreover, this solution is ineffective so long as the root cause of the problem is the party and not the individual minister. The likely punishment is therefore the dissolution of the coalition government itself; but this form of brinksmanship is a blunt, and often unsuccessful, tool. The effectiveness of such threats depends on the ability of coalition members to find alternative partners to replace any defectors. This requires some dynamism in party system structure. Coalition theorists tell us about the likelihood of a new coalition forming. Laver and Shepsle (1996) argue that some parties cannot be excluded, because they have electoral strength combined with a middle position in the country's political spectrum.[14] Other coalition partners cannot punish such strong parties in the perspective presented here. Fiscal contracts in the presence of a strong party are unlikely to work. Countries with a history of strong parties are likely to have fiefdom governments.[15]

The final question concerns renegotiation of the contract. One can imagine situations in which one or more party is no longer satisfied with the original contract. If a coalition partner expects to do much better after new elections, the contract and the coalition itself are probably at their end, and renegotiation will not be possible. Early elections are the result and there is no bargaining. A more interesting case is one where an unforeseen event places a burden on the budget. How are the consequences of the burden distributed among the coalition partners? Grilli et al. (1991) concentrate on the effects of economic downturns, and they argue that all coalition governments (not just commitment governments) face gridlock during economic downturns because they cannot negotiate the distribution of costs (both budgetary as well as political) across coalition partners. The result is policy drift and, during an economic downturn, large budget deficits.

The Grilli scenario probably describes well the situation facing fiefdom governments, but it is not satisfactory for explaining the functioning of commitment governments. First, parties can write detailed provisions into the contracts to assure that there are very few "unforeseen" effects. Provisions in the original contract for across-the-board spending cuts during negative shocks or provisions that require that all additional revenue during a positive shock go to reducing the overall debt level (what today's commitment government in Belgium refers to as the Golden Hamster Rule) take the decision out of the hands of the coalition. Second, governments can make negative shocks less likely by writing contracts based on intentionally conservative estimates of future economic growth. If the expected annual real growth rate of the economy over a four-year term is 3% per year, the government may write fiscal contracts that estimate a growth rate of only 2.5%. As Hallerberg et al. (2001) showed in their survey of fiscal rules in EU countries during the period 1998–2000, commitment states regularly employ both tactics to try to avoid contract renegotiations in the middle of a coalition's term. There is a clear role for the finance minister, but it is not the same as in delegation states. The finance minister is one guarantor of the fiscal contract,

14. In particular, Laver and Shepsle (1996, 69–71) differentiate between two types of strong parties. A very strong party is one where no majority in parliament prefers an alternative coalition that excludes it. A merely strong party, in contrast, can threaten to veto certain alternative cabinets.

15. I will return to the point more formally later in the chapter when I consider a multiperiod game that allows borrowing from the future.

but she does not have the same powers as a delegation minister to introduce the budget or to change it during its execution.

Mixed Governance

Both delegation and commitment forms of governance assume that governments can pass their budgets through parliament relatively unchanged and with little difficulty. This assumption may be realistic in Western European countries with majority governments, but it does not describe the passage of legislation in countries with minority governments. By definition, minority governments do not have the votes in parliament to pass legislation without the help of the opposition. Since just under a third of all postwar European governments have taken a minority form, this point is not trivial (Tsebelis 1995). Moreover, minority governments have received less attention in the literature than majority governments and there is little consensus about how such governments affect the making of budgets. Some authors consider them to be highly unstable and incapable of passing significant legislation. Edin and Ohlsson (1991), in their reanalysis of Roubini and Sachs's (1989) data set, found that minority governments are more likely than any type of majority government to run large budget deficits. In contrast, Strøm (1990) insists that such governments are relatively stable and that they are at least as effective as majority parties. Tsebelis (1995, 1999, 2002) even argues that there is no functional difference between one-party minority and one-party majority governments.

For the purposes of this book, which deals with budget policy, minority governments can take one of two forms of governance. Like majority governments they can lapse into fiefdom modes. To the extent that minority governments consider a smaller share of the overall tax burden than majority governments, one can anticipate that the common pool resource problem may be even worse in minority governments than in majority governments.

Yet there is a way that minority governments can avoid this fate, which in practice is a combination of the ideal types of delegation and commitment. The strong finance minister solution to the common pool problem is possible in minority situations at the cabinet level in one-party governments and in minority coalition governments where the coalition partners are close to one another ideologically. While a finance minister may coordinate the budget-making process within the government if there is one dominant party, as in delegation, this step is not enough. Centralization at the governmental stage can come to naught if the budget unravels in last-minute deals with the opposition that simply "buy" support from this or that party on key dimensions. As we shall see in chapter 7 Swedish Finance Minister Kjell-Olof Feldt learned this lesson in the late 1980s when it proved difficult for the minority Social Democratic government to pass its budget.

A more effective method is to include selected opposition parties in budget negotiations early in the process and, as in Denmark after 1982, reach agreement with them on all dimensions of the budget. This type of agreement, of course, resembles very much the agreements reached under commitment. The key difference is that the agreement is not negotiated with coalition partners. The government's negotiations with the opposition are instead functionally equivalent to the coalition negotiations necessary under multiparty majority governments. The government agrees to fiscal contracts with certain opposition parties. In Sweden in 2001, for example, the minority Social Democrats negotiated a spending agreement with the Left Party as well as with the Green Party across twenty-seven different spending categories that, together, constituted the entire budget.

Consistent with the data presented in Strøm 1990, one would expect parliamentary committees to be especially strong in countries with frequent minority governments. As in the commitment case, these committees would monitor the government's implementation of the budget to assure that it kept its part of the fiscal contract.

Factors in the Choice of Fiscal Governance

The underlying party system is the crucial factor for understanding why states adopt a given form of governance. The two features that matter are the level of competition in a political system and the ideological location of parties.

If there is low competition, there is little incentive for parties to centralize the budget process. Individual cabinet members have an *ex post* incentive to spend more than either the finance minister (under delegation) or the fiscal contract (under commitment) would prescribe. If there is no punishment for overspending, there is no reason to constrain it. The ultimate punishment comes from the electorate. A given political party must fear an electoral sanction if it mismanages the budget, and, by extension, the economy.

The location of parties in ideological space relies on a long tradition in political science that maps the positions of parties. If the parties can be grouped together in two distinct blocs, then any coalition that forms will have parties that have few ideological differences. If the parties are not grouped together, then coalitions will have parties that have wider ideological differences.

Two factors, in turn, affect the likelihood that parties will bunch up in two distinct ideological camps. The first is the party system's dimensionality. Lijphart (1999, 80–81) mapped the number, as well as the intensity, of different dimensions of the political system. A country such as Greece, for example, has a main left-right cleavage and a less dominant regime-support cleavage. In comparison, Finland has several social cleavages with high salience, the left-right cleavage on economic issues and an ethnic cleavage (Swedish-speaking minority). Additional cleavages exist along religious, urban-rural, and regime-support dimensions.

The second factor concerns the electoral system. As Neto and Cox (1997) persuasively argue, there is an interaction effect between the number of relevant political cleavages in society and the electoral system. Following Duverger (1954), they argue that a plurality electoral system leads to a two-party political system, regardless of the number of underlying political cleavages. At the other end of the spectrum, a true proportional representation system leads to more political parties in rough proportion to the number of political cleavages plus one (Taagapera and Grofman 1985; Lijphart 1999). A political system with two dominant cleavages, for example, should have, on average, three main political parties. There are also proportional representation systems that have institutional rules to limit the number of parties in a political system. In Sweden, for example, a party must win 4% of the vote to qualify for entry into parliament. This type of system would fall between the two polar positions mentioned above.[16]

This research is important for predicting the form the party system will take. If there is one cleavage, or if there is a plurality electoral system, there will be two main parties that face each other in elections. The governments that form under such a system will have cabinet ministers with few ideological differences. A political system with multiple relevant dimensions and a proportional representation system is likely to have several political parties that gain representation in parliament. No one party will be able to form a one-party majority government, and the coalitions that emerge will have parties with different ideological views. The case study chapters will consider this framework in more detail.

Why Forms of Governance Matter

Empirical evidence illustrates differences among the four models. The fifteen European Union states can be classified according to the different possible forms of fiscal governance for the time period 1973–2000 (table 2.1). One of the first things to notice is that the forms of fiscal governance do change. Eleven of the fifteen countries have changed their form of fiscal governance at least once during that period. The timing of changes is also relevant. Several states, including Austria, Denmark, Ireland, and the Netherlands,

---

16. Lijphart (1994) has created a threshold index, which represents the percentage of votes a party would need to win in order to gain parliamentary seats. The higher this index, the fewer parties receive representation.

Table 2.1. Categorization of states, 1973–2000

Country	Form of Fiscal Governance
Austria	Fiefdom 1973–86, Commitment 1987–94, Fiefdom 1995, Commitment 1996–97, Fiefdom 1998–99, Delegation (attempted) 2000
Belgium	Fiefdom 1973–92, Commitment 1993–2000
Denmark	Fiefdom 1973–81, Mixed 1982–2000
Finland	Commitment, strengthened mid-1990s
France	Delegation
Germany	Delegation
Greece	Fiefdom 1975–96, Delegation 1997–2000
Ireland	Fiefdom 1980–87, Mixed 1988–91, Commitment 1992–2000
Italy	Fiefdom 1980–95, Delegation 1996–2000
Luxembourg	Commitment
Netherlands	Fiefdom 1980–82, Commitment 1983–2000, strengthened 1994
Portugal	Fiefdom 1975–2000 (some elements of Delegation 1993–95)
Spain	Fiefdom 1977–93, Mixed 1994–2000, Delegation 2000
Sweden	Delegation 1973–75, Fiefdom 1976–96, Mixed 1997–2000
United Kingdom	Delegation

had moved away from fiefdom before the Maastricht treaty was agreed to in December 1991. The EMU process did not cause the domestic changes in the budget process in these states. At the same time, there are a number of states that either introduced a new form of fiscal governance or strengthened a preexisting one in the mid-1990s. One question the case study chapters will ask is whether the changes in the budget process are due to EMU or to other reasons. Finally, the table reveals that delegation states tend to be more stable. Three large countries—France, Germany, and the United Kingdom—have had delegation forms of fiscal governments for the entire period studied here.

Does the delegation-commitment-fiefdom theory accurately predict which states will choose which type of fiscal institution? There are three hypotheses to test:

H1. Uncompetitive party systems are likely to have fiefdom governments.
H2. Countries with unstable party systems that generate several different types of government (one-party majority, multiparty coalition, and minority) will have fiefdom governments.
H3. Governments made up of coalitions with few ideological differences are appropriate for delegation, while those with many ideological differences are appropriate for commitment.

The countries have varying forms of fiscal governance. To capture the competitiveness dimension, the first column in table 2.2 shows the amount of time the party that was in government the longest remained in government. Note that the theory predicts that fiefdom will exist where there is at least one party that is always in government.[17] A party that has no fear of being replaced has little incentive to stick to any type of fiscal contract or to unite behind a strong finance minister. Moreover, if one party has no intention of sticking to budget agreements, there is little reason for others to do so. The second column displays a Herfindahl index that measures the concentration of a given type of government system.[18] Finally, to predict what form of fiscal governance is adopted to centralize the budget process, which is a test of H3, one can consider the ideological distance among the parties in government. The prediction is that the greater the distance the more difficult it is for delegation to function in majority governments and the more likely it is that a commitment form of fiscal governance will be used. Moreover, under a mixed form of fiscal governance, one would expect the ideological distance to resemble the level of distance found in delegation states. The reason is that the finance minister centralizes the process within the government, but because of the government's minority status it must make agreements with one or more opposition parties. The finance minister's effectiveness would presumably decrease as the ideological distance increases.

The three hypotheses are largely confirmed (see table 2.2).[19] Countries that have had fiefdom forms of fiscal governance have, with one exception, either had one party dominate the government (as in Italy) or had instability in the type of government (Portugal). The one exception is Spain. Delegation and commitment states, in contrast, have had both more competitive party systems and little or no rotation in the type of government. The clear exception in these two groups is Austria. In fact, the lack of competition undermined the functioning of commitment in the mid-1990s (chapter 8). An examination of the veto-player data largely confirms H3. A t-test indicates that the average for the commitment states is significantly different from both the delegation states and the mixed states.

17. An alternative measure would be a Herfindahl index to measure party concentration (Skilling 2001; Wibbels 2003). Yet it is difficult to conceptualize how to use this measure in coalition governments. How should one code the variable if only some of the parties leave the government while others remain? Skilling (2001) treats coalitions in Belgium and Italy the same, where some parties rotate in and out, yet he does not follow the same practice for Finland. Wibbels (2003) looks at only what amount to two-party systems in the United States and does not confront this problem. The theoretically relevant measure here is simply the greatest proportion of time that any one party remains in power.

18. This is measured as $1-\Sigma g_i$, where g_i represents the proportion of time the country has a given type of government.

19. Veto-player data are based on Tsebelis's Web page as well as the coding rules in Tsebelis 2002. The value is an average of three indices that measure party positions on a left-right dimension that is then averaged with Laver and Hunt's (1992) score for the foreign policy position of the party. The indices used in the left-right average are from Castles and Mair 1984, Warwick 1994, and Laver and Hunt 1992. Note that the Portuguese president is not a relevant actor in fiscal policy decisions, so the figures used for this country differ somewhat from those reported in Tsebelis 2002.

Table 2.2.   Party dominance, rotation of type of government, and veto players

Country	Party Dominance	Rotation of Type of Government	What Is Missing	Veto Player
Fiefdom				
Austria, 1973–86	1	.26	Competition	.08
Belgium, 1973–92	1	.00	Competition	.28
Denmark, 1973–81	.78	.00	Competition	.04
Greece, 1977–96	.70	.30	Competition (after '81)	.13
Ireland, 1973–87	.80	.46	Stability	.15
Italy, 1973–94	1	.43	Both	.22
Netherlands, 1973–82	1	.00	Competition	.27
Portugal, 1975–2000	.72	.69	Stabililty	.14
Spain, 1977–93	.80	.00	Neither	0
Sweden, 1976–96	.67	.42	Stability	.07
Average	.85	.25		.14
Delegation				
France	.61	.20	Neither	.08
Germany	.93	.00	Neither (high number FDP)	.15
United Kingdom	.71	.12	Neither	0
Italy, 1996–2000	Not enough data	—	Not enough data	—
Average	.75	.11		.08
Commitment				
Austria. 1987–95	1	0	Competition	.29
Belgium, 1993–2000	Not enough data	—	Not enough data	—
Finland	.89	0	Neither	.50
Ireland, 1992–2000	.78	0	Neither	.26
Netherlands, 1982–2000	.79	0	Neither	.28
Average	.87	0		.14
Mixed				
Denmark, 1982–2000	.63	.20	Neither	.18
Spain, 1993–2000	.62	0	Neither	0
Sweden, 1996–2000	Not enough data	—	Not enough data	—
Average	.63	.10		.09

Source: Author calculations from Woldendorp et al. 1998, Tsebelis Web page (http://www.polsci.ucla.edu/tsebelis/), and Müller and Strøm 2000.

Note: Rounded to nearest year. Countries with fewer than two elections under a given form of fiscal governance are excluded. Finland data exclude the small Swedish Party.

Do differences in forms of fiscal governance have a tangible impact on policy outcomes? It would be most desirable to test the formal model directly, but "ideal" spending preferences cannot be measured in practice. What we can observe are strategies that individual parties and ministers pursue, but the strategies are not the same thing as preferences. A way around this difficulty is to consider a multiperiod game instead of a one-period game that allows government borrowing. As the formal models in Hallerberg and von Hagen 1999 and Velasco 1999, 2000 suggest, governments with serious common pool resource problems should run larger budget deficits, all else being equal. According to this book's framework, fiefdom governments should run larger budget deficits than the forms of government that address the common pool resource problem.

A regression analysis involving the current European Union states for the time period 1973–97, from the first oil shock through the year used to determine participants in EMU, shows the economic and political factors that influence government debt (table 2.3). The dependent variable is the change in the gross debt burden. This measure is used because it is more consistent over longer periods of time than changes in the budget balance. States did not necessarily use the same accounting standards to determine their budget balances, but there are few differences across countries in measuring gross debt. The analysis includes two groups of independent variables, explicitly political variables and economic variables that are included as controls. To test the effects of forms of fiscal governance, there are dummy variables for each form that address the common pool resource problem. Fiefdom exists when the dummy variables all equal zero. One might anticipate that a change in government would lead to paralysis (or drift) in budget policy, so the fourth political variable codes changes in government. The fifth political variable measures the partisanship of the government in a two-dimensional policy space as coded in Tsebelis 2002. Increases in the partisanship variable represent a move rightward. The sixth political variable is the ideological distance among party veto players in government. Tsebelis (2002) argues that countries with larger ideological distances among veto players are likely to have fixed fiscal policies while parties with smaller ideological distances are likely to have more flexible fiscal policies. While Roubini and Sachs (1989) and Grilli et al. (1991) do not use the term "veto player," their contention that coalition governments perform worse than one-party governments would imply that increases in the ideological distance among veto players should lead to increases in the gross debt burden over time. The data for veto players is the same as in Tsebelis 2002 with the exception of Portugal, which I recoded to take out the possible role of the Portuguese president.[20] For both variables, I standardized them so that they range from 0 to 1. A dummy variable for whether a country has a fixed exchange rate tests whether fixed exchange rates imposed discipline on European Union countries. The data for the variable are from Clark and Hallerberg 2000. I also included a set of economic variables that one would expect would affect the gross debt burden, including changes in economic growth and unemployment. For robustness reasons, I included a lagged dependent variable to address auto-correlation and I calculated panel-corrected standard errors (Beck and Katz 1995; Beck 2001). Year dummies were

---

20. Portugal's president has little role in the budget process and is not a true "veto player." I therefore adjusted the Tsebelis figures for years where the president's party was not included in the government.

Table 2.3.   Fiscal performance of European Union States, 1973–97

Independent Variable	Coefficient (Standard Error)
Political Variables	
Delegation	-1.33** (0.53)
Commitment	-1.63** (0.54)
Mixed	-1.89** (0.85)
Change in government	-0.25 (0.40)
Partisanship (Tsebelis two-dimensional coding)	0.08 (0.15)
Ideological distance, veto players (Tsebelis two-dimensional coding)	1.85 (0.31)
Fixed exchange rate	0.59 (0.48)
Control Variables	
Intercept	1.68** (0.71)
Change in debt$_{t-1}$	0.42** (0.07)
Debt$_{t-1}$	0.47* (0.07)
Growth	-0.57** (0.11)
Change in unemployment rate	0.40* (0.23)
N	304
R-Squared	0.60

Note: Dependent variable: change in the gross debt burden. * $p < .05$ ** $p < .01$

included (but not reported) to control for year-specific fiscal shocks, and the regressions results were computed using Stata 8.1.

The results show that the forms of fiscal governance have real effects on budget outcomes. The intercept term indicates that debt levels are expected to grow at around 1.7% of GDP per year in fiefdom countries. All the forms of fiscal governance variables are statistically significant in the expected direction. Introducing any of the forms of governance to address the common pool resource problem reduces the growth of the debt level in the fiefdom case. This means that swings in the economy in the form of output growth or changes in unemployment largely dictate increases or decreases in the debt burden.[21]

The remaining political variables have little impact on budget discipline. An increase in the veto player ideological distance has the correct sign but is not statistically significant. Partisanship seems to have no impact on the debt burden, while fixed exchange rates do not serve as a way to impose fiscal discipline.

21. The question is: Does a country expand the debt burden in years when it is experiencing average growth? One can test for the linear combination of a given form of fiscal governance with the intercept term and with the average level of growth times the coefficient of growth to determine expected changes in the debt burden given an average growth year. If year dummies are included, one is technically testing for the effects of fiefdom in the excluded year (1980 in the reported results), so it is necessary to exclude the year dummies. With standard errors reported in parentheses, the expected growth of the debt burden in an average growth year under fiefdom is statistically significant at 1.68 (0.60), while there is no expected growth in the debt burden under average growth under any of the three forms of fiscal governance meant to address the common pool resource problem (coefficients of 0.28 (0.47) for delegation, 0.13 (0.70) for commitment, and -0.13 (1.00) for mixed).

✧

The case study chapters that follow are organized by type of party system, the crucial variable in determining the form of fiscal governance a country will adopt. Four countries have systems either where one party consistently wins a majority of seats (Greece, United Kingdom) or where groups of parties with minor ideological differences run in elections as blocs (France, Germany). From them one would expect delegation forms of fiscal governance. Four countries (Belgium, Finland, Luxembourg, and the Netherlands) have regular majority coalition governments where partners routinely run against each other, and commitment would be expected to develop in these countries.[22] Denmark and Sweden have minority governments, and they should be expected to have mixed forms. Austria, Ireland, Portugal, and Spain do not have stable party systems that yield one form of government (one-party/coalition, minority/majority). Their forms of fiscal governance, while often taking root, are not as well institutionalized as in countries with more stable party systems. Finally, Italy is a wonderful test case. It changed its electoral system in 1994, which has had notable effects on the country's party system. The predicted type of fiscal governance that would be appropriate for Italy shifted from commitment to delegation.

The competitiveness of the party system is crucial—states remain stuck with fiefdom governments when they have uncompetitive elections. Moreover, the EMU framework can be interpreted as a set of rules as well as a set of requirements to monitor budgetary performance. Economic and Monetary Union is consistent with a rules-based form of fiscal governance, and it has enhanced the fiscal performance of commitment states such as Belgium, Finland, and the Netherlands. It is not, however, consistent with a discretion-based form of fiscal governance. It is no surprise that delegation states such as France, Germany, and (today) Italy are having difficulties abiding by the provisions of the Stability and Growth Pact in 2002–2004, years that are beyond the focus of this study.

22. Because of data limitations for Luxembourg, however, I do not consider Luxembourg in this chapter.

3

European Union Fiscal Policy Coordination and Domestic Budget Making

Since the end of the Bretton Woods system in 1973 macroeconomic policy coordination among industrial countries has been rare and, when it has existed, short-lived. Two clear cases of policy coordination emerged after the Economic Summit in Bonn in 1978 and the Plaza-Louvre efforts in the mid-1980s. The agreements reached at these G-7 economic summits had some success in managing exchange rates, but they soon collapsed because governments did not match domestic policy adjustments to their international agreements (Willett 1999a).

As difficult as international coordination of monetary policy has been, the coordination of fiscal policies has been even more difficult. Germany and Japan did both pledge at the Bonn summit to initiate fiscal expansions, but there has been no explicit agreement to coordinate fiscal policies over any length of time at the G-7 level. Given the clear externalities of fiscal policy on monetary policy (and vice versa) it could be argued that one should accompany the other. Willett (1999a) provides a seemingly convincing political economy explanation for the lack of coordination: although few domestic actors are involved in the formation of monetary policy (generally a central bank and sometimes the treasury or finance minister), making it relatively easy to adjust policy and to adjust it quickly, fiscal policy requires the approval of a legislature and is subject to more domestic pressure and, as a result, is not easily or quickly adapted to international agreements. He therefore predicts that it will be easier for countries to coordinate their monetary policies than their fiscal policies.

The behavior of European Union countries in the past decade would seem to challenge the notion that fiscal policies cannot be effectively coordinated. In 1991, the year that twelve member states signed the Treaty of Maastricht, fiscal policies differed significantly (see fig. 1.1). The range of deficit positions has decreased notably since then, and the median position in the

European Union moved from below –3% in 1992 to exact budget balance in 2000. Even in 2002, when the economy notably declined, most European Union countries maintained budgets that were at least in balance, if not in surplus. Even the big countries that have received the most press in 2003 about their budget positions are mostly better off than they were a decade before. The French budget balance of –3.1% of GDP in 2002 is almost half the –5.5% of 1993, while Italy's –2.3% in 2002 is a clear improvement over the –10.3% of GDP in 1993. The glaring exception is Germany, where the deficit was higher in 2002 than in 1992 (3.6% versus 3.1% of GDP) (European Commission 2003).

To what extent can one attribute the undeniable harmonization of budgetary positions to explicit fiscal policy coordination at the European Union level? One thing that coordination has going for it within the European Union—which is missing at the G-7 level—is an elaborate supranational institutional framework to evaluate and, potentially, coordinate member state macroeconomic policies. A directorate general of the European Commission has, under various names, been responsible for monitoring economic policy within the Union for decades. Within the Council of Ministers two committees, the Economic Policy Committee and the Monetary Committee, were forums for ministries of finance and/or the economy to discuss macroeconomic issues at the subcabinet level among themselves, members of the commission, and, more recently, with representatives from the European Central Bank. At the same time, the Council of Economic and Finance Ministers (ECOFIN) meetings have brought cabinet-level ministers together. The European Monetary Institute (EMI) and its successor, the European Central Bank (ECB), created a European Union–level bureaucracy that works explicitly on European macroeconomic policy. Finally, Eurostat collects statistics and produces harmonized measures that could be used to compare the performance of member states. Although all of the institutions but the EMI/ECB existed before Maastricht, each was either created (EMI/ECB) or given expanded power under successive treaties (Maastricht and Amsterdam) and European Council agreements to assist in the coordination of member state fiscal policies.

To answer the question of "why fiscal policy harmonization" requires an examination both of the supranational record at the European Union level and the national record at the member state level. The rest of this book deals with the member state level. This chapter evaluates the role of EU institutions in the coordination of national fiscal policies. It argues that direct fiscal policy coordination at the EU level was, and remains, limited in its direct effect. Ignoring for the moment the issue of credibility, the only parts of the overall European Union–level framework with true punishment mechanisms for "defections" from efforts at coordination were the requirements that states not have "excessive deficits" if they were to become members of

EMU, and that, once they joined, they not run "excessive deficits" after the beginning of Stage Three of Economic and Monetary Union. Yet it is also clear that European Union institutions have become more involved in monitoring member state budget policies since the beginning of Stage Three of EMU and in issuing country-specific recommendations for corrections.

Theoretical Background: Why Fiscal Policy Coordination?

Before evaluating whether there has been fiscal policy coordination it is useful to consider why one would expect it to exist in the first place and why the Union would want it. The level of fiscal policy coordination needed at the European Union level is not at all self-evident. One only has to consider the recommendation of the Werner Report (1970) that the European Community take control of the essential features of national budget policy, such as the size of budget deficits, the financing of budgets, and how they are spent to grasp the range of possible options there were for guaranteeing an effective monetary policy under a common currency—from no coordination at all to centralization of budget decisions in Brussels (Gros and Thygesen 1998).

The overall theme has not changed; the usual explanation European Union officials provide for why there should be some fiscal policy coordination concerns the effective management of monetary policy within Economic and Monetary Union. The main concern is with how domestic decisions can have inflationary consequences. As a 1997 European Council resolution put it, "To the extent that national economic developments have an impact on inflation prospects in the euro-area, they will influence monetary conditions in that area. It is for this basic reason that the move to a single currency will require closer Community surveillance and coordination of economic policies among euro-area Member States" (December 13, 1997, resolution of the European Council on economic policy coordination in Stage Three of EMU and on Treaty Articles 109 and 109b of the EC Treaty). Moreover, uncoordinated fiscal policies can make it difficult to achieve a proper policy mix under a common currency. Efforts to increase demand in one state have effects in other states as well. Domestic fiscal expansions to stabilize budgetary positions can be potentially counterproductive. Finally, uncoordinated policy can make it more difficult for the European Central Bank to provide a consistent monetary policy.

The reason for the original fiscal criteria in the Maastricht treaty was, primarily, fear of insolvency. The concern was that a country would rely too much on the one policy tool available to governments after the creation of a common currency. Additional externalities concern the effects of large budget deficits. Higher levels of borrowing may raise interest rates and put pressure on the interest rates of other EU countries. Moreover, the inevitable economic slowdown from higher rates would lead to lower exports for the other EU countries and lower growth throughout the euro-zone. There is some question whether higher interest rates would spread (Kenen 1995, 92), but nevertheless the argument fits the general concern that economies are more interconnected in a monetary union.

There are, however, concerns that stabilization policies and restrictions on the ability of states to run deficits are incompatible. According to some, it is precisely because fiscal policy is the one remaining tool available to policy makers that restrictions on deficits should be loose or nonexistent (Kenen 1995). This issue is far from clear, however. Leeftink (2000) argues that the deficit restrictions embodied in the Stability and Growth Pact increase the effectiveness of fiscal policy as a stabilization device. In his empirical analysis, EU countries with lower levels of debt are more successful at stabilizing their economies. By requiring that debt burdens be low or that they move lower, the Stability and Growth Pact increases the ability of countries to smooth out economic shocks (see also Buti and Onega 1998; Buti 2000). In the view of these scholars, restrictions on deficits are therefore a requirement rather than a hindrance to effective stabilization policy.

It is useful to compare the official reasons for policy coordination with reasons provided in the economics literature for economic policy coordination more generally. Willett (1999a, 222–23), in his summary of the literature on international policy coordination, describes four reasons why coordination may be beneficial:

(1) avoidance of beggar-thy-neighbor policies; (2) the exchange of information and analysis to improve national policy making (often termed "cooperation"); (3) the actual mutual adjustment of national policies to promote balance of payments adjustment and exchange rate and macroeconomic stability (coordination per se); and (4) the promotion of external discipline to help induce countries to adopt more prudent macroeconomic policies.

Clearly not all of these goals fit fiscal policy coordination in the European Union—there are no concerns for beggar-thy-neighbor devaluations or the need to adjust exchange rate policies to promote balance of payments adjustments. Yet, the list provides some insights that are often overlooked, such as the role of the exchange of information and analysis and the use of external discipline to adopt more prudent domestic policies. The following list rephrases these four reasons to fit fiscal policy coordination instead of macroeconomic policy coordination more generally:

1. Avoid moral hazard problems
2. Exchange information and analysis to improve policy making

3. Mutually adjust national fiscal policies to improve macroeconomic stability
4. Promote fiscal discipline to induce countries to adopt more prudent macroeconomic policies

Instead of beggar-thy-neighbor policies for point 1, the more appropriate concern within a monetary union especially is moral hazard. Also, under point 3 the focus is explicitly on the adjustment of fiscal policy to promote macroeconomic stability.

The exact level of fiscal coordination that the European Union wants within the euro-zone is still not decided. The European Commission has been pushing for tighter coordination than what is formally prescribed in the treaties. Member states are naturally concerned because fiscal policy is the one remaining tool at their disposal, and they are hesitant to give it up. The commission's response, as a member of commission president Romano Prodi's staff puts it, is that "if you do not give us your tool, you lose it"; if states do not coordinate, their efforts to manage their own economies will cancel out (author interviews in Brussels, April 2001).

Treaties and Institutions

Before discussing the future shape of fiscal policy coordination, however, we need to understand the history of coordination within the European Union. Maastricht represented a potential sea change in the role of the European Union in the fiscal affairs of member states. Yet many of the key institutions were already in place, even if they did not have the competencies they would have after Maastricht.

The European Commission had been involved at some level in the coordination of economic policy for decades, either writing reports on what coordination should exist or, more actively, monitoring the behavior of states. Since 1960 there had been country-specific desks at the commission with staff who monitored member state economic conditions. After the Werner Report, their responsibilities were revised.

The Council of Economic and Finance Ministers had also met for decades. It was, and is, the forum where member state ministers meet to resolve remaining conflicts that have not been sorted out below it, as well as to approve legislation and other measures that fall under its responsibility.

Under ECOFIN was the Monetary Committee. It too was first established at the beginning of the 1960s, and its role as an advisory committee to the council was spelled out in Article 105 of the Treaty of Rome. It had two members from each member state, with one from the country's central bank and one from either a ministry of finance or ministry of the economy. Verdun (2000) notes that, unlike the Committee of Permanent Representatives

(COREPER), the Monetary Committee was to be composed of "independent experts" from these countries, not representatives of member states. The Monetary Committee helped to prepare the Council of Economic and Finance Ministers, as well as COREPER.

Although there was, of course, no European Central Bank before Maastricht, there was a general forum for the bankers from the individual states to meet, the Committee of Governors of Central Banks (CGCB). This committee was established in 1964. The ECOFIN called for its creation so that there would be a committee similar to the Monetary Committee where central bankers could meet. The Community's central bank governors composed the committee (Verdun 2000). It generally did not have a formal voice on fiscal policy.

The Economic Policy Committee was established in 1974 after the merging of the Short-term Economic Committee, the Budgetary Committee, and the Medium-term Planning Committee. Each member state could send up to four members. In the 1970s it was more involved in budgetary policy than was the Monetary Committee. There was a gradual, but persistent, shift of fiscal policy responsibilities from this committee to the Monetary Committee in the 1980s.

The Treaty of Maastricht changed the fiscal policy roles of all these institutions except the Economic Policy Committee. To summarize briefly the fiscal requirements embodied in the treaty, states were required to have general government deficits at or below 3% of GDP and general government debts at or below 60% of GDP. Yet there were two clear reservations to this, for states that had a "ratio [that] has declined substantially and continuously and reached a level that comes close to the reference value" and states that had high ratios that were "only exceptional and temporary" (Article 104(2a)).[1] These qualifications left room for interpretation beyond the simple "3% and 60%" so often cited in the press. The European Commission would be responsible for monitoring the budgetary positions of member states and be expected to report on member states that were running "excessive deficits." The recommendations of the European Commission would then go to the Monetary Committee for its comments. After hearing the recommendation of the commission and the advice of the Monetary Committee, the council (ECOFIN) would, by qualified majority, decide whether an "excessive deficit" existed in a given country. Once a country had this status it would take commission action to abrogate its status.

The Treaty of Maastricht also included provisions concerning economic coordination that have become more important after the start of Stage Three of EMU. The treaty noted that "Member states shall regard their economic policies as a matter of common concern and coordinate them in the

---

1. All article numbers cited in the text, unless they are part of an official title, are from the latest version of the treaties.

Council" (Article 99 (1)). A tool for economic coordination, the Broad Economic Policy Guidelines (BEPG), would be passed each year. The commission would draft a recommendation on the contents of the BEPG and give it to ECOFIN, which would then draft a proposal with qualified majority approval for the European Council (the heads of government and, for France, state). Once the council adopts its version of the BEPG by qualified majority, the treaty states that it must inform the European Parliament.

Yet consideration of the BEPG does not end here. ECOFIN, with the assistance of commission reports, is required to monitor the member states to determine whether their economic policies are in line with the BEPG. If ECOFIN decides that a member state's policies "prove to be not consistent with the broad economic guidelines referred to in Paragraph 2 or that they risk jeopardizing the proper functioning of economic and monetary union, the Council may . . . make the necessary recommendations to the Member State concerned" (Article 99(4)). By a qualified majority and based on a proposal from the commission, the council may also choose to make its recommendation to a member state public. Since 2000, the council also has provided a regular mechanism to check compliance through the annual Implementation Report, which is presented shortly before the BEPGs are passed (European Commission 2002).

Maastricht also provided for the establishment of the European Central Bank. It integrated the Committee of Governors of Central Banks into the European Monetary Institute on January 1, 1994. Although the EMI did not have a formal role in fiscal policy making, it and its successor institution, the European Central Bank, do monitor policy developments.

Finally, there is a statement in the treaty that some have interpreted as a "no bailout clause." Article 103 explicitly states that neither the Community nor the member states are liable for the commitments of other governments. Yet there is some concern that this clause is only as credible as the former pledge that the German federal government would not bail out its *Länder* (state governments). As Rodden (2000) has shown, both Bremen and the Saarland, which are financially weak Länder, have taken advantage of the incentives of the German system to receive clear bailouts.

In sum, Maastricht provided two separate procedures for European Union–level institutions to monitor the behavior of states. The excessive-deficit procedure existed to determine whether states had deficits beyond the reference values. Although some interpretation of the reference values in the treaties was required, at least the reference values were clear. There was also a clear punishment for states that were found to have an excessive deficit, which was exclusion from Stage Three of EMU. The BEPG, on the other hand, were more vague. Their contents could change from year to year. Moreover, the ultimate explicit punishment was that a council recommendation to a member state be made public.

Evolution between Maastricht and Amsterdam

There was a general feeling after the Treaty of Maastricht was signed that the progression to the various stages would be a smooth one. This illusion, however, was quickly shattered by two events. The first was the European Monetary System crisis in September 1992 when the British pound and the Italian lira fell out of the exchange rate mechanism, while the Portuguese escudo and Spanish peseta were forced to realign. The second event was a recession that had ominous effects on the budget balances of member states. Because the EMS crisis is the subject of many excellent histories, as well as analyses, this section deals primarily with the second event. Yet before continuing it is worth noting that the two events were not wholly unrelated. The Italian and Spanish currencies came under pressure in part because of what was perceived to be runaway public finances. My interviews of government officials in Madrid and Rome indicate that the determination to get deficits under control in the two countries in the early 1990s was framed almost exclusively in terms of a response to the EMS crisis rather than any concern about Maastricht criteria.[2]

The 1992–93 recession's effects on the member states' budget balances was perhaps to be expected, but the result was that all countries except Ireland and Luxembourg had deficits above 3% in 1993. This was a change from the Maastricht year of 1991 when only the Mediterranean countries, Belgium, and Portugal had deficits above 3%. In this climate, the European Union moved to Stage Two of EMU. There were several practical details that were missing in Maastricht that were decided on at the beginning of Stage Two. At the end of 1993 the Council of the European Union passed regulations on the reporting requirements of member states (Official Journal L332, Dec. 31, 1993, pp. 7–9). From the beginning of 1994 onward, the states were required to report twice a year to the European Commission both their planned and their actual budget deficits and levels of government debt. They were also expected to report investment expenditure, expenditure on interest payments, and gross domestic product figures. States were asked to submit programs that explained how they planned to reach their medium-term objectives.

The European Union first initiated its excessive deficit procedures after the beginning of Stage Two. In spring 1994, the commission decided that ten of the twelve members had excessive deficits, with Luxembourg and Ireland the exceptions. The procedure was for the commission's recommendation to be discussed in the Monetary Committee and then the council would vote on the commission's recommendation after receiving the Monetary Committee's advice. There was no debate about Luxembourg in the council, but the decision on Ireland was not what the Germans had wanted because

2. The interviews were conducted in both capitals in December 2000.

of the size of Ireland's debt, which was clearly well above 60% of GDP. Yet the commission proposed to the council that Ireland met the criteria because the Irish debt ratio was moving in the right direction, and the council unanimously agreed (author interviews in Brussels, April 2001). This set an important precedent. From thenceforth the deficit level was the crucial marker, not debt. This made it easier for Belgium and Italy to later qualify with debt ratios well in excess of 60%.

The Maastricht treaty also stated that a determination should be made in 1996 as to whether a majority of states were ready for Stage Three of EMU. The European Commission's report stated that a majority of states were not ready, and indeed most continued to receive a judgment of having an "excessive deficit."

The story of March–May 1998 is by now a familiar one. The European Commission decided to rescind the "excessive deficit" status of all the states that found themselves in that position except for Greece.[3] The commission recommended that eleven of the fifteen member states join Stage Three of EMU in March, and at the beginning of May the European Council agreed. Greece joined on January 1, 2001, to become the twelfth member.

The Maastricht Treaty and Fiscal Coordination

I use the four possible gains from economic coordination from Willett (1999a) to evaluate the provisions and the practice under Maastricht. Point 1, which considers the avoidance of moral hazard problems, is not relevant until after Stage Three of EMU because running large budget deficits only meant exclusion from EMU and would not hurt the group as a whole. Yet the so-called no bailout clause that appears in the treaty was an attempt to allay concerns about solvency issues. It is also clear that the Maastricht framework did not lead to overt coordination of fiscal policy (point 3), or economic policy more generally. As one observer noted when expressing frustration at the prospects of European Union countries attacking low growth and high unemployment within the Union, "The [Maastricht] Treaty creates no institutional capacity for collective action in economic policy that might enable the member states participating in EMU to redress those problems, and there seems to be little desire in the EU as a whole to create that institutional capacity" (Cameron 1997, 15).

Yet the Maastricht treaty did result in some success along the lines of points 2 and 4. The exchange of information was especially important for the harmonization of statistical standards, and more important than most observers

3. Technically, Sweden also did not qualify because it did not make its central bank independent and because it had not participated in the Exchange Rate Mechanism (ERM). Denmark and the United Kingdom had opt-outs.

suspected. Before the treaty only the United Kingdom and the Scandinavian countries regularly reported data in a format close to the general government figures known as the "Maastricht definitions." The Italian case is illustrative of problems other states faced. Italy maintained its statistics in terms of "the public sector," which could not be changed effortlessly into general government terms. After the EMS crisis the Italian government requested a loan from the European Union. The Union initially demanded that Italy commit to deficit targets in general government terms as a condition of the loan. The Italian response, however, was that it was technically impossible at the time to convert the statistics. As a consequence, it could not commit to targets when it was not possible to provide the statistics to verify the meeting of the targets. The Union then backed off from the deficit requirement (author interviews, Brussels, April 2001). Work with Eurostat, however, led to the production of general government statistics in Italy by 1996. Indeed, one member of the Italian treasury told me that the harmonization of statistics was the most important thing the European Union did to help Italy qualify for EMU. It made it easier for the government to understand where money was being spent and what could be, and should be, cut (author interview, Rome, December 2000).

With respect to point 4, an evaluation of how the Maastricht treaty made it easier for countries to impose fiscal discipline on themselves cannot be answered at length here. Yet it seems clear that identifying states with excessive deficits made it easier for domestic reformers to argue that fundamental changes were needed. The 3% deficit target was especially useful for states that relied on the commitment to fiscal contracts type of governance (see Hallerberg and von Hagen 1999; Hallerberg, Strauch, and von Hagen 2001). States such as Belgium, Finland, and the Netherlands write their fiscal policy targets into coalition agreements. The Maastricht treaty helped set the parameters of these fiscal contracts and provided some monitoring through the commission so that violations of the contract are clear to coalition partners. Indeed, von Hagen, Hughes-Hallett, and Strauch (2001) found that contract states were more effective in reducing their debt burdens in the 1990s than delegation states, where governments relied on a strong finance minister to maintain fiscal discipline.

Amsterdam and the Stability and Growth Pact

The Treaty of Maastricht did not have clear provisions for how "excessive deficits" would be avoided once Stage Three of EMU began. At the 1995 Madrid European Council there was an agreement to have some sort of "stability pact." The German finance minister, Theo Waigel, is the person most identified with the pact. He originally pushed for automatic sanctions on countries that ran excessive deficits.[4] Yet other (mostly northern European) states were also concerned about the moral hazard risk and pushed for some sort of pact as well. The French emphasized the importance of taking action to increase employment at the European Union level, and what emerged from the negotiations became known as the Stability and Growth Pact.

The most noteworthy, and most controversial, part of the pact was its punishment mechanism. If ECOFIN, acting on a recommendation from the commission, and after receiving the advice of the Economic and Financial Committee (the renamed and strengthened Monetary Committee as of 1999) by qualified majority, decides that a member state in EMU has an excessive deficit and is not making necessary corrections, it can require the state to make a deposit in a noninterest-bearing account of up to 0.5% of its GDP.[5] If ECOFIN decides that the deficit has not been corrected, the deposit can become a fine. Exceptions do, however, exist—a deficit can go over 3% and not be judged "excessive" if the deficit is considered "exceptional." A decline in economic growth of 2% or more makes this automatic; for a decline of between 0.75 and 2% ECOFIN will make a decision; if growth is more than $(-)0.75\%$ then a state cannot claim exceptional circumstances.

When the treaty was first signed, there was a debate in both the policy and academic communities about whether the threat to fine states was credible, and whether states would even agree to make an initial deposit in the first place (Buti and Ongena 1998; DeGrauwe 1997; Eichengreen and Wyplosz 1997; Willett 1999b). Based on events between 2001 and 2003, it is clear that the sanctions under the Stability and Growth Pact are by no means automatic when a country's deficit exceeds 3%. Portugal's deficit in 2001 was over 4%, while France and Germany both had deficits above 3% of GDP in 2002. Portugal did successfully get its deficit below 3% again in 2002, and there was hope in Paris and Berlin and in Brussels as well that an economic recovery in these two large states would make the issue go away. As of this writing, both countries are expected to have similar deficits in 2003 and 2004, and whether this behavior will lead to sanctions on the two largest economies in the eurozone is open to question. What is undisputable is that the "stick," however brittle, is certainly a first in the postwar history of fiscal policy coordination. It is also a blunt device—it is only usable if a state's deficit exceeds 3%. It cannot be used to coax a state to take a different course of action so that it will not break the excessive deficit barrier.

There was also general dissatisfaction (especially at the commission) with the submittal of convergence programs and more generally with the paucity

---

4. See Buti, Franco, and Ongena 1998 for a comparison of Waigel's original proposal and the Stability and Growth Pact.

5. The amount of the deposit depends on how much the deficit is above 3% of GDP. There is a fixed amount of 0.2% plus 0.1% for every 1% of deficit over 3%. The maximum deposit is therefore reached when a country has a deficit of 6%.

of information gathered from the member states. The member states were required from 1994 on to submit certain economic figures. A justification of those figures through convergence programs, while encouraged, was not required, however. There were also only loose guidelines as to what should be included in convergence programs. There was a general feeling that the countries that took seriously the opportunity to submit convergence programs, and that revised them frequently, were the countries that were likely to meet the Maastricht criteria in any event (author interviews at the European Commission, July 1999).

In July 1997 the European Council passed a regulation that established the procedures for monitoring the fiscal behavior of member states. All states would be required to submit programs to the European Commission on a yearly basis beginning before March 1999, with EMU participants to submit "stability programmes" and nonparticipants to submit "convergence programmes." The programs were required to provide both medium-term objectives for reaching the goal of deficits "close to balance or in surplus" and to explain what policy measures the state would take to reach those goals. Budget forecasts were to cover at least three years into the future. The programs were also supposed to provide an analysis of how changes in the underlying economic assumptions would affect deficits and debt levels in future years. Finally, member states were required to make their programs public (Council Regulation (EC) No 1466/97 of July 7, 1997). While the titles of the two types of programs differed, the reporting requirements were the same.

These regulations again changed the role of the European Union–level institutions. Both the European Commission and the Economic and Financial Committee are required to produce assessments of the programs. ECOFIN's assessment must be based on "whether the medium-term budget objective in the stability programme provides for a safety margin to ensure the avoidance of an excessive deficit, whether the economic assumptions on which the programme is based are realistic and whether the measures being taken and/or proposed are sufficient to achieve the targeted adjustment path towards the medium-term budgetary objective" (Article 5; virtually identical text that covers convergence programs appears under Article 9). The council also should evaluate whether the programs "facilitate the closer coordination of economic policies and whether the economic policies of the Member State concerned are consistent with the broad economic policy guidelines" (Article 5). The council, after considering the recommendation of the commission and after consulting with the Economic and Financial Committee, issues an opinion on each program.

The regulation also establishes procedures for the commission, the Economic and Financial Committee, and ECOFIN to monitor member state execution of their programs. If the council finds a problem, it can make a recommendation to a member state for a correction of its policy. If it then judges that the problem remains, the council makes a recommendation to the member state for corrective action based on Article 99(4) of the Treaty on European Union. The council can also decide to make its recommendation public, which is meant "to increase pressure" on the member state to comply (European Commission 1999, 3). What is of note here is the integration of the submittal of stability or convergence reports with the Broad Economic Policy Guidelines. The BEPG provisions in the treaty allow some action to be taken so long as the budget position is not consistent with them. This means that the restrictions are tighter than those mentioned explicitly in the Stability and Growth Pact, which provides for action only if a member state is in an "excessive deficit."

The explicit mandate of the BEPG was also expanded through a council regulation passed six months after the Stability and Growth Pact (Resolution of the European Council of December 13, 1997, on economic policy coordination in Stage Three of EMU and on Treaty Articles 109 and 109b of the EC Treaty). The articles of the resolution emphasize that the BEPG should play an enhanced role after the beginning of Stage Three. Sensitive to political concerns about high unemployment, the resolution states that the BEPG "should provide more concrete and country-specific guidelines and focus more on measures to improve Member States' growth potential, thus increasing employment" (Article 4). The scope of the BEPG should include such fields as labor markets, education, and taxation; indeed, in theory any policy that is deemed to affect potential economic growth. Structural reforms would thenceforth explicitly be on ECOFIN's agenda.

The resolution also attempted to strengthen the monitoring role of ECOFIN. The emphasis would be on early warning of potential problems in all fields, not only fiscal policy. The resolution encouraged ECOFIN to meet "in restricted sessions (Minister plus one)" in order to "stimulate an open and frank debate" (Article 5).[6]

In sum, the BEPG were no longer to be just bland documents with general recommendations on economic policy that member states should consider. Although the general recommendations would remain, each BEPG would include country-specific recommendations, and ECOFIN would be expected to monitor whether member states were adhering to the recommendations. The council would not do this work alone, however. In addition to commission reports the council has two institutions to assist it, the Economic and Financial Committee and the Economic Policy Committee.

The Economic and Financial Committee is at its core simply the renamed Monetary Committee. The Maastricht treaty called for the committee's transformation at the beginning of Stage Three, and indeed an article in the treaty (Article 114) covers its responsibilities. The Economic and Financial

6. The expansion of the role of the BEPG was first agreed to at the Cardiff European Council Meeting in June 1998.

Committee's primary duty is to assist ECOFIN in its work, which was the same job the Monetary Committee had before Stage Three. Yet there has been a change in the importance of the committee within the council. Although the internal institutional battles do not seem to be completely done, the Economic and Financial Committee has replaced COREPER as the body that does the background work for ECOFIN on most short-term economic issues. Traditionally, COREPER has set the agenda for council meetings and done the behind-the-scenes preparation work for ministerial meetings.

To understand the significance of this change, one should keep in mind who appoints the members of COREPER and the Economic and Financial Committee. COREPER members are ambassadors from member states, that is, representatives from foreign ministries. Member states, the European Commission, and the European Central Bank each appoint two members to the Economic and Financial Committee. A member state generally appoints one person from its finance ministry and one from its central bank. Thus at the EU level there is a shift in importance from the foreign ministries to the finance ministries. Moreover, the members are more explicitly representatives of their home countries. Verdun (2000) notes that the Monetary Committee's members were supposed to be "independent experts." The new statutes of the Economic and Financial Committee remove the stipulation that members be independent. They state merely that "Members of the Committee and alternates shall be guided, in the performance of their duties, by the general interests of the Community" (Article 3, Statutes of the Economic and Financial Committee, Official Journal L 005, Jan. 9, 1999, p. 71).[7]

In practice, the Economic and Financial Committee remains the mysterious body that Verdun (2000) described in her analysis of the Monetary Committee. There is no Web page for the committee to disseminate information to the public and no press releases that explain the recommendations the committee makes to ECOFIN. This contrasts with the second committee that works with the council on the BEPG, the Economic Policy Committee. The Economic Policy Committee evaluates the BEPG according to longer-term economic priorities and is responsible for structural issues. Its coverage includes fiscal policy issues if they impact structural reforms—for example, the Economic Policy Committee will address any taxes that have an impact on labor markets. The committee also deals with the long-term consequences of ageing populations on employment and government spending, and works on long-term budget issues such as the financing of pensions. Unlike the Economic and Financial Committee, the Economic Policy Committee is more

---

7. Similarly, Article 2 of 98/743/EC, the council decision of December 21, 1998, on the composition of the Economic and Financial Committee, notes only that "the members of the Committee and its alternates shall be selected from among experts possessing outstanding competence in the economic and financial field." There is no mention that these experts should be "independent."

transparent. It maintains an active Web page, and some of its reports are available to the public.

There is a final institution that deserves discussion, namely the Euro Group. The Conclusion from the Luxembourg council meeting in 1997 provided the initial legal basis for the Group when it stated that "the Ministers of the States participating in the euro area may meet informally among themselves to discuss issues connected with their shared specific responsibilities for the single currency. The Commission, and the European Central Bank when appropriate, will be invited to take part in the meetings" (http://europa. eu.int/council/off/conclu/dec97.htm#EMU). Several parts of the design of the Group reinforce its "informal" nature. Although it is composed of the economic and finance ministers of the euro-zone, it is much smaller than ECOFIN. Each state sends only two persons (the minister and an additional staff person). The European Commission and the European Central Bank, usually represented by the bank's president, are also included. When they meet, the number of people in the room does not exceed twenty-seven. There is no secretariat for this group, and the staff members from the country that has the presidency at the time are responsible for any preparation. The discussions focus on matters that are of common concern to countries that circulate the euro. Peer pressure is sometimes brought to bear on a finance minister from a country that the others think is not performing as it should. The discussions are secret and are expected to remain secret, although there have sometimes been press conferences after meetings where the country that had the presidency at that time presented comments in general terms. There is also an international dimension to the Euro Group. At G-7 meetings, the country with the presidency of the euro-zone represents the euro-zone and participates (with the president of the European Central Bank) in meetings that discuss either the world economy or exchange rate policy.

Although the high level of secrecy about the content of discussions makes it difficult to ascertain what exactly the Euro Group has done since its creation, there are several issues that have arisen since the Group's creation. First, there is some frustration among non-euro-zone members that more policy is made in the Euro Group than should be made, and that this freezes out the three countries—Sweden, Denmark, and the United Kingdom—that have chosen not to join the common currency. The Swedish government response was to hold a referendum, which was unsuccessful, on euro membership with the hope of becoming one of the "insiders," while the British position has been to restrict the policy-making abilities of the Euro Group where possible (author interview, Swedish finance ministry, June 2001; author interview, United Kingdom treasury, January 2003). Second, some argue that the role of the Euro Group should be formalized. Institutionally, annex 2 of the European Convention's draft constitution, volume 2, proposes that ministers from euro-zone countries elect a president of the Euro Group for a two-and-a-half year term. Press reports characterized this position as the "Eurozone's Finance Minister" (*Financial Times,* May 26, 2003). Yet among current members of the Euro Group there is clearly a concern that any formalization of its organization and its responsibilities may reduce its effectiveness, especially if "formalization" means the end of secret discussions. The Euro Group is the only setting where finance ministers discuss issues directly with the president of the European Central Bank, and, while there is no *ex ante* coordination between the bank and the ministers, there is a sense among participants that these meetings are useful. There is also a fear that ministers would be reluctant to be frank with fellow participants if they thought their comments would appear publicly. As an anonymous Euro Group finance ministry official put it, "Simply formalizing the group does not solve anything; on the contrary, it would be more difficult for the ministers to have open and frank debates, and the ECB certainly would shy away from the discussions if it feared that confidentiality would be endangered" (author interview, April 2003).

Evaluation: Stage Three and the Irish Reprimand

The Stability and Growth Pact, together with the agreements at the Cardiff European Council in June 1998, increased the role of European Union–level institutions in fiscal coordination. How much change in fiscal coordination occurred?

Returning to the modified list of Willett's (1999a) summary of the goals of fiscal policy coordination, it is clear that the Stability and Growth Pact attempted to address the fears of moral hazard (point 1) once Stage Three began. The punishment mechanism is meant to increase the costs of states running deficits over 3% of GDP. Moreover, the expectation that states will maintain balances that are "close to balance or in surplus" is supposed to provide a safety margin, so that the 3% deficit level is not tripped immediately even during economic downturns. All these measures reinforce the "no bailout clause" in the Maastricht treaty and make it less likely that debt burdens will grow to a point where a bailout will be needed. It is still too early to assess how well the excessive deficit procedure works to prevent deficits larger than 3%. Eichengreen and Wyplosz (1997) predict that states will do just enough to stay below 3%, and the European Commission will fudge the figures just enough so that there is doubt and the punishment mechanism is not invoked. A real test will come with negative economic growth. No member state has experienced negative economic growth since 1993, and economic growth has been robust in the two years under Stage Three.

There has also been an increase in the exchange of information on budgets (point 2). The standardization of the stability and convergence programs, along with their regular evaluation, has provided more information than was available before the beginning of Stage Three. Yet there is some question whether the member states are using this information effectively and whether they are integrating their programs into their domestic budget processes. It is one thing to report to the commission and to ECOFIN a medium-term budgetary framework. It is another to use this framework in the annual budget process.

The real question concerns whether there has been explicit mutual adjustment of fiscal policies to maintain economic stability (point 3). Given the benign economic climate during 2000 and 2001, this point is difficult to evaluate. Yet the reprimand of Ireland at the beginning of 2001 provides a good test case of the effectiveness of the BEPG in keeping states in line.

The 2000 Broad Economic Policy Guidelines, as drafted by the commission, following recommendations from the Economic and Financial Committee and ECOFIN, recommended that Ireland "be ready, already in 2000, to use budgetary policy to ensure economic stability given the extent of overheating in the economy; gear the budget for 2001 to this objective" (see ECFIN/209/00 and 2000/517/EC). Based on a recommendation from the commission, ECOFIN decided to reprimand Ireland. The text is worth quoting at some length:

> Given that the monetary policy is now set for the euro area as a whole and no longer available as an instrument at national level, other policies, including budgetary policies, must be used more actively. Against this background, the Council finds that the planned contribution of fiscal policy to the macroeconomic policy mix in Ireland is inappropriate. The Council recalls that it has repeatedly urged the Irish authorities, most recently in its 2000 broad guidelines of the economic policies, to ensure economic stability by means of fiscal policy. The Council regrets that this advice was not reflected in the budget for 2001, despite developments in the course of 2000 indicating an increasing extent of overheating. The Council considers that Irish fiscal policy in 2001 is not consistent with the broad guidelines of the economic policies as regards budgetary policy. The Council has therefore decided, together with this Opinion, to make a recommendation under Article 99(4) of the Treaty establishing the European Community with a view to ending this inconsistency.[8]

The circumstances of the reprimand provide evidence for the shift from the Stability and Growth Pact provisions to the use of BEPG to evaluate the budgetary positions of states. The same council opinion cited above also noted that Ireland is expected to have a budget surplus of 4.2% in 2001, more than 7 percentage points of GDP higher than the figure that trips

8. Council Opinion of February 12, 2001, on the 2000 update of the Stability Programme of Ireland, 2001–2003.

the excessive deficit procedure under the Stability and Growth Pact. This suggests that the expectations for fiscal policy coordination within the European Union have become higher since the beginning of Stage Three.

There are two issues that are relevant when considering the implications of the Irish reprimand. The first is why Ireland was singled out in February 2001. The second concerns the enforcement effects, that is, whether failing according to BEPG standards has any effect on member state behavior.

The initial Irish reaction to word that a reprimand was coming was anger. The Irish complained that, given their large surplus, they should not be singled out. They contended behind closed doors that if a large country had had the same fiscal profile as they had, no reprimand would be forthcoming. In March 2001, the Irish finance minister, Charlie McCreevy, came to the European Parliament in Brussels to offer a public defense of his fiscal record before the Economic and Financial Committee; there he described the achievements of Ireland's fiscal consolidation since the 1980s.

My interviews with officials at the European Commission and the Economic and Finance Committee and with member state representatives indicate several plausible motives for reprimanding Ireland. Commission members stressed that Ireland has known for some time, and been urged in private for some time, to reduce the inflationary consequences of its fiscal policy. The recommendation for the reprimand came only after the passage of the 2001 Irish budget that included both increases in spending and cuts in taxes, which were clear violations of the 2000 BEPG. If the commission did not recommend action against such a flagrant violation of the BEPG, the process would lose its credibility. Similarly, one person added that the reprimand sets an important precedent for future action—"If you cannot reprimand the best pupils, you cannot reprimand the worst."

The second issue concerns the meaning of the reprimand in the first place. The most ECOFIN can do is publicize the recommendation, which indeed is what occurred in the Irish case. The reprimand appeared on the front pages of Irish newspapers and in the *Financial Times*. The expectation is therefore that populations will put pressure on their governments if their governments receive bad notes from the European Union. This is probably an optimistic expectation. There may even be some governments that would proudly boast of any sanctions from Brussels so that the reprimand would backfire. One EU official the author spoke to in Brussels in April 2001 indicated that he had no doubt that Ireland "would lose something" at the EU level if it did not get its budgetary affairs in order. This more diffuse threat is reminiscent of the treatment Austria received after the formation of a People's Party–Freedom Party coalition, when it lost the opportunity to fill EU positions and the like.

More recent events involving the deficits of the largest states in the euro-zone have overshadowed the Irish reprimand. Whether France and Germany (and maybe Italy) will continue to violate the Stability and Growth Pact, and whether they will receive real punishment under the pact's terms, is the subject of debate. Yet the Irish reprimand remains of interest because it signals the attempt of the commission in particular to use a non–Stability and Growth Pact tool, the Broad Economic Policy Guidelines, to influence domestic fiscal policy.

Conclusion

There is a clear sense among Eurocrats that the importance of the European Union–level institutions in the making of domestic economic policy has increased. Although the European Union has become more involved, true fiscal coordination (point 3)—where states explicitly adjust their fiscal policies to one another—is not a reality. Brussels does, however, pay increasing attention to fiscal policy developments in member states. The European Commission monitors budgetary behavior in all member states and not just Economic and Monetary Union members. ECOFIN, together with the Economic and Financial Committee, receives yearly recommendations from the commission on the performance of states and evaluates member state programs that are designed to maintain medium-term budgets that are "close to balance or in surplus."

At the same time, any explanation of why most European states have improved their budgetary performance since the early 1990s cannot stop with an examination of the European-level framework. The "carrot" of participation in EMU was a one-time event, and it cannot explain why countries generally have performed well since the single currency was introduced. Once Stage Three of EMU began, the Stability and Growth Pact was meant to provide a "stick" to be used only if deficits climbed above 3% of GDP. But the move of deficits above 3% in France and Germany in 2002 and 2003, together with the reluctance of the European Commission and the Council of Ministers to punish them, suggests that the Stability and Growth Pact cannot explain the change in fiscal behavior in some states. The following case study chapters will examine the development of domestic fiscal policy and will evaluate explicitly to what extent the European Union–level incentives affected decision makers.

4

The Delegation Form of Fiscal Governance

The delegation form of fiscal governance works best when there are no ideological differences among ministers in a cabinet. It is also possible when the ideological differences are minor. Governments with these types of ideological profiles are expected where party systems enable either single parties or blocs of parties to form majority governments.

In this chapter I focus primarily on the development of forms of fiscal governance in the United Kingdom and in Germany. The United Kingdom is a classic case, with competitive elections pitting two main parties against each other. It has regular one-party governments and competitive elections. It has developed the practical application of the delegation form of fiscal governance. The chancellor of the exchequer coordinates the budget process on behalf of the cabinet. Germany, in contrast, represents the limits to which delegation can be applied. Rather than two political parties facing each other, elections usually pit two blocs of parties against each other in competitive elections. This arrangement of parties can still lead to stable delegation (chap. 2), but in Germany the finance minister has difficulty centralizing the budget process when coalition partners have serious policy differences. Moreover, in Germany there are additional institutions, such as an upper house of parliament with tax powers and subnational governments with budget powers, that can reduce the effectiveness of the finance minister.

This chapter also provides shorter case studies for France and Greece. France has competitive elections, but it has had no true one-party governments through 2002. Instead, two or more parties with similar political views traditionally form coalition governments. France does not face the same institutional complications as Germany, however, and delegation functions better as a result. The difficulties arise primarily when coalition partners do not work well together on budget issues. Greece, like the United Kingdom, traditionally has one-party governments, but for much of the period after the restoration of democracy in 1974, it did not have a truly competitive party system. The Socialist Party, PASOK, dominated the political landscape. This changed in the 1990s, however, as New Democracy (Greece's conservative party) gathered more votes. Since the mid-1990s, Greece has used delegation to maintain tighter fiscal discipline than it had in the previous period.

In this chapter I illustrate some subtleties of the functioning of delegation in practice. Close ideological alignment of parties is necessary for delegation to function well. Splits between the Free Democrats and Social Democrats in the early 1980s, for example, eroded the power of the finance minister in the Helmut Schmidt government in Germany. The relative power of a given finance minister can also vary from government to government. One key question concerns the support of the prime minister for his watchdog over the budget. When the support is virtually nonexistent, as was the case under Prime Minister Andreas Papandreou in Greece in the 1980s, then finance ministry calls for fiscal rectitude fall on deaf ears. In contrast, British Prime Minister Tony Blair has provided Chancellor Gordon Brown with unstinting support, not only on economic matters but also on some social ones as well.

These countries provide a useful contrast with one another when considering the role of Maastricht in the making of domestic budgets. France and Germany are at the very core of Economic and Monetary Union, and an EMU without these two countries is scarcely imaginable. Both countries made short-term adjustments to their budgets to get them below the critical 3% level for 1997, but otherwise there is no discernable Maastricht effect. The United Kingdom had an opt-out for EMU and every intention to use that opt-out. Impressively, it brought a large deficit under control by 1997, but the reasons for the fiscal success had nothing to do with Maastricht. In only one case, Greece, can one argue that the Maastricht effect was there, albeit later than in other countries. Greece was the only country not to qualify for EMU because it failed the fiscal criteria. Yet it did make adjustments to the way it made budgets, and Maastricht proved useful in 1997 to gather both party and public support behind reforms of the budgetary process.

United Kingdom: The Ideal Form of Delegation?

Political Background

The United Kingdom is generally perceived politically as a land of strong prime ministers, strong chancellors of the exchequer, and strong political parties. The primary political cleavage in the twentieth century has been an economic left-right divide. The Conservative Party anchors the political right. It was often the party of government in the twentieth century. The Labour

Party, founded in 1900, has been the main party in opposition to the Conservatives since the demise of the Liberal Party shortly before World War I. Until Tony Blair's landslide victory in May 2001, a Labour government had never been reelected. A second cleavage, a regional one, has gained increasing prominence since the 1970s, and regional parties such as Wales's Plaid Cymru and the Scottish National Party now regularly win seats in the House of Commons. Partly in response to the increasing relevance of this cleavage, Blair's Labour government initiated a limited form of devolution in the form of new regional parliaments in Wales, Scotland, and Northern Ireland in 1999. Although the parliament in Scotland does have some limited tax authority, the United Kingdom remains a centralized country in terms of fiscal policy. The important decisions on the budget continue to be taken in London.

Since World War II, the country has almost always had a one-party majority government. In the time period covered in this study, exceptions occurred midterm when governments with thin majorities lost by-elections for the House of Commons and fell into minority status. James Callaghan's Labour government existed from 1977 to 1979 under Liberal Party toleration, while John Major's Conservative government survived with Ulster Unionist toleration at the end of his term. These short-term exceptions aside, prime ministers enjoy the luxury of one-party majority governments. One reason is the electoral system. The United Kingdom uses a plurality electoral system, which, as Duverger (1954) explains, generally leads to a two-party system. The party that wins the most votes usually wins more than a majority of seats. The only exception to the rule was the February 1974 election, when neither major party won a majority. Since the situation was not stable, elections were held again eight months later and Labour won a thin majority.

The regularity of one-party majority governments suggests that delegation to a strong finance minister is the appropriate form of fiscal governance. Indeed, some form of delegation has existed in the United Kingdom since the end of the nineteenth century.

Fiscal Policy and Fiscal Actors

The British cyclically adjusted budget balance and the overall debt level since 1973 reveal two "troughs" in budget performance (fig. 4.1). The first was in the mid- to late-1970s when the cyclically adjusted budget balance hovered around –5% of GDP. The budget balance improved steadily from 1979 through 1981, and it even experienced a surplus in 1982. The balance suffered a serious decline at the beginning of the 1990s, reaching a low of –6.1% in 1993. Afterward, it progressively improved until it reached surplus again in 1998. When examining the debt figures, one characteristic that stands out is that they do not show particularly wide swings, especially when compared with other countries in the European Union. The debt level is also never

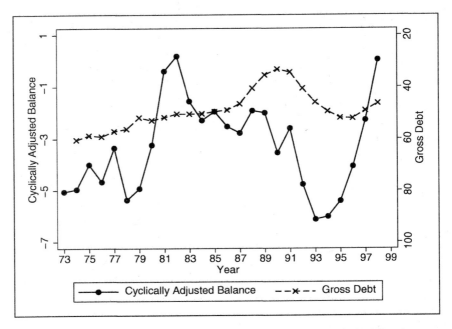

Fig. 4.1. Cyclically adjusted budget balance and gross debt level in the United Kingdom, 1973–98. The debt figures cover April of a given year through March of the following year. Source: European Commission 1999a.

large when judged by the Maastricht criteria—the only time that the United Kingdom had a debt level above 60% of GDP was in 1974.

The key institutional participant in the budget process is the Treasury. Officially, the prime minister is the first lord of the Treasury, and she bears ultimate responsibility for Treasury actions. In practice, there are two actors at the top of the hierarchy that are of primary interest in budgeting issues: the chancellor of the exchequer (or second lord of the Treasury) and his chief secretary.[1] The chancellor's position is more public than that of finance ministers in most countries. He announces the annual budget, and he is the person the press and the public hold responsible for budgetary successes as well as failures. Before meetings of Parliament, the chancellor has his own "question time," which, under the Blair government, falls on Thursdays. Because of its importance, the chancellorship has often served as a stepping stone to the the prime ministership. H. H. Asquith, David Lloyd George, Stanley Baldwin, Winston Churchill, Neville Chamberlain, James

---

1. Although this account focuses on the budgetary aspects of the Treasury, the chancellor has other roles as well. He has broad responsibility for the economy, performing functions that would be reserved for a minister of economics in other systems, and he sets monetary policy.

Callaghan, and John Major all served as chancellors in No. 11 Downing Street before moving next door to No. 10.[2]

The chancellor's chief secretary also plays an important role in the budget process that, while less public, involves him more directly in day-to-day policy making. He usually is the most junior member of the cabinet, which makes the Treasury the only department with two cabinet ministers. He is the person responsible for the expenditure side of the budget within the Treasury. From the creation of the position in 1961 until 1998, the usual practice was the following: Spending ministers negotiated bilaterally with the chief secretary through the Public Expenditure Survey. While the Public Expenditure Survey set budgets for the departments for the next three years, in practice negotiations took place annually, and the focus was on the following year's budget (HM Treasury 2002b, 231). An agreement between a spending minister and the chief secretary was supposed to be the norm. What followed if the negotiations failed to produce an agreement has varied over time, with some form of cabinet committee often making the final decision after 1981. The chief secretary's power relative to the spending minister's came at its height in the early Thatcher years when the Treasury was able to set budgets more or less autonomously. This strength faded, however, and other institutional devices were needed to shore up the chief secretary's ability to determine budgets for spending ministers. Since 1992, there has not been an expectation that bilateral negotiations should, as a rule, determine the spending limits for a department in a given year. Since 1998, moreover, most departments receive multiannual budget allocations instead of annual budget allocations.

The British central bank is irrelevant in regard to fiscal policy. It was not independent from government, and it did not set monetary policy, until Gordon Brown gave the Bank of England partial independence in 1997. The chancellor of the exchequer was the main monetary policy maker until then. Today, the chancellor sets the inflation target while the bank determines what combination of policy instruments to use to reach that target. In fiscal policy, the bank's role is limited to occasional working papers from its staff.

Parliament's role is primarily one of scrutiny. What the chancellor proposes passes the House of Commons essentially unchanged. Opposition members of Parliament and, less often, backbenchers in the government may express public disappointment in one or more elements of the budget. Yet Parliament has little opportunity to change the government's proposal. Amendments to the government's budget are not allowed, and the vote on the budget is an up-or-down vote (correspondence with parliamentary staff person, October 2000).

2. Indeed, the question on Fleet Street in 2003 was not when the Tories would replace Labour but when Gordon Brown would replace Tony Blair.

Delegation

The following section traces the development of fiscal policy and fiscal institutions in the United Kingdom from 1973 to 2002. The goal is not to explain every nuance of the budget process; there are three books on the formation of budgets that explain the system at a level of detail that is not possible here (Heclo and Wildavsky 1974; Thain and Wright 1995; on the Treasury and social policy, Deakin and Parry 2000). Rather, I use the theoretical framework put forward here to explain the development of the Treasury's role in the budget process. The United Kingdom traditionally has a form of delegation that comes closest to an ideal form of fiscal governance. It relies on the discretionary power of a finance minister. The power of the chancellor in the United Kingdom during the last thirty years has not been uniform. When the chancellor has failed to rein in costs, new institutions have been introduced to reinforce either his power directly or to achieve the more general goal of a full consideration of the tax burden in budgetary decision making.

1973–79

The first oil crisis, in 1973–74, quadrupled oil prices, hitting the United Kingdom hard. The economic difficulties came at a time when there was little economic leadership from the government. The February 1974 election produced no clear winner. As sometimes happens in close elections under a plurality electoral system, Labour won four more seats in aggregate but the Conservatives won slightly more votes, and neither party had a majority in Parliament. Labour formed a brief, unstable, minority government under Harold Wilson that lasted only a matter of months. The new chancellor, Dennis Healey, proposed a budget that he considered "broadly neutral" and not expansionary. He had set the public sector borrowing requirement, a main target of the Treasury, at £2.7 billion, which would have been a reduction of £1.6 billion from the previous year (£.60 = $1).[3] Yet the actual public sector borrowing requirement nearly tripled to £8 billion (Burk and Cairncross 1992, 181–82). The political situation made all attempts to control spending difficult. The government did not have a majority in Parliament, and this meant that "unpleasant and difficult measures tended to be avoided or postponed" (Harmon 1997, 81). There could not be corrections to the budget that would potentially hurt key constituencies. If anything, budget items were introduced that were meant to gather additional votes, such as the end of

3. The public sector borrowing requirement establishes the total borrowing requirement of the public sector in a given fiscal year, which includes all levels of government. U.S. dollar equivalents for this and other currencies are approximations at the end of 1998 from http://www.oanda.com/convert/fxhistory. "Billion" here and elsewhere means thousand million, not million million.

statutory pay controls and the extension of automatic cost-of-living adjustments to parts of the public sector that had not had such guarantees before (Burk and Cairncross 1992, 14). As a former Treasury official put it in his minutes of a meeting with the chancellor in July 1974, there was a sense that "government policies are more directed to winning the next election than to the needs of the economic situation" (Dell 1991, 86).

Those elections would come soon. In October 1974, Labour captured a slim parliamentary majority of three seats that allowed the government to stay in power. One of the first tasks the government confronted was to gain control of the economy and of the budget. By 1975, "stagflation" had set in, with inflation running at 22% while growth was negative. The balance of payments plunged into negative figures because of the sharp rise in oil prices in 1973, and the pound, which had floated since 1972, was under almost constant pressure. The budget during this time was also precarious. Public sector net borrowing increased from 2.8% of GDP in the last fiscal year before the elections (1972–73) to 7.0% in fiscal year 1975–76. In cyclically adjusted terms, the deficit remained above 4% of GDP in this period, indicating that the deficit was consistently worse than what one would expect given the state of the economy (European Commission 1999a).

The chancellor was not able to take firm measures to control the deficit until James Callaghan succeeded Harold Wilson as prime minister in April 1976. Three months after the change at No. 10 Downing Street, Healey imposed firm cash limits on expenditures. The chancellor placed these limits on top of the volume-based budgets. If inflation were higher than forecast, the money would simply run out. The cash limits had an almost immediate effect. Public borrowing dropped in the third and fourth quarters, and this drop "was plainly associated with the introduction of cash limits" (Burk and Cairncross 1992, 184).[4] While the fiscal side of the ledger had stabilized and even somewhat improved, this came too late to save the pound. On September 29, 1976, Chancellor Healey announced that the United Kingdom had no choice but to approach the International Monetary Fund (IMF) for a loan.

Healey used the approach to the IMF to justify additional measures on the budget. He announced to the cabinet that the IMF would like to see a cut in the public borrowing requirement of between £2–3 billion. He proposed a combination of public expenditure cuts and value-added tax increases. Yet what followed showed that both sides of the budget debate could try to use the IMF. A majority of the cabinet, including the prime minister, objected to Healey's plans, and Callaghan authorized an approach to the Gerald Ford administration outside of Treasury channels to ask Treasury Secretary William Simon and Secretary of State Henry Kissinger for more lenient

4. While limits were in cash terms, spending plans remained in volume terms until 1982 (Deakin and Parry 2000, 39).

terms (*Economist,* December 4, 1976). These efforts proved to be of little effect. The IMF team then negotiating in London continued to press for expenditure cuts. Healey eventually got the cabinet to agree to a reduction in public expenditure of £1 billion in 1977–78 and another £1.5 billion in 1978–79, and to provisionally agree to cut another £500 million in 1978–79 (Burk and Cairncross 1992, 105). This episode was deeply embarrassing to the Treasury. As a senior Treasury official put it, when the IMF came in 1976 to advise the country, "it was the worst moment in Treasury history" (author interview, January 2003, London).

Healey needed to draw on only half of the loan offered, or $3.9 billion, but the political damage had been done (Morgan 1997, 560). There was no split of the party as some had feared, but the episode did not boost the government's standing among voters either. Dissatisfaction with Labour eroded the party's already thin majority in Parliament. In November 1976, Labour lost two of three by-elections in constituencies that had traditionally been safe, leaving the party with a one-seat majority. In March 1977, another by-election resulted in a Conservative gain, and Labour faced an imminent vote of confidence. The government survived the vote later that month only after agreement on the "Lib-Lab pact," which provided the government with the backing of the small Liberal Party's thirteen seats. There was nothing explicit in the pact concerning the budget, but there was an agreement that the chancellor and the Liberal economics spokesmen would meet regularly (Morgan 1997, 567). Confident of Liberal support at least in the short-term, six days after the confidence vote Healey presented his budget proposal to Parliament. It included additional spending cuts as well as wage restrictions. It also proposed to limit the public borrowing requirement for the next fiscal year to £7.5 billion. Indeed, the government was able to keep to this limit for fiscal year 1977–78 (HM Treasury 2003).

Healey's budget situation was again precarious the following year. He proposed a tax cut to Parliament to spur the economy. Margaret Thatcher's Conservative Party harshly criticized the budget and argued that the tax cuts were too small to have any real effect on the economy. The Liberal Party agreed with the Conservatives and broke from the Lib-Lab pact to support two amendments that the Conservatives made to the finance bill to reduce the standard rate of income tax. Labour could not block this tax cut, so, to make up the revenue, Healey proposed a 2.5% surcharge on employers' national insurance contributions. The Liberals balked initially at the surcharge and backed it only after Labour agreed to cut it almost in half, to 1.5% (*Economist,* July 1, 1978).

Even with this compromise, however, the government was on its last legs. In March 1979, Callaghan lost a vote of confidence by one vote, with the Liberals voting against the government, and the prime minister asked the queen to call new elections. Margaret Thatcher swept to power two months later with a majority of twenty-one seats.

Before moving on to the Thatcher years, it is worth considering how the development of fiscal policy under the Wilson and Callaghan governments is consistent with the theoretical perspective presented here. One reason for the weak fiscal performance was a lack of support from the prime minister for fiscal measures to rein in the deficit. A clearly frustrated Treasury man, Edmund Dell, wrote that Harold Wilson rarely addressed economic matters. Wilson did not back his chancellor in defense of the budget, and Callaghan offered only lukewarm support. This situation undercut the power of the chancellor to rein in spending. The government's loss of majority status further complicated the chancellor's efforts. As I suggested in chapter 2 (and illustrate in chapter 6 with examples from minority governments in Denmark and in Sweden), a comprehensive fiscal contract with one or more opposition parties can maintain fiscal discipline. Yet British parties had little experience with minority governments. The Short Parliament in 1974 was preoccupied with the next general election, and the Lib-Lab pact said little about the budget. Government disputes with the Liberals over tax policy indicated that the Liberals were willing to oppose the government on budget issues when they thought they could garner electoral support by undercutting the government. As the *Economist* commented after the refusal of the Liberals to support a small tax hike on gasoline in 1977, "The real damage had been done to the government's never-strong backbone" (May 14).

1979–83

The first Conservative budget came five weeks after the election. The Conservatives made a campaign promise that they would cut taxes as well as public expenditure to pay for the tax cuts. In practice, while the expenditure cuts were made, Chancellor Geoffrey Howe focused on the deficit problem and received backing from Margaret Thatcher to push through his priorities. In a speech before Parliament a month after the election, the new chancellor proposed £3.5 billion in expenditure cuts and an income tax cut as well. Yet the consequences to the health of the budget balance were clear, and, to make up the revenue that would be lost on the income side, Howe also proposed an increase in the value-added tax (VAT) rate. The slogan that the Conservatives had adopted was "pay as you spend rather than pay as you earn," which represented what Chancellor Howe (1995, 129) later characterized in his memoirs as a "tax switch" rather than a true tax cut. Another way that Howe characterized it was, "Finance must determine expenditure, not expenditure finance."[5]

5. Attributed to the Second Permanent Secretary, HM Treasury, Sir Anthony Rawlinson and repeated by Chancellor Geoffrey Howe on Budget Day (June 12) in 1979.

In total, £3.5 billion in cuts stuck and fell primarily on the Labour spending priorities of nationalized industries and social programs. In March of the following year, Howe proposed an additional £1.5 billion in spending reductions for the upcoming budget, which included restrictions on civil servant pay increases.

In 1981, the deficit stubbornly remained above 4% of GDP. Howe pushed through a combination of new spending cuts with increases in consumption taxes on items including liquor, tobacco, and gasoline. The increase in the gasoline tax was unpopular in the country and unpopular even within the Conservative Party, and, in the parliamentary vote, eight Tories broke party ranks to vote against the tax (Associated Press, March 17, 1981). There were also sporadic civil servant strikes to protest the government's offer of a 7% pay increase at a time of double-digit inflation. As a response both to the strikes and to a more general dissatisfaction with the ability of the government to control personnel costs, Thatcher abolished the thirteen-year-old Civil Service Department.

There was some gloating in the Treasury after this move. Prior to 1968, the Treasury had maintained the responsibility of "employer" within the civil service. In the late 1960s, there was general dissatisfaction both in academic and in governmental circles with the quality of civil servants. A committee report argued that the Treasury was largely to blame for the failings of the civil service, and the personnel parts of the Treasury were merged with minor non-Treasury personnel organizations to form the Civil Service Department in 1968. The new department was expected to work with the Treasury, which continued to set general expenditure targets for civil service spending, but in practice there was little formal coordination between the two departments. By 1981, the Civil Service Department had grown to include over three thousand civil servants, and Thatcher agreed with Treasury officials that the department was an obstacle to maintaining control over spending (Chapman 1997, 49–53). In November 1981, in a statement before Parliament, Thatcher announced that most of the functions of the department would, henceforth, return to the Treasury. As Thain and Wright (1995, 62) note, "The Treasury, with its control of pay and manpower restored, could now more easily devise and implement strategies for manpower planning and for controlling the costs of both state and non-staff administrative structure."

The following month, Chancellor Howe announced increases in social security taxes as well as in municipal housing rents. Unemployment was running near 14% by October 1982, and there were repeated calls from the opposition Labour benches, as well as from some Conservative dissenters such as former Prime Minister Edward Heath, to abandon the austerity course, but Thatcher continued to back her chancellor. The 1982–83 budget did make some minor concessions. There were some increases in unemployment insurance, child benefits, and pensions. Howe also included some tax breaks for industry. To keep the impact of these measures on the borrowing requirement to a minimum, however, he also increased taxes once again on liquor, tobacco, and gasoline. The austerity measures had some success in controlling the budget. While the general government deficit level remained mostly stable between 1979 and 1983, between 3% and 4% of GDP (HM Treasury 2003), the cyclically adjusted deficit came down from almost 5% in 1979 to a surplus of 0.2% by 1982 (European Commission 1999a).

Why was the first Thatcher government successful at getting the cyclically adjusted budget back in balance? Certain procedural changes contributed to an improvement in fiscal discipline. The first was that the Treasury was again firmly in control of the making of the budget. There was little debate within the cabinet on the content of the budget between 1979 and 1981, giving the chancellor the freedom to propose what he wanted. In debates within the cabinet on spending, the prime minister consistently backed her chancellor against the protests of all spending ministers but one, Francis Pym, who was sometimes successful in persuading the prime minister to preserve some additional spending on defense (Howe 1995, 145). There were also two procedural changes in the making of the budget. With some fanfare, the chancellor introduced the Medium-Term Financial Strategy in 1980. The primary focus was on the monetary side, but there were some efforts to introduce medium-term planning on the fiscal side of the chancellor's responsibilities as well. The Medium-term Financial Strategy stipulated that the public sector borrowing requirement would decrease from 4% of GDP in 1980–81 to 1.5% of GDP in 1983–84. The use of such planning reinforced the chancellor's efforts to focus the government on the entire budget, not just specific spending categories. As Thain and Wright (1995, 23) note, "The annual exercise in setting out the PSBR, public expenditure, and revenue figures provided the Treasury with a useful weapon in containing public-spending pressures." The second measure was a move from volume-based budgeting to cash-based budgeting. Volume-based figures had been included since the 1961 Plowden Report. Such figures stipulated that a given budget item, once approved, would be provided more or less regardless of cost. This meant that inflation would necessarily increase government expenditures. The move to cash terms broke the direct link between inflation and expenditure increases.

Though there is little evidence that the austerity measures made the government more popular, neither did they undermine support for the government. In a 1982 poll, the Conservatives were ahead with 42%, followed by Labour at 30% and the new Liberal–Social Democratic Alliance at 27%. Indeed, in June 1983 the Conservatives won a landslide in the general election with a new majority in Parliament of 144 seats. Thatcher's popularity, in part because of the Falklands war, and the disarray of the opposition parties, certainly contributed to the result.

The Rise of the Star-chamber Committee

The Treasury's relative autonomy over the budget was at its highest during the economic crisis years of 1979–81. Chancellor Howe's 1981 budget was unpopular even among many Tories, and there were several ministers who requested full cabinet meetings to discuss their budgets. When the economy resumed growth in 1982, there was pressure to increase spending from both inside and outside the party. Bilateral negotiations between the chief secretary and the respective spending ministries continued as before during the preparation of the budget, but spending ministers were more willing to stand by their initial spending bids. The process to follow when there was no agreement played an increasingly significant role.

In the Thatcher years, the main body that ruled on budget disputes was the Star-chamber Committee. Thain and Wright (1995, 296–303) provide an excellent discussion of the functioning of this committee. It was a cabinet committee, which meant that only ministers sat on it. It was intentionally composed of people who were political heavyweights but who generally did not have large portfolios themselves, or, if it did on occasion include a minister from a heavy-weight department, the minister's budget had to have already been settled in bilateral negotiations between the minister and the Treasury. In his memoirs, Thatcher's second chancellor, Nigel Lawson, noted that the committee needed to have "three public spending hawks and one public spending dove" to assure some balance on the committee (Lawson 1993, 290, as cited in Thain and Wright 1995, 298). In October 1984, for example, the committee included Home Secretary Leon Brittan, Leader of the House of Commons John Biffen, the Scottish Secretary George Younger, Lord William Whitelaw, and Chief Secretary Peter Rees (*Financial Times,* October 25, 1984). Both Brittan and Biffen had served as chief secretary already under Thatcher, and only Brittan had a budget of his own of any note.

The committee was conceived as a reconciliation committee. It was to be called whenever it was clear that there would not be a resolution of a given budget within the bilateral negotiations. The Star-chamber Committee was expected to consider the arguments of both sides. The chief secretary would present the Treasury's case while the minister would make his case. There was a crucial difference: unlike the bilaterals, where he usually had his staff with him who knew the financial details, the minister was alone. After hearing the cases, the Star-chamber Committee would then make a ruling. An appeal to the prime minister was possible, and, if the prime minister did not resolve the issue, finally to the full cabinet.

The course of events in fall 1984 is illustrative of the process. The cabinet approved a total spending target of £132 billion in July. Bilateral negotiations ensued between the Treasury and the individual spending ministries. By October, there were still eight spending categories on which there was no agreement. Those eight went to the Star-chamber Committee. Three were resolved in the committee, but an unprecedented number, four, were resolved only on appeal to the prime minister, and one, funding for the Housing ministry, faced resolution in the full cabinet. The Treasury originally wanted a £600-million cut in housing investment, and the Star-chamber Committee had decided on a £572-million reduction. Having gotten as far as the full cabinet, the Housing minister triumphed with a cut of only £65 million (*Economist*, November 17, 1984; *Financial Times*, November 9, 1984). In a total budget of £132 billion, however, Chancellor Lawson could justifiably argue that spending had been kept in line with plans.

The Star-chamber Committee played an important role in settling budget disputes until its demise in 1992. As Thain and Wright observe (1995, 300), "The Star Chamber . . . was seen by Ministers as a means of appealing over the head of the Chief Secretary to wider interests in the cabinet, yet its existence kept public spending haggling away from the formal Cabinet." From the theoretical perspective developed here, the committee proved a useful arena for reinforcing the operation of a delegation form of fiscal governance for three reasons. First, the rules for membership on the committee meant that ministers would have little stake in a particular spending outcome. They were likely to consider the broader implications of spending decisions. Second, the Treasury's chief secretary knew that the body likely to rule on a spending dispute was predisposed to favor his position. Spending ministers understood this as well, which meant that they were more willing to reach an agreement at the first stage with the chief secretary. For this reason, most disputes never made it to the Star-chamber Committee.[6] Third, in the rare instances when a dispute made it to the full cabinet, there was little opportunity for spending ministers to log roll support for higher spending across ministries, because only specific issues were subject to debate.

This system, therefore, worked moderately well. The general government budget balance improved from a deficit –3.8% of GDP in 1980–81 to a budget surplus in 1988–89 of 0.9% of GDP (HM Treasury 2003). The surplus was the first the United Kingdom had experienced since the oil crisis of the early 1970s. Yet a review of the cyclically adjusted balance numbers in figure 4.1 suggests that much of the improvement in the raw figures was due to economic growth. Cyclically adjusted figures in the late 1980s, in fact, remained negative. The recession that hit all European Union countries revealed some weaknesses of this system for setting the annual budget.

The Remaining Conservative Years

The Conservative Party entered the 1990s behind Labour in the opinion polls. One of the principal reasons was Margaret Thatcher's insistence on

6. During its existence from 1981 to 1992, the Star-chamber Committee was not convened in 1982, 1988, 1990, and 1991 (Thain and Wright 1995, 297, 300).

instituting the highly unpopular poll tax. The tax shifted the burden from property owners to a per-head tax, with the rate varying according to expenditures in a given locality. The political calculation was that people would see how much their local governments spent and apply pressure on those governments to cut costs. People did object, but they protested the introduction of the tax, which, as a per-head tax, fell disproportionately on the poor. In November 1990, a former defense minister, Michael Heseltine, challenged Margaret Thatcher in a leadership vote among Conservative MPs, and he pledged to abolish the tax. Although he did not win the election outright, he did force a second ballot, and it was likely that the prime minister would lose in the next round. Margaret Thatcher then resigned. Her chancellor, John Major, who had succeeded Nigel Lawson just a year earlier, won the leadership election and became prime minister. His chief secretary, Norman Lamont, succeeded him as chancellor.

The new government soon found itself dealing with debt levels higher than those at any time under the Labour governments of the 1970s. The general government balance was a healthy –0.3% of GDP in fiscal year 1989–90, but it ballooned to –3.7% by 1991–92 and –7.4% of GDP a year later.

There were several reasons for the poor fiscal performance. The first was the recession. The United Kingdom experienced negative real economic growth in 1991 and essentially no growth in 1992. Yet the cyclically adjusted balance figures indicate that the deficit grew much larger than one would have expected given purely economic effects.[7]

The second reason was the upcoming election. Although Major's replacing Thatcher gave the Conservative Party a healthy bounce in the polls, it was by no means clear who would capture a majority in the next parliament. The prime minister had to call an election by 1992. At the prime minister's insistence, health spending in particular increased, but other budget items also received increases.

The third reason was the poll tax. The initial reaction of the Tories to the large protests was to approve a series of exceptions. Almost half the taxpayers received some sort of tax relief, and another quarter initially balked at paying the tax. The poll tax fiasco cost £10 billion in expected revenue over two years (Lamont 2000, 43). The "solution" to the problem was to increase the national value-added tax and to replace much of the poll tax with grants from the central government, but in the meantime the poll tax hurt general government revenue.

A final reason was the budget system in place. The bilateral negotiations worked well when the chancellor was politically strong and when the

---

7. One could argue that it is unfair to set the standard as one of a cyclically adjusted budget balance. Yet the chancellor himself made this a goal. As Norman Lamont (2000, 144) wrote in his memoirs when discussing fiscal policy in the early 1990s, "It was our intention to balance the Budget over the [business] cycle."

prime minister supported the Treasury in most internal battles. By the early 1990s, however, the system was under serious strain. John Major was more likely to side with spending ministers. Fears about the upcoming election contributed to pushes for higher expenditures, and the Treasury understood that it could do little until after the elections. The wait, however, was not advantageous. The reputations of Norman Lamont and, indeed, the Conservative Party for managing the economy were tarnished by the Exchange Rate Mechanism (ERM) crisis in September 1992.

Although my focus is on fiscal policy, the ERM crisis had consequences for the budget, so some background information is useful. When several European countries established the ERM in 1979, the United Kingdom initially chose to stay out. Largely based on the hope that ERM membership would reduce inflation, Margaret Thatcher heeded John Major's advice to join just two months before her resignation. There appeared to have been little foresight about what ERM membership would mean for the British economy. German reunification led to higher interest rates in Germany, and, if the British government wanted to remain in ERM, it needed to match those rate hikes. In September, there were runs on the pound, and the pound was stuck at the bottom of the band in which the currency was allowed to fluctuate. A series of events both inside and outside the country eroded market confidence that the pound could remain in the system, and, on a day that has become known as Black Wednesday, Chancellor Lamont announced the suspension of Britain's membership in the Exchange Rate Mechanism.

The ERM crisis was not the reason why revisions to the budgeting system were introduced in 1992, but it certainly contributed to the institutionalization of a new system. The first new development was the use of the New Control Total, a predetermined maximum amount that aggregate expenditures could reach. Over the medium term, aggregate spending on noncyclical elements of the budget was not to grow more than 1.5% in real terms, while general government expenditures in total were not to grow more than the estimated trend growth of the economy, which was then expected to be 2% in real terms (Thain and Wright 1995, 241–42). These totals represented a conscious use of top-down budgeting. A clear aggregate target is expected to make trade-offs among different spending categories explicit.[8] This represented a change from the previous period when the focus was on the bilateral negotiations between the chief secretary and the spending ministers. Although the Treasury had some general sense of a maximum amount of spending it wanted, usually these figures were not made public.

The second element of the reform was the replacement of the Star-chamber Committee with another cabinet committee known as the EDX Committee. The committee was designed to have senior ministers as its predecessor did, but it was larger, with seven cabinet members instead of three or four. The

8. See, for example, Schick 1986 and OECD 1987.

Treasury had two members: the chief secretary was a voting member instead of the "prosecutor" of Star-chamber days, while the chancellor was directly involved as the committee's chair. The mandate of EDX was broader than that of the former Star-chamber Committee. Rather than simply ruling on disputes between the chief secretary and a particular spending minister, it would present to the cabinet a package of spending proposals that, together, would fall under the New Control Total. Negotiations between the chief secretary and the spending ministers continued on a bilateral basis as before, but there was no longer an expectation that the chief secretary and the minister would usually come to an agreement (Thain and Wright 1995, 304–6). Once the committee had heard testimony from all spending ministers, it would propose a total spending package to the cabinet for consideration. The secretariat for the committee came from the Treasury as well as from the cabinet office.[9]

Together, these reforms represented an acknowledgment that the previous system was not working as well as the Treasury would have liked and, indeed, that the budgetary outcomes were getting worse. There was a sense in Treasury circles that the spending ministers were getting too much in the bilateral negotiations. Moreover, the star-chamber process did not allow one to weigh relative spending priorities (interview with senior Treasury official, London, January 2003). The EDX Committee provided a way for the Treasury to secure its goals without ceding too much control. It forced a consideration of explicit budgetary trade-offs without going to the full cabinet. Moreover, the chancellor chaired the committee, and his staff provided much of the committee's staff. The EDX Committee was also useful because it gave the chancellor, weakened by the ERM crisis, useful political cover.

Although Norman Lamont was chancellor when EDX came into being, he chaired the committee only once. The year following the ERM crisis, John Major replaced him with Kenneth Clarke. Clarke was an enthusiastic supporter of the EDX Committee, and he found it a useful forum for setting government spending priorities. Only rarely was the committee overruled. As with previous chancellors, one of the few times a spending minister successfully lobbied the full cabinet to overrule Clarke's EDX was when Defence Minister Malcolm Rifkind averted the lion's share of proposed defense cuts in the 1994–95 budget (*Financial Times*, October 29, 1993). Yet, this exception aside, the new process, combined with tax increases under both Lamont and Clarke, was seemingly a success. The cyclically adjusted budget balance improved from a low of –6.1% of GDP in 1993 to –2.2% of GDP in 1997. Using the Maastricht treaty definitions of deficits, with a deficit of 2.0% of GDP, the United Kingdom would have qualified for EMU in 1997, had it, of course, chosen to apply. Compared with the state of the budget in the

---

9. There was a third element to the reform, the so-called unified budget that meant that taxation and expenditure decisions were made at the same time. This practice lasted only until the mid-1990s (interviews with Treasury officials, London, January 2003).

early 1990s, the Conservatives were leaving a relatively healthy budget to the Labour Party after its May 1997 landslide victory.

Labour's Iron Chancellor and Constrained Discretion

It had taken Labour eighteen years to return to power. There was a sense in the leadership of the party that it was essential for the party to earn a reputation as a good manager of the economy if it was to gain reelection. To make the point that the electorate could trust Labour, the shadow chancellor, Gordon Brown, pledged during the campaign to honor Tory spending plans for the first two years if Labour won. He added that Labour would not increase the basic or top rate of the income tax for the life of that Parliament.[10]

The ascent of Labour restored luster to the Treasury. After Labour's victory, there was little doubt that Gordon Brown would become Tony Blair's chancellor. Moreover, the chancellor would have clear autonomy over economic policy. As a recent journalistic account of the relationship between Blair and Brown notes, while in the opposition they had already decided their roles in a future government, with "Blair as a quasi-presidential figure directing government strategy, making treaties and fighting wars and painting the big picture, [and] with Brown as the all-powerful economic overlord" (Naughtie 2002, 81). The Labour government maintained this division of power, and indeed Brown became known in the press as the Iron Chancellor. His authority on economic issues, including the state of the budget, was largely unquestioned both within the party and in the country.

Under Labour, the EDX Committee continues largely as before, albeit as the PSX (Public Services and Public Expenditure) Committee. The committee now includes ten people instead of seven, with the prime minister's chief advisor on delivery also invited to attend, so that the number of people at a committee meeting can be as many as eleven. As before, the members are expected to have little stake in the budget process. The committee in 2002 included Secretary of State for Work and Pensions Alistair Darley, for example, whose budget responsibility is essentially set on automatic, as well as the Lord Chancellor, Lord Irvine of Lairg, whose main responsibility was the law and who had a small budget of his own. The Lord Chancellor established a reputation for finding the weaknesses in the cases that spending ministers put before the committee (Treasury interviews, January 2003).

10. This pledge led to a nice twist in budgeting. The Tories had originally planned to increase public spending to 40% of GDP. Tax increases in the mid-1990s did not lead to as much revenue as anticipated, and, rather than raise taxes again before an election, the Tories kept spending at around 38% of GDP. When Labour came to power, it kept the level of spending as before. Tory plans, however, were to raise spending to 40%. Overall public spending was therefore lower under Labour during its first two years in government than it would probably have been had John Major held on to power (author interview with senior Treasury official, January 2003).

The chancellor remains the chair, and the chief secretary continues to present an overview of the expenditure case for every department.

The goal of the revised committee remains setting priorities for the budget. The overall framework, however, differs in at least three important respects from that under the Conservatives.[11] First, the committee discusses spending priorities in the context of the more general expenditure review. This review establishes spending targets for the following three years. The review occurs every two years, however, so the process in practice sets spending at two-year intervals. The initial review occurred in 1998, and it was really an occasion for the new team at the Treasury to get a full sense of the different parts of spending while Labour kept to its pledge to execute the Conservatives' spending plans. A review followed in 2000, which set spending for 2001–2003. What was the third year of the 1998 plan became the first year of the 2000 plan. The nature of these targets is a natural extension of the practices under the Conservatives. The so-called DELs, or Departmental Expenditure Limits, are targets on noncyclical expenditure. The DELs represent approximately 70% of all spending, and there is a budget reserve to deal with possible unforeseen shocks to a given spending category. The second targets are on Annually Managed Expenditure, and they represent targets on cyclical components of the budget such as social security and interest payments, as well as European Union–level payments to the Common Agriculture Policy (HM Treasury 2002b, 235–36). There is also a reserve that backs the AME. When expenditures in this category are less than anticipated, the extra funds go directly into the reserve. When there is an economic shock that leads to greater expenditures, the reserve is drawn down.

The second change is the focus of the review. Instead of a focus on inputs, the review is meant to critique each department on the quality and quantity of its outputs. Each department is expected to set general goals as well as more specific, and generally quantifiable, targets to reach those goals. This system is an application of what the public administration literature refers to as "performance-based management."[12]

The final change is the introduction of what the Treasury refers to as the "government's two fiscal rules." The first rule is the "Golden Rule," which under the current government means that there is to be a balanced budget over the economic cycle and that borrowing can occur for capital investment.[13] The second rule is the Sustainable Investment Rule, which states

11. A complete review of the current budgetary framework can be found in HM Treasury 2002.

12. There is a large academic literature on performance-based management. For an overview of its application to the United Kingdom, see National Audit Office 2001.

13. The most basic definition of a "Golden Rule" states that a government must finance all current spending so that there is indeed a budget balance. Capital spending is financed through borrowing. The notable variation under Labour is the stress on "over the economic cycle," which provides some flexibility to run a deficit when the economy is weak.

that public sector debt will remain at a stable and sustainable level, again, over the business cycle. The target figure of "less than 40% of GDP" is more stringent than the Maastricht treaty's 60% of GDP.

There has been only one complete term of office under this new system, but Treasury officials are, on the whole, content with the new system. By almost any standard, fiscal performance has been exemplary. As an independent report produced by the Institute for Fiscal Studies noted, the government has easily kept to its two fiscal rules (Emmerson and Frayne 2002). From the Labour government's ascent to power in 1997 through 2002, the cyclically adjusted current budget remained in surplus (HM Treasury 2003). According to Maastricht definitions, general government deficits have been mildly negative while the overall debt burden has dropped from 48% of GDP in 1998 to 39% in 2001 (HM Treasury 2002a).

Is this performance due to the personal power of a chancellor intent on keeping public finances in order or to the form of fiscal governance in place? The functioning of one of the institutions in particular, the PSX Committee, is the subject of some speculation. The committee's meetings are not open to the public, and there is less leaking to the press than was the case when the Star-chamber Committee was in session.[14] The government publishes only the final conclusions of the committee's deliberations. Yet, based on a series of interviews conducted in London in January 2003, I believe that the committee is less important to the Labour government than EDX was in the last years of John Major's government. One reason may be that Gordon Brown has the power of the purse firmly in his hands. A second, related reason could be that the chancellor is so dominant that it is difficult to disentangle his objectives from the objectives of the PSX Committee. As a Treasury official commented to me, "The chancellor is so powerful at the moment that the process becomes something of a ritual" (London, January 2003).

Indeed, the operation of the PSX Committee and the new system in general are relevant to the discussion of the theoretical model presented here. A close advisor to the chancellor, Ed Balls, has referred to the new multiannual spending plans as constituting "constrained discretion" (HM Treasury 2002b). The phrase seems to imply a further, and intentional, erosion of the powers of the chancellor in the budget process. Moreover, in the theoretical framework presented here, constrained discretion seems to represent a move away from delegation to commitment, that is, a move away from a finance minister as the budget gatekeeper to Dutch-style multiannual budget

14. A senior Treasury official explained to me that leaks might damage a spending minister's case before EDX or PSX. These committees essentially took testimony from the different ministries and then produced a recommendation for the entire budget. Leaking the discussions could anger one or more committee members before decisions were made on spending priorities. This contrasted with the experience under the Star-chamber Committee, where spending ministers could hope that the committee would appear unreasonable if the budget figures were leaked.

plans. This interpretation is mistaken. If anything, the new framework strengthens the chancellor's position. Consider the following responsibilities that the chancellor maintains: First, he sets the aggregate amount of spending allowed in a given year. Second, he chairs the PSX Committee, which reviews the spending proposals from each department. Third, after discussion in the committee, he sums up the sense of the committee, and his statement is usually the decision (interviews in London, January 2003). Finally, he has the power to rewrite the targets. There would certainly be some political cost to rewriting them, but spending departments as well as the Treasury are aware that the chancellor has this ability. As I will show in the next chapter, this process of formulating and executing targets varies considerably from the practice in a commitment state such as the Netherlands where the finance minister has none of these powers.

The Evolution of Delegation in Britain and the Maastricht Treaty

Some general lessons emerge from this discussion of the evolution of fiscal rules and fiscal performance since 1973. First, there have been periods when the chancellor was stronger and others when he was weaker. When the budget is seemingly spiraling out of control, new fiscal rules are often introduced to strengthen the chancellor's hand. The implementation of Treasury cash limits in 1976, the abolition of the Civil Service Department in 1981, and the introduction of a top-down approach in 1992 all gave additional power to the Treasury. Yet there is little doubt that this power alone did not suffice when the chancellor himself was not politically powerful. The Star-chamber and the EDX Committees gave the chancellor political cover when it was not possible for him (or, more accurately, his chief secretary) to maintain tighter fiscal policy. These committees did not die away, but they became less important after the budget recovered and the chancellor became strong politically.

Indeed, whether the Treasury has control of the budget process is the subject of debate among British political scientists. Heclo and Wildavsky (1974) argue that, while the Treasury does not always get its way, it is certainly the critical player in the budget game. Thain and Wright (1995) are more skeptical. As they note in their introduction to *The Treasury and Whitehall,* "The central argument of this book is that the Treasury failed to achieve both the short-term and medium-term objectives for public spending set by successive governments through the years 1976–93. It failed also to achieve its historic mission to restrain the growth of public spending" (5).

Delegation in the United Kingdom does indeed have political limits. First, each party has some sacred cows. No matter how strong the chancellor, there are some budget items that are more difficult to cut than others. For Labour, there was reluctance in the mid-1970s to cut expenditures that labor unions wanted. For the Conservatives, the sacred cow was defense, and both Margaret Thatcher and John Major sided with the defense minister in spending battles. Second, the effectiveness of delegation eroded in the year before an election.[15] External shocks, such as the oil crisis and the recessions that hurt all of Western Europe in the early 1980s and early 1990s, also damaged the health of the budget balance.

There is, therefore, general agreement that the Treasury is not all-knowing, and that the deficit sometimes spikes upward because of shocks both internal (e.g., an upcoming elections) and external (e.g., a slump of the world economy). Yet, given these limitations, the delegation form of fiscal governance in the United Kingdom has provided a measure of fiscal discipline. Except for 1974, when the debt level was almost exactly at 60% of GDP, the overall debt burden has not been over Maastricht's 60%. Significant deviations from a balanced budget have occurred, but there was usually a correction that came afterward that brought the budget back in balance (at least in cyclically adjusted terms). Importantly for the argument in this book, the evolution of the British budget system has been one that has made explicit trade-offs on spending more transparent to decision makers. As a senior Treasury official told Deakin and Parry (2000, 67), "With EDX we've made much more progress than ever before in getting a collective view of priorities." The process has therefore confronted the common pool resource problem discussed in chapter 2.

Another question to ask after *how* the United Kingdom performed is *why* it chose the fiscal institutions that it did. One question concerns the role of the Maastricht treaty. The United Kingdom chose not to join EMU, and it received an explicit opt-out in the treaty. A priori one would think that the treaty could not in any sense "bind" the government, yet the treaty may have had some effect. As the Treasury and Civil Service Committee noted in 1992 (as cited in Thain and Wright 1995, 27), "A strategy for deficit reduction in the medium-term is required under the terms of the Maastricht treaty, whether or not the UK joins the ERM, and will be required for domestic policy reasons even if the UK does not ratify the Maastricht treaty." Parliament did eventually ratify the Maastricht treaty despite the vocal protests of some Tory Euroskeptics, and the timing of the introduction of the EDX Committee in 1992 is consistent with a Maastricht-based argument.

Yet it is probable that the "domestic policy reasons" mentioned in the Treasury and Civil Service Committee's report were much more important. There was certainly no explicit attempt to link reforms of the budget process with Maastricht. As Treasury officials told me (London 2003), the British tabloids

---

15. The erosion was especially noticeable prior to the one election (1992) in which the United Kingdom effectively had a fixed exchange rate. As Clark and Hallerberg (2000) suggest, fiscal political business cycles are more likely when there is a fixed exchange rate and open capital mobility.

would have attacked any effort to link budgetary reform with anything having to do with Brussels. The Conservative government in power then also would have lost further credibility with its own backbenchers. Even under the Blair government, there is reluctance to admit any connection between government policy and the meeting of European-level requirements. In December 2002, in testimony before the House of Commons Treasury Committee, Chancellor Gordon Brown refused to state that the United Kingdom was abiding by the Maastricht restrictions. He stressed instead that he was sticking to the government's fiscal rules, and those rules would mean that the United Kingdom would have a deficit below 3% of GDP.[16]

This is not to say that Maastricht had no effect at all on domestic budgeting. As a senior Treasury official emphasized to me, the Maastricht process certainly improved the transparency of British government accounts. The public sector borrowing requirement, which had been on a cash basis, was replaced with the resource counting budgetary system. Although the new system was not an exact copy of Maastricht accounting definitions, it was nevertheless much closer to them. This shift made it easier to convert domestic accounts into the figures that the United Kingdom filed in its annual convergence program.

Yet a domestic electoral, rather than a European Union, logic for the changes in 1992 seems most persuasive. British electorates are known to punish governments that mismanage the economy. Going to the IMF in September 1976 was a fatal blow to the credibility of the Labour Party. The Conservatives knew in the 1980s that when electoral fortunes looked bad, a Tory offensive based on Labour's economic record was a surefire way to shift the political winds (Howe 1995; Lamont 2000). Similarly, the ERM crisis in September 1992 tarred the Conservatives. The Labour Party knew that it had only to bide its time until the next election (Naughtie 2002). Incumbent governments know that they will lose if they appear to mismanage the economy.

The Federal Republic of Germany: Checked Delegation

In the postwar period, Germany developed a reputation for sound economic management. An "economic miracle," guided by Economics Minister Ludwig Erhard in the 1950s, transformed a country devastated by World War II into the economic engine of Europe. The German mark became the strong currency on the Continent, and the Bundesbank, together with occasional

16. A Liberal Democrat, David Laws, asked the chancellor, "So you are committed to keeping borrowing under the 3% Maastricht limit?" Gordon Brown responded that "we are committed to our fiscal rules . . . and these fiscal rules, as you see from the figures, show that we will be below 3%." Despite repeated questioning about the connection between Maastricht and Treasury behavior, Gordon Brown never made the direct connection in his testimony. House of Commons Treasury Committee 2003, Ev 56–57.

support from the German government, worked to ensure low inflation rates. Sound management extended to fiscal policy. The country was considered a "hawk" that advocated tight adherence to the Maastricht fiscal criteria. Its insistence in 1996 and 1997 that euro-zone members maintain fiscal discipline after the creation of the euro took institutional form as the Stability and Growth Pact.

Given this seemingly stellar economic record, one would expect, if an argument about the effectiveness of fiscal forms of governance had any validity, that Germany would have a particularly developed form of fiscal governance. Indeed, like the United Kingdom, Germany has developed a delegation model of decision making on the budget. The finance minister is clearly the most important person in the budget process. Yet the ability of the finance minister to affect the budget is less consistent than in the United Kingdom, and it depends on four factors that do not appear in the British system. Two of these factors, the presence of coalition governments and the requirement that some types of bills pass the upper house of parliament (or Bundesrat), potentially undermine the finance minister's role in the budget process. Another, more infrequent, check on the finance minister is the Constitutional Court. It is not clear a priori whether the court will make decisions that help or hurt the finance minister's role. Finally, although it has no formal role in the making of fiscal policy, the Bundesbank does make its views on the state of German fiscal policy known. It generally takes a tougher line than the finance minister. In addition to these outside checks on the finance minister, a relative decline in the institutional capacity of the finance minister after German reunification in 1990 has led to growing budget problems. The general picture is one of a finance minister who has more checks on his power than the chancellor of the exchequer does in the United Kingdom. This leads to a more or less effective finance minister depending on the absence or presence of each of these checks at any given time. Indeed, Germany no longer has the same reputation for fiscal prudence as it once did. For 2002, the budget deficit in general government terms was above 3% of GDP, and the Council of Ministers initiated an excessive deficit procedure against Germany in January 2003. The irony that the excessive deficit procedure was introduced against the country that insisted on the procedure in the first place is not lost on commentators both inside and outside the country.

Political Background

Germany has become a more complex polity in the past twenty years. Lijphart (1999) identifies three relevant political cleavages in Germany. The first is the traditional left-right divide. The second is a religious dimension. The third is a modernist-postmodernist one. One could add a fourth cleavage that has arisen because of reunification, an east-west divide.

The electoral system has allowed several parties to form along these cleavages, although it has restricted the absolute number of parties (at the national level) to no more than six at any one time. Germans know the electoral system as "personalized proportional representation." For the lower house of parliament, the Bundestag, half the seats are filled according to an electoral system that approximates the plurality system in the United Kingdom and half according to proportional representation. In practice, this means that voters see two ballots on one ballot form. They first cast a vote for an individual. The candidate who wins the most votes in an electoral district wins the seat. Voters also have a second ballot for a political party. The party vote is, ultimately, the crucial one. The final distribution of seats is supposed to correspond directly to the distribution of party votes. The seats awarded through the party vote, therefore, are used to "fill in" the gaps left by the first ballot. A party that wins 35% of the vote on the second ballot is supposed to get 35% of the seats in parliament regardless of how well it does on the first ballot.[17] An important part of the electoral law is that a party must receive either 5% of the party vote or win three seats outright on the first ballot in order to receive its proportion of seats under the second ballot. This limitation is the most important reason why there is a cap for the number of parties that can hold Bundestag seats. The history of the Party of Democratic Socialism (the former East German Communists) in a reunified Germany illustrates how this law functions in practice. In 1994, the PDS received 4% of the party vote but won four direct seats in its strongholds in East Germany. It therefore received 4% of the seats. In 1998, it passed the 5% hurdle on the second ballot, so the results from the first ballot were not relevant. In 2002, it won less than 5% of the party vote and only two direct seats. It obtained no additional seats in parliament on the second ballot, so only two representatives from the PDS are now in the Bundestag.

Since the restoration of democracy in 1949, one of the mass-based political parties has formed every government. Moreover, with the exception of the "grand coalition" that brought the major parties of the left and the right together from 1966 to 1969, the norm is that a mass-based party forms a coalition with a smaller partner. The party that has spent the most time in government is the Christian Democratic Union. The party runs candidates in all parts of Germany except Bavaria, where its sister party, the Christian Social Union, is firmly entrenched. Both parties represent the center-right of the political spectrum, with the CSU somewhat more conservative than the CDU.

17. An additional complication to the system is that the seats are distributed at the Land, or state, level rather than at the federal level. There are occasions, therefore, when a party wins most or all of the first ballot seats but less than 50% of the second ballot votes. Because a person cannot be removed from parliament once elected, and because the number of party seats to be distributed is fixed, there are sometimes so-called overhanging seats, or *Überhangsmandate*. In the 2002 elections, there were five such seats, so the number of (federal) parliamentarians in Berlin was 603 instead of 598.

The mass-based party that opposes these two parties from the center-left is the Social Democratic Party of Germany (SPD). There are three smaller parties that have won seats in the Bundestag since 1973. The Free Democratic Party traces its heritage from the liberal parties founded in Wilhelmine Germany. During the period considered here, they combined a free market outlook on the economy with a policy of active engagement with Communist Eastern Europe in foreign policy. They have formed coalitions at various times with both the SPD and the CDU/CSU, and they have therefore been in government more often than any one of the mass-based parties. The Green Party first entered the Bundestag in 1983. It arose out of the peace movement's opposition to the stationing of U.S. nuclear short-range missiles on German territory, and it combines a decided streak of pacifism with a pronounced concern for the environment. This party entered government for the first time in 1998. Finally, the Party of Democratic Socialism arose after reunification from the remnants of the East German Communist Party (which had been known officially as the Socialist Unification Party of Germany or SED). It is even more pacifist than the Greens, and it receives its support primarily in areas of the former East Germany. It has never been in government at the national level, although it does participate in government at the state (or *Land*) level, including Germany's capital city, Berlin.

The party system that emerges from the confluence of the cleavage structure and the electoral system that exists in Germany has led to a "clumping" of parties as blocs on the center-right or the center-left. These blocs generally run against each other in elections, although there is often internal tension within a given electoral alliance over specific issues. In the period beginning in 1973, there was a "red-yellow," or SPD-FDP, coalition first under Chancellor Willy Brandt and then under Chancellor Helmut Schmidt that lasted through 1982. The FDP then left the coalition to form a new one with the CDU/CSU under Chancellor Helmut Kohl, the "black-yellow" coalition. This coalition lost the 1998 election, and a "red-green," or SPD-Green, coalition replaced it.

Given that the parties in coalition are generally close together ideologically, one would expect that a delegation form of fiscal governance would be the appropriate form for Germany. Indeed, German coalitions have used delegation, yet the effectiveness of the finance minister has varied over time. Politically, coalition tensions can undermine the finance minister's ability to maintain fiscal discipline. Institutionally, the powers of the finance minister decreased after reunification but increased again when the Social Democrats returned to power in 1998.

Fiscal Policy and Fiscal Actors

In cyclically adjusted terms, Germany's fiscal performance included two periods when the budget balance deteriorated below –3% of GDP (fig. 4.2). The

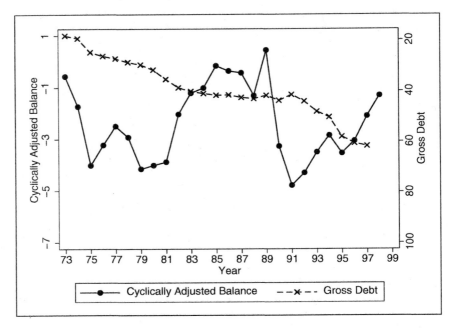

Fig. 4.2. Cyclically adjusted budget balance and gross debt level in Germany, 1973–98.
Source: European Commission 1999a.

first period was in the late 1970s, and it lasted three years. The second period began after German reunification, and, including 1994 when the balance stood at –2.85% of GDP, it lasted twice as long, or seven years. In cyclically adjusted terms, in fact, the balance did not move above –3% of GDP until 1997, the year that the Council of Ministers used to determine membership in Stage Three of EMU. The gross debt figures, which are according to Maastricht definitions, similarly indicate a marked deterioration in the 1990s. The debt level jumped from 41.5% of GDP in 1991 to 58.1% in 1995, and in both 1996 and 1997 the gross debt level was slightly above Maastricht's 60% threshold. What is noteworthy is that this is the only time since 1973 that the debt level has been this high. One reason for the deterioration of the fiscal accounts was certainly German reunification, which has been much more expensive than even independent observers such as the Bundesbank expected. Yet, there was also a shift in the balance of power on fiscal issues within the Kohl government that undermined the finance minister.

The chancellor is formally the most important actor in the budget process. Article 65 of the Basic Law (or Grundgesetz, the German equivalent of a constitution) grants him responsibility for the policies of the government. He is required legally to issue policy guidelines to the various ministries, a power known in German as the *Richtlinienkompetenz*.[18] In principle, this extends to all aspects of policy making, which includes the budget.

In practice, the key person in the budget process is usually the finance minister. Once the chancellor has made his policy statement, the finance minister's job is to ensure that what the spending ministers eventually receive accords with the chancellor's policy statement. The role of the finance minister in Germany is similar to the role of the chancellor of the exchequer in the United Kingdom. The finance minister writes five-year plans that provide aggregate figures for the budget on items such as the budget balance and total amount of spending. Twelve months before a budget is to come into effect, or January of a given year, the finance ministry circulates a brief to the spending ministers that forecasts the aggregate spending caps for each ministry. These caps are then the basis for bilateral negotiations between the finance ministry and spending ministries. Although a dispute could reach the full cabinet for an airing if it is not resolved in bilateral negotiations, under such circumstances the finance minister has an institutional advantage. Formally, Paragraph 28(2) of the rules that regulate the passage of the budget (*Bundeshaushaltsordnung*) states that the finance minister can veto any proposal in the cabinet that has budget implications. It takes a vote of a majority of the cabinet plus the chancellor to overrule this veto. There are no known cases of a successful override (Sturm 1994; interviews at the finance ministry, Bundestag, Berlin, October 2000; interview at the Bundesbank, Frankfurt, March 2002). Although this record is indeed impressive, such a vote would probably lead to a finance minister's resignation. There is therefore an incentive on both sides for ministers in a dispute to resolve an issue before it comes to a formal cabinet vote.

Under the black-yellow coalition, Chancellor Kohl made clear that he wanted disputes to be resolved outside the cabinet. The only time this rule was broken was when the FDP wanted to "lose" a vote in cabinet in order to signal to voters that it preferred a different course of action. A vote in the cabinet was then allowed (interview with former cabinet member, Berlin, October 2000). More recently, in 2000 under Gerhard Schröder's chancellorship, a public dispute over the level of defense spending between Defense Minister Rudolf Scharping and Finance Minister Hans Eichel was resolved after a temporary commission appointed to study the issue brought the two sides closer. Once again, a formal cabinet vote was not necessary. The more general lesson is that the finance minister is effective only so long as she enjoys the chancellor's confidence. In 1971 and 1972, two finance ministers,

18. As Article 65 of the Basic Law states, "The Chancellor determines and is responsible for the general policy guidelines. Within the limits set by these guidelines, each Minister conducts the affairs of his department independently and on his own responsibility" (as translated in Tschentscher 2002, 47).

Alex Möller and Karl Schiller respectively, resigned when Chancellor Willy Brandt refused to back their proposed expenditure cuts (Strauch and von Hagen 2001, 10).

Besides the lack of backing from the chancellor, there are additional factors that can undermine the finance minister. The first concerns the nature of coalition governments. There are coalition agreements that set the priorities of the government. For electoral reasons coalition partners are usually concerned that they be identified with certain items in the budget (Horst 1995). This makes them more likely to resist cuts in items that are most dear to them. As a consequence, it is more difficult for the finance minister to cut the budgets of ministries that are controlled by a coalition partner.[19] Parties also have appointed state secretaries who serve immediately below the respective ministers in each ministry. The coalition agreement determines the absolute number of state secretaries. This procedure can even check the finance minister. Horst (1995) reports that the CSU's political boss at the time, Franz-Josef Strauss, made sure that his confidant, Friedrich Voss, was appointed as a state secretary in 1982 to watch over the CDU's Gerhard Stoltenberg.

Unlike the unitary British system, the German political system is federal. The governments of states (Länder) have representation in the Bundesrat, and any law that affects the Länder governments must pass this chamber. The Bundesrat's approval is not required on the annual federal budget, but tax matters usually do involve Länder affairs and do require Bundesrat approval. When the government does not have a majority in the upper house, its control of fiscal policy is limited to the expenditure side of the ledger.[20] Each Land government has between three and six votes, and the votes are not divisible. This means that coalition governments at the Land level must make decisions on how they will vote as a bloc. In the 1980s and 1990s, party cleavages usually dictated the course of votes in the upper chamber (Tsebelis and Money 1997). Divisions according to small versus large Länder and the like were more common in the 1950s, but since then they have become more infrequent—although since reunification the East German Länder have sometimes cooperated closely across the party loyalties of their respective governments. There have also been occasions when the government seemed successful at "buying" the votes of some Land governments, as Chancellor Schröder did in 2000 to pass his tax reform. Yet it is fair to say that the Bundesrat must be taken into account when devising policy, especially when the government does not have a majority in the upper chamber.

19. Former cabinet members from the SPD and the FDP independently confirmed this difficulty in conversation with me (telephone interview, December 1996, and interview in Berlin, October 2000).

20. König and Tröger (2001) make this same point in a detailed statistical study of German fiscal policy from 1961 to 1998.

Indeed, the government has lacked a majority more often than not in the period covered in this book. The SPD-FDP coalition lost its majority in the Bundesrat in 1972, and it continued to hemorrhage seats in the upper house after losing elections at the Land level until the FDP switched coalition partners in 1982. Helmut Kohl's government enjoyed a majority in the upper house until it lost it in 1992. Gerhard Schröder's tenure with a government-friendly Bundesrat lasted only months, until the CDU won the elections in Hesse in early 1999.

Another peculiarity of the German system is that its constitution has explicit provisions concerning public finance. The Basic Law restricts public borrowing according to the so-called Golden Rule discussed earlier. As Article 115 states, "Revenue obtained by borrowing may not exceed the total of expenditures for investments provided for in the budget; exceptions are permissible only to avert a disturbance of the overall economic equilibrium" (as translated in Tschentscher 2002, 87). This constitutional provision would seem to empower the finance minister. Yet, as a senior staff member of the Bundesbank told me (Frankfurt, March 2002), this article is in practice a "toothless tiger." Governments must propose budgets that are expected to follow this restriction, but there is no requirement that the government make adjustments if actual budget performance deviates from expected performance. Indeed, *every* budget but one in the 1990s violated Article 115 (Kreber 2002, 322).

As a review of German fiscal policy during the time period 1980–2000 will show, fiscal policy is less effective when the finance minister has weaker institutional control.

Development of Fiscal Policy

Germany's fiscal history can be broken into three distinct periods. The first period is from 1973 until the collapse of the SPD-FDP coalition in 1982. Differences between the coalition partners on the budget contributed to the coalition's demise. The second period, 1982–89, is one of fiscal consolidation under Helmut Kohl's government. During the third period, 1990–2002, the budget situation deteriorated sharply through 1996 and then stabilized. This is not a comprehensive overview of German fiscal history. Rather, I focus on distinct episodes that illustrate how the delegation form of governance did or did not function effectively in Germany.

Fiscal Policy under Chancellor Schmidt

The oil crisis in the early 1970s led to higher prices and higher unemployment in Germany than at any other time in the postwar period. Yet the country began the period in good financial shape. The gross debt burden was less than 20% of GDP. Moreover, the budget balance did not deteriorate to the extent that it did in other European countries. Germany had a budget surplus in 1973 of 0.7% of GDP, and the balance deteriorated to a low of only –2.8% in 1975 (European Commission 1999a). There was growth in expenditures, with overall transfers to households in particular increasing from 19% of GDP in 1974 to 24% of GDP in 1977.

Yet, despite the expenditure pressure, budget deficits did not become a chronic problem as in other countries. The deficit did reach a peak of –5.6% of GDP in 1975 but was quickly cut back. The strength of the finance minister in the budget process at the time was certainly one reason. Politically, the social-liberal coalition began the period facing a Bundesrat under opposition control. Control of the budget on the spending side was easier than on the tax side. Helmut Schmidt, chancellor since May 1974, generally backed his finance minister, Hans Apel, in budget matters. An illustrative case comes from preparations for the 1975 budget that Apel reported in his memoirs. The finance minister was committed to slowing the growth of expenditures, and he took a hard line on ministerial spending requests. When fellow cabinet member Erhard Eppler refused to accept cuts in spending on Third World development, Schmidt signaled that he would support his finance minister. Eppler then resigned (Apel 1991, 22). In the run-up to the general election, the government targeted the unemployment insurance fund, which had a large deficit because of increasing unemployment, and it both cut the level of benefits and raised the contribution levels (Scharpf 1991, 141). It also restricted increases in public service pay (Bundesbank 1981, 21).

The coalition did not flinch from raising some taxes, and particularly the value-added tax, to keep the budget deficit under control when it could get the votes either in the Bundesrat or in the Reconciliation Committee (Vermittlungsausschuss), where compromises could be struck between government and opposition. The amount of money collected from indirect taxes increased two percentage points of GDP from 1974 to 1977 (European Commission 1999a). Schmidt was Willy Brandt's last finance minister, and, while Schmidt did not involve himself in the detailed formulation of tax policy, he did oversee a tax reform that readjusted tax rates and increased allowances to families. The expenditure cuts as well as the tax increases had some success, as the budget balance improved from –2.8% of GDP in 1975 to –0.8% in 1977.

At a political level, the electoral consequences of such fiscal austerity are debatable. A federal election was scheduled for the latter part of 1976, and the weak economy was a real cause for concern. The SPD, nevertheless, made clear during the campaign that it would again need to raise taxes. Despite (or because of) the austerity measures, the coalition held on to power in a tight election in 1976, when the CDU/CSU had the best electoral result since 1957. A thin majority of ten seats proved to be even more precarious the day the Bundestag reelected Helmut Schmidt as chancellor. He received only one more vote than absolutely necessary. This demonstrated that he would have to fear defections of members of parliament from his coalition during the next four years. The situation was also made more difficult for the Schmidt government in the Bundesrat. Earlier that year, the blocking majority for the opposition in the upper house had been just one vote (twenty-one to twenty). Moreover, one Land, Saarland, had a Christian Democratic government that the FDP tolerated in exchange for an informal agreement that Saarland would not block any legislation the FPD considered important in the second chamber. This arrangement had given the Schmidt government some flexibility. In February, however, the opposition's majority increased to eleven when Lower Saxony changed from a social-liberal coalition to a Christian Democratic minority government.

With a razor-thin majority in the lower house and firm opposition in the upper house, gaining government tax reforms was difficult. Continued economic weakness, in fact, led to growing pressure both at home and abroad for a stimulative package of fiscal measures. At home, the FDP saw its political fortunes tied to large tax cuts. The SPD also favored some tax cuts, but it wanted to couple these with additional spending on such budget items as research and technology. Abroad, the government faced pressure both from the United States and from its European neighbors to increase economic growth. The hope was that Germany would act as a "locomotive" that could pull the rest of the developed world into greater prosperity.

Despite the misgivings of Schmidt's new finance minister, Hans Matthöfer, and Schmidt himself, the government caved in to pressure and agreed at an international economic conference in Bonn in July 1978 to stimulate the economy at least 1% of GNP. The promise of increased budgets quickly spread through Bonn's ministries. Spending ministers had the opportunity to push for projects that the finance minister would normally not approve. As Fritz Scharpf (1991, 145) noted, "Minister of Labor Ehrenberg pushed [additional maternity leave benefits] through in the heat of the moment. The unanimous opinion at the time was that he would not have had the chance of succeeding in a regular budget process." Moreover, the tax cuts included in the package lasted through 1981, past the upcoming general election (Bundestag 1981).

The big winner of the 1980 Bundestag elections was the FDP. Its support jumped from 7.9% to 10.6% and came primarily at the expense of the CDU/CSU, which fell from 48.6% to 44.5%. Yet despite this increase in support for the two coalition partners among the voters, the coalition was soon in trouble as the economy deteriorated. In 1981, budget negotiations became increasingly divisive and drawn out. The opposition's control of the Bundesrat left expenditure cuts as the only option available for the government.[21] Finance Minister Matthöfer signaled that he wanted cuts in "all areas

21. When discussing this period, Fritz Scharpf (1991, 155) notes that "since the opposition was able to block unpopular tax increases in the state chamber of the Bundesrat, the self-imposed obligation to reduce the deficit made additional budget cuts necessary."

of public spending, including social security programs" in order to reduce public borrowing (*New York Times,* July 20, 1981). The rest of the SPD, with labor union backing, wanted large government expenditures. The Free Democrats, in contrast, argued for cuts in social security spending and tax relief for businesses. In the version of the budget that passed, both Matthöfer and the FDP won. The budget honored Matthöfer's deficit limit while avoiding any new employment schemes that the SPD wanted (*Washington Post,* September 4, 1981).

Yet fiscal matters continued to deteriorate. Matthöfer's successor as finance minister, Manfred Lahnstein, was a technocrat who had worked his way through the finance ministry with few ties to the Social Democrats. He assumed office in April 1982 with a commitment to an early passage of the 1983 budget. He expected that an agreement before the summer break would avoid the previous year's "summer theater" in which the coalition partners routinely attacked each other in the press. At first Lahnstein seemed to succeed, with the coalition partners reaching agreement on a budget at the beginning of July. The proposed budget would have cut spending in real terms and reduced the government's borrowing to DM 28.4 billion from almost DM 34 billion the previous year (DM 1.68 = $1) (*Financial Times,* July 8, 1982). Economic forecasts produced over the summer, however, suggested that the original figures used in the budget draft were too optimistic. The Bundesbank set the tone of the debate at the end of August when its president, Karl Otto Pohl, stated on German TV that he thought government borrowing would again increase in 1983 if the proposed budget was not modified.

Tensions had been growing within the coalition over other issues, such as foreign policy, but the budget situation proved to be intractable. Given the economic conditions, the Social Democrats wanted higher welfare spending financed through increased taxes on the wealthy. The FDP, in contrast, wanted higher subsidies to industry, new tax breaks for business, and deep cuts in welfare spending. The four FDP ministers in the government walked out after Helmut Schmidt's refusal to accept the deep welfare cuts demanded by FDP Economics Minister Otto Lambsdorff (*New York Times,* September 20, 1982).

The new government formed with the CDU's Helmut Kohl as chancellor. One of the first legislative actions the coalition took was to withdraw the SPD-FDP draft budget. The budget's replacement included several items that the FDP originally wanted, such as increased subsidies for business and cuts in welfare programs. Sensitive to a large budget deficit, which would hit 3.3% of GDP in 1982, the coalition also agreed to increase the value-added tax.

Fiscal policy under the Schmidt governments illustrates two points about the effectiveness of the finance minister in imposing fiscal discipline. The first is that the finance minister can work effectively only on the expenditure side of the budget when the opposition controls the Bundesrat. The second is that the ability of the finance minister to set budget policy is dependent on the relationship of his party with his party's coalition partner. There were more negotiations, which in tone were also more divisive, in the early 1980s than under the coalition in the 1970s. Delegation was no longer functioning well. The reason why negotiations became so intense seems clear. The policy preferences of the SPD and the FDP diverged in the early 1980s, making it unlikely that the FDP would allow a Social Democratic finance minister to have too great a role. The existence of the "exit option" also mattered. The fate of the FDP in government was not tied to the fate of the coalition. In the 1980 elections, the CDU and CSU together won more seats than the SPD, and they could easily form a new government with majority status.

Although it was less obvious, there was also a growing alternative for the SPD as well. The party leadership initially treated the Green Party as a competitor that could only take votes from its left flank. Yet, in the first Land elections after the change in government, in Hesse, the Greens entered parliament with 8% of the vote, while the FDP failed to cross the 5% hurdle. The Greens were not yet ready to enter a coalition with the SPD at even the Land level, but the party system was evolving from one in which the FDP was the exclusive king-maker to one with two clear blocs opposing one another.

Fiscal Policy under Kohl: From Discipline to Profligacy

Soon after he replaced Helmut Schmidt, Helmut Kohl made reducing the budget deficit one of the primary goals of his government. In his inauguration speech before the Bundestag, he stated that "our goal is to return to an ordered state through ordered finances" (as quoted in Sturm 1998; my translation).

In practice, Kohl and his coalition partners delegated considerable responsibility for the budget to the new finance minister, Gerhard Stoltenberg. He had served as the youngest member of Ludwig Erhard's cabinet in the early 1960s, and he left his position as minister-president of Schleswig-Holstein to assume his new position in Bonn. Stoltenberg began with cuts in social and education spending as well as increases in indirect taxes. He coupled these changes with tax cuts for business, which was popular within the coalition and which met a demand of his coalition partner, the FDP. New elections were called for March 1983 to confirm the new coalition, and Stoltenberg made clear that further belt-tightening would be needed after the election as well (*Financial Times*, November 11, 1982). After the coalition won these elections, Stoltenberg kept his promise. He cut social spending further, froze public sector pay, and reduced some subsidies for the agriculture sector.[22]

22. While not directly endorsing Stoltenberg's proposals, the Bundesbank's monthly report agreed at the time with the general need for social spending cuts (Bundesbank, April 1983). It argued that the public sector needed to curb social spending.

The government's consolidation efforts were largely a success. The structurally adjusted budget balance improved from –3.9% of GDP in 1981, the last full year of the social-liberal coalition, to near balance (–0.2% of GDP) by 1985. This is not to say that the finance minister was always successful—he lost some battles with coalition partners on some issues, such as the fight with the FDP on the timing and size of some tax cuts and with the CSU on state subsidies for Lufthansa (*New York Times,* June 22, 1984, and *Financial Times,* May 16, 1987). Yet Stoltenberg's efforts to control the deficit were by and large successful. They also proved to be popular. As Sturm (1994, 90–91) observes, "He won credit for restoring credibility to public finance." For a time the finance minister was even more popular than his chancellor, and there were rumors in the press that the CDU would use him to replace Kohl before the next election.

Yet political scandals undermined the finance minister and removed him as a political threat to the chancellor. Stoltenberg was implicated in the Barschel Affair and was also accused of selling secret submarine blueprints to South Africa; in April 1989, he was forced to resign. The budgetary situation Stoltenberg left his successor, Theo Waigel from the CSU, was a healthy one. Measured either in actual or cyclically adjusted terms, the budget was in surplus for the first time since 1973. Much of the progress was due to cuts in expenditure, which fell from 45% of GDP in 1982 to 41.5% in 1989.

German reunification in 1990, however, quickly changed the fiscal landscape. In July 1990, three months before reunification, a confident Finance Minister Waigel predicted that the central government's net borrowing requirement would increase only DM 300 million in 1991, to DM 31.3 billion, but that it would then quickly fall to DM 24 billion in 1992 and DM 11 billion in 1994. Central government spending would increase only around 4% in real terms in 1991 and then fall again below 3%. His chancellor promised during the election campaign that year that no new taxes would be needed. The opposition leader, Oskar Lafontaine, countered that the budget deficit would rise above DM 200 billion and warned that the Kohl government was "lying" about the real fiscal impact of reunification.

Actual fiscal outcomes were not as dire as Lafontaine had predicted, but they were certainly much worse than what Waigel had predicted. Two months after the triumph of the "reunification chancellor" in the December 1990 elections, the coalition admitted that tax increases would be necessary because of the worsening fiscal picture (*Financial Times,* February 21, 1991). The most visible tax increase was the so-called solidarity surcharge, which was levied on income tax payments as a one-off tax in 1991 before its reintroduction in 1995; but taxes also increased on mineral oil, gas, and tobacco. The rates for contributions to social insurance programs also increased. Yet the fiscal conditions would continue to worsen. The cyclically adjusted budget went from a surplus in 1989 to deficits of –3.3% of GDP in 1990 and –4.8% of GDP in 1991. The cyclically adjusted deficit remained around –3% of GDP through

1996. The debt figures were much worse, with the overall debt burden increasing from 40% of GDP in 1991 to 59.6% by 1996.

There are several possible explanations for the deterioration of German finances in this period. An economic recession that hit all of Western Europe in the early 1990s also hit Germany. Yet, as the cyclically adjusted figures illustrate, public finances worsened more than one would expect based only on economic conditions. Reunification was also clearly expensive, more expensive than most observers anticipated.[23] The Bundesbank (March 1997, 17, 19) estimated that more than half the over DM 1 trillion increase in debt from 1989 to 1996 was due to the costs of reunification.

One can also argue that government policy exacerbated the fiscal costs. First, the accounts for paying for the rebuilding of East Germany were not subject to the normal budget process. While the national deficit remained around 3% of GDP, off-budget debts related to reunification bulged to 12% of GDP, while the organization responsible for privatizing the East German economy, the Treuhandanstalt, had its deficit swell from 0.6% of GDP to 6% (Strauch and von Hagen 1999, 16–17). In addition, when the East German economy contracted in the early 1990s, the government passed a series of investment incentives including some tax breaks. These incentives also were generally off-budget.

As I indicated in chapter 3, the Council of Ministers' decision on which countries would join the euro was to be made based on the budget figures from 1997, and the figures for 1996 were ominous. The country that was so insistent on the need for countries to qualify based on actual macroeconomic performance was in danger of missing the critical deficit target of 3%. In 1996, the budget deficit was 3.3%. In an effort to gain greater control over spending, Finance Minister Waigel decreed that his personal approval would be needed for all spending decisions over a certain size.[24] Moreover, in the preparations for the 1997 budget, he proposed expenditure cuts in eighteen of twenty-six spending areas and a total cut in spending of 2.5%. Finally, there were some tax increases that were coupled with a cut in the unpopular solidarity surcharge.

The course of events the following year illustrate both the strengths and the weaknesses of the finance minister. The expenditure cuts passed the Bundestag on the first reading, and, later in 1996, as it became clear that the proposed budget for 1997 would not fall below 3%, Waigel added another DM 3 billion in spending cuts before the final version of the budget passed the lower house. These changes did not require upper house approval, and Waigel was able to carry through the expenditure cuts he wanted. In contrast, the tax measures did require Bundesrat consent, and they ran into

23. Even the usual watchdog of the economy, the Bundesbank, underestimated the true costs. Author interview with Bundesbank official, Frankfurt, March 2002.

24. The thresholds ranged from DM 500,000 for administrative costs to DM 5 million for military procurement and construction (*Financial Times*, March 14, 1996).

immediate problems. The SPD had held a blocking majority in the upper house since 1992, and the opposition blocked the proposed tax increases. Without the corresponding tax increases, it would be difficult to pay for the reduction in the solidarity surcharge, and, despite complaints from the FDP, the government delayed the cut for another year.

In 1997, tax revenues were initially lower than forecast, and Waigel was again on the prowl for additional revenue. Rather clumsily, he attempted to revalue the Bundesbank's gold reserves and to use the resulting profit to reduce the debt burden, and, correspondingly, the interest payments that appeared in the current year's budget. The Bundesbank strongly objected, and Bundesbank President Hans Tietmeyer criticized the government's move. The press sided with the Bundesbank and derided the plan as "creative accounting." There were persistent rumors that President Tietmeyer would resign in protest. Waigel then backed down and reached a compromise with the Bundesbank. The gold would indeed be revalued, but the money would count only in 1998 and would not be the reason why Germany would qualify for Stage Three of EMU (*Financial Times*, May 29, 1997; *Frankfurter Allgemeine Zeitung*, June 4, 1997).

The news for the government worsened in the fall, when it became clear that the Länder would experience a tax shortfall. Moreover, an attempted tax reform, which would not have increased revenue in the short term, nevertheless failed again to pass the Bundesrat. With no real alternative left on the revenue side, Waigel again pushed for spending cuts. He imposed a spending freeze on all German ministries. He also instituted one-off spending cuts for the Labor Office. In total, Waigel announced, the budget freeze and the Labor Office reductions would save another DM 7 billion (*Financial Times*, November 12, 1997).

When the official figures were released the following spring, Germany had a budget deficit of 2.7% of GDP, 0.3% below the critical 3% level in the Maastricht treaty. Much of Europe breathed a sigh of relief. Germany would lie at the heart of the euro-zone and realistically could not be excluded, yet admitting a Germany with a deficit above 3% might have decreased confidence in the euro before the common currency was created. There is still some debate today about whether the budget figures were legitimate (Strauch and von Hagen 2001). There is also some confusion about where the money ultimately came from.[25] Yet public spending undoubtedly dropped a full percentage

25. Zohlnhöfer (2001), for example, attributes much of the fiscal improvement to a wave of privatizations in 1996 and 1997, which included such prominent firms as Lufthansa and Deutsche Telekom. Although the privatizations certainly occurred, Maastricht definitions of deficits and debt did not allow such asset sales to count against the current deficit. The only way they could affect the deficit was indirectly, through a reduction of the deficit and concomitant interest payments. Yet the overall debt burden actually increased from 1996 to 1997, from 59.7% of GDP to 60.8%. The drop in the deficit, therefore, cannot be attributed either directly or indirectly to the privatizations.

point of GDP, from 49.6% of the economy to 48.6% (European Commission 1999), and this drop in spending contributed to the lower deficit.

Red-Green Fiscal Policy

Helmut Kohl did not remain in power to see the euro in circulation. In fall 1998, the coalition lost power to the Social Democrats and the Greens. Kohl's rival for the chancellorship in the 1990 elections, Oskar Lafontaine, became finance minister. He immediately proposed large spending increases in ministries he thought vital to Social Democratic constituencies. Overall spending was to increase 6.8%, with a 12% increase in social spending. Yet Lafontaine did not work well with his chancellor, Gerhard Schröder, and he resigned from office only six months into his term. His successor, Hans Eichel, immediately took Lafontaine's spending back, and more generally he cut overall expenditure 1% from 1999 to 2000 rather than increase it (Zohlnhöfer 2001, 1565). Eichel soon became the coalition's star, gaining a reputation as an "Iron Hans" who maintained fiscal discipline (*Die Zeit*, number 7, 2000). Indeed, the budget deficit in 1999 was only 1.5% of GDP, and it even went into surplus with the help of debt reductions due to the sale of mobile telephone licenses (European Commission 2002).[26]

Chancellor Schröder was not immune to problems with an intransigent upper house. Months after winning the lower house, the new coalition lost the election in Hesse, and, with it, its majority in the Bundesrat. Unlike Helmut Kohl, however, he had some success getting his tax reform through the upper house in 2000 when some Länder with the CDU as a coalition partner voted for the government's proposal after Schröder essentially "bought" them with a package of targeted side payments, such as additional spending for Berlin to mollify the CDU mayor there, Eberhard Diepgen.

This success was not to last. In 2002, Germany experienced a budget deficit above 3% of GDP, and the European Union initiated an excessive deficit procedure against Germany in January 2003. Finance Minister Eichel complained that most of the increase in the general government deficit was due to additional spending at the Länder level. Although exact figures on the deficit breakdown are difficult to verify, the figures for the debt burden support Eichel's assertion. As a percent of GDP, the federal government's debt burden increased only 0.3% of GDP in 2002, from 33.7% of GDP to 34.0%. In contrast, the debt of the West German Länder increased a full percentage point, from 14.5% of GDP to 15.5%. The combined debt burden of the

---

26. Readers should note that the European Union 2002 database calculates budget balance figures according to the standards of the European System of Accounts established in 1995 (ESA 95). Most figures in this book are based on the European Commission (1999a) database, which uses the ESA 79 accounting standards. There are minor differences between the two standards, but there is no clear bias toward smaller or larger deficits under one or the other.

remaining governments, the East German Länder as well as the East and West German local governments (*Gemeinden*), increased another 0.8% of GDP. The growth in the debt burden was therefore six times larger as a percentage of GDP below the central government than at the central government level (Bundesministerium der Finanzen 2003, 113).

Review of the German Case

What can explain the evolution of German fiscal policy? In broad brushstrokes, fiscal discipline was tight in the mid-1970s, from the mid-1980s through reunification, and in the late 1990s. Does the Maastricht treaty explain the fiscal tightening in the late 1990s? The answer is yes, but Maastricht's effects were limited. There was clearly pressure to bring the deficit below 3% for the 1997 budget, and the finance minister responded to this pressure with a series of proposals. When the Bundesrat and Bundesbank in turn blocked some of these, he succeeded in imposing even deeper expenditure cuts. Yet it is hard to find any "Maastricht" effect either before or after this critical year. In terms of outcomes, Germany exceeded the 3% limit in both 1995 and 1996. A Maastricht effect was also missing in terms of rhetoric. In introducing his 1994 budget proposal to the Bundestag and stressing the need for fiscal discipline, Theo Waigel did not even refer to Maastricht (Zohlnhöfer 2001, 1557 n. 7). Civil servants in the finance ministry as well as a senior staff member of the Bundesbank similarly do not trace any budget reforms directly to the Maastricht process (author interviews, Berlin, October 2000, and Frankfurt, March 2002).

Explicit market effects to rein in the budget are similarly difficult to find. Most discussions of market effects, in fact, compare the spread in bonds between a given country's bonds and German bonds. While the interest rate premium on, for example, Italian bonds diminished, German bonds themselves remained stable. There may have been an indirect effect of markets because of worries about the credibility of the euro if Germany were to be a founding member of the common currency with a deficit above 3%. To the extent that even this pressure existed, however, it existed only in 1997.

One can, however, trace the relationship between the power of the finance minister in the budget process and budgetary outcomes. When the finance minister had a privileged position in the formation and execution of the budget, deficits were lower. This was the case under Hans Apel in 1975, Gerhard Stoltenberg in the 1980s, and Hans Eichel during the 1999–2000 time period.

Several factors absent in the prime example of the delegation form of fiscal governance, the United Kingdom, restrict the power of the finance minister in Germany. First, coalition governments are the rule in Germany. When the political parties hold similar views on budget priorities, there are fewer disputes within the coalition, and the finance minister is more autonomous.

Second, the upper house of parliament, the Bundesrat, can restrict the government's ability to use changes in tax policy to balance the budget. All of the governments during the period studied encountered Bundesrat resistance. Third, federalism affects general budget outcomes. In this chapter I have largely focused on the activities of the central government, and Maastricht's focus is on general government deficits and debts. In 1997, however, Theo Waigel needed to make additional budget cuts at the central level to compensate for smaller than expected tax collections at the Land level. In 2002, it was additional spending in the West German Länder that pushed the general government deficit above 3% of GDP.[27]

The final issue concerns the design of the finance ministry. The structure of fiscal policy after reunification undercut the ministry's traditional role as, to use the British phrase, "the guardian of the treasury." Most of the initial borrowing to rebuild East Germany did not go through normal budget channels and was officially "off budget." Decisions on what to spend on the "new Länder" were often made at various roundtables that included the new Land governments as well as the chancellery but not the finance ministry. This lack of oversight extended to the new institutions with spending powers created in this period, such as the Treuhandanstalt. As Strauch and von Hagen (1999, 17) explain, "Requests of the [Finance] Ministry concerning the usage of funds *Treuhand* borrowed in the capital markets or received from other sources were not necessarily answered." The tax incentives introduced to lure investment to the former East Germany also did not appear as expenses according to the budget law. The exclusion of the finance ministry from most decision making on the former East Germany was one reason why fiscal discipline slipped precipitously in the early and middle 1990s.

In terms of its structure and responsibilities, the finance ministry did benefit in one important respect from Oskar Lafontaine's brief tenure. Lafontaine wanted a more powerful ministry, and when the new government was formed, he ensured the transfer to his own ministry of the economics ministry's European experts as well as the economic staff that writes the government's yearly Economic Report. This structural change remained in place after Lafontaine resigned, and, as a civil servant at the finance ministry explained to me, it consciously made the ministry more similar to its counterpart in France (author interview, Berlin, October 2000). This change had an effect especially on the European stage. Eichel was better prepared than before for ECOFIN meetings, and finance ministry officials agreed that this change increased his effectiveness.

A final word should be said about the role of voters and the stability of the party system. It seems clear that all parties consider management of the budget, and more generally management of the economy, as basic prerequisites for

27. For more on Länder issues, see Seitz 1999 and Rodden 2001.

remaining in power. In resisting American efforts in the 1980s to get Germany to stimulate its economy as it did in the late 1970s, German officials told their American counterparts that they saw voter displeasure at the size of deficits at the end of the social-liberal coalition as one of the primary reasons why the Schmidt government fell (*New York Times*, November 5, 1987). Theo Waigel's attempt to use proceeds from the revaluation of the Bundesbank's gold reserves similarly tarnished the reputation of the Kohl government. Concern with the state of the economy was one of the primary reasons why Kohl was voted out of office. The party system was clearly competitive enough to lead to changes in government when the public was dissatisfied with a given government's economic management. The failures of the Kohl government, in fact, contributed to a commitment in the Schröder government under Eichel's tenure to keep deficits under control.

Contrasting Cases: France and Greece

France and Greece provide useful contrasting cases to the United Kingdom and Germany. France represents a case with two blocs of parties that face each other and where delegation generally works well. It represents an intermediate case between the United Kingdom, which has the most effective form of delegation, and Germany, which has a functioning but less effective form. Greece allows one to explore a different dimension of the party system, namely its competitiveness. With one exception that lasted only two years, the country had regular one-party majority governments. Unlike in the United Kingdom, however, it did not have similarly competitive elections. There was not the same punishment mechanism for governments that had lax fiscal discipline. This changed in the mid-1990s, however, when competition in the electoral system increased, and the government installed its own form of delegation. Given greater centralization of the budget process around the minister of the Economy and of Finance, Greece was able to get its budget in order and to qualify for the common currency in 2001.

Because France and Greece are discussed to emphasize certain parts of the argument, I will not review the general fiscal history of these countries as I did for the United Kingdom and Germany. The political dynamics are important, however, and an abridged review of the party system and the key actors in the budget process as well as a look at specific episodes from each country's fiscal history is in order.

French Politics and Fiscal Institutions

France was one of the founding members of the European Coal and Steel Community. European integration has generally been popular, and there seemed to be little question inside or outside the country that it would be one of the founding members of the euro as well. In terms of economic policy, inflation had sometimes been a problem during the Fifth Republic, but by the early 1990s the inflation dragon had been slain. Fiscal policy had become more conservative, and budget deficits moved above 3% consistently only in the 1990s in the period that followed the end of the Bretton Woods system (after 1973). To understand the course of French fiscal history as well as the underlying institutional structure requires some knowledge of the underlying political structure.

Politically, France is considered a centralized country, perhaps one of the most centralized countries in the world. Most politics revolves around what happens in Paris. This focus on Paris, combined with differences in traditions and history in regions as diverse as Normandy, Provence, and Alsace-Lorraine, might lead to a center-periphery political cleavage to complement the usual left-right cleavage. Lijphart (1999, 80–81) does not acknowledge a center-periphery cleavage for France but does add medium cleavages along religious, regime support, and foreign policy divides.

How these multiple cleavages translate into a party system depends on the electoral system (Neto and Cox 1997). If there were a proportional representation system in France, the multiple political cleavages would translate into multiple parties with divergent ideologies as in a country like the Netherlands. If a plurality electoral system like the United Kingdom's were in place, one would expect just two dominant parties. The particular form of plurality used in elections to the French lower house, the National Assembly, leads to several parties that are nevertheless tied together.[28] There are two rounds of balloting. If a candidate wins 50% of the vote, that candidate wins the seat outright on the first ballot. If no candidate wins an absolute majority, all candidates with at least 12.5% of the vote move on to the second ballot. The candidate who wins the most votes on this ballot wins the seat. In practice, this system rewards parties that make tactical agreements across different electoral districts. A Socialist Party candidate, for example, may withdraw from one district in exchange for a Communist (or Green) candidate withdrawing from another. Similarly, on the political right, an RPR candidate may drop out of a race to benefit a UDF candidate, as long as the reverse happens in another district. This electoral system binds coalition partners together in two ways. First, the parties must coordinate their candidate slates if they wish to maximize their own electoral chances. Second, voters must see the parties in alliance in order for the party's tactical measures to work. If Socialist voters feel more sympathy toward the UDF than the Communists, for example, the withdrawal of a Socialist candidate in a district could lead to

28. The electoral system described here was used in all elections from 1973 to 2002 except for the 1986 elections, when proportional representation was used to elect the lower house.

the election of someone from the center-right. In practice, personal rivalries as well as differing party calculations about which candidates should be swapped in which districts often lead to suboptimal outcomes.[29]

Largely because of the type of party system that the electoral system encourages, coalition governments in France have been majority coalitions either of the left or of the right. The only exception to this rule was 1988–93, when the Socialists maintained a one-party minority government. The dynamics of the budget process during these years differed because of the need to gain opposition support, and one illustration below of budget making comes from this period. Because the parties in coalition are close to one another ideologically as a rule, one would expect a delegation form of fiscal governance. Yet there are reasons why, at least superficially, France would seem to have the same sorts of institutional actors on budget policy as in Germany, which would lead to checked delegation. The French political system has a president with real policy-making power in some areas, and, for this reason, some observers classify it as a "semi-presidential" system (Duverger 1980). France has an upper house, the Senate, and it has regular coalition governments.

Yet, in practice, the French budget process is more streamlined and comes closer to the British version. The president has no formal role in the making of budgets. The formation of the budget and the budget's execution are the purview of the prime minister. This is not to say that the president has no role at all. The president often sets the general tone of "his" government. Moreover, the president may insist that specific spending issues be included in the budget. In 1991, for example, President François Mitterrand demanded that his prime minister, Michel Rocard, include an additional FF 4.5 billion in the education budget (FF 5.62 = $1) (Knapp and Wright 2001, 108). Finally, the president sometimes appoints ministers directly and without the prime minister's approval.

Yet these examples all come from periods when the same party controlled both the presidency and the prime ministership. Under what is known as cohabitation, which exists when different parties control the two executives, the president's role in the budget process is nonexistent. Even in periods with a unified government, the president's involvement in the budget process is usually exceptional and affects only a small portion of the overall budget.

Under all forms of government, the pivotal person is the finance minister, who has the formal title today of minister for the Economy, Finance, and Industry. The April before the start of the budget year, which coincides with the calendar year, the prime minister sends to the spending ministers what is known as the "framework letter." This letter is based on the finance minister's recommendations, and it provides the proposed spending caps for

29. Many on the political left blame discord among the left parties for the dramatic losses they incurred in the 1993 and 2002 parliamentary elections.

each ministry. Bilateral negotiations between the finance ministry and the individual spending ministers then take place the following month. If the two sides cannot reach agreement, the prime minister is expected to resolve the dispute. At no time does the issue appear before the full cabinet for debate (von Hagen 1992; author interview, Ministry of the Economy, Finance, and Industry, Paris, October 2000).

Other actors in the budget process are not prominent. The French central bank until the 1990s was politically dependent on the government, and it has never played a role like the Bundesbank's in monitoring government fiscal policy (author correspondence with official at the Bank of France, December 2000). Parliament also has little direct input on the budget. According to Article 40 of the French Constitution, the National Assembly is not allowed to increase spending or decrease taxation in the government's draft. Article 49.3 also gives the government a blunt tool to pass the budget when necessary. The article states that, when the government invokes it, debate on a given bill ends immediately and the government's version is considered passed unless the Assembly censures the government within twenty-four hours. In addition to having little input into the design of the budget, the National Assembly traditionally has little ability to monitor budget developments. This has changed recently, however, with a reform in 2001. The government must now provide the National Assembly with more detailed information more frequently about budget execution. Also, while Article 40 remains firmly in place, the Assembly may redesignate some spending among programs so long as the total amount to be spent does not change (Ministry of the Economy, Finance, and Industry 2001).

Three Illustrative Episodes from French Finance

In reviewing the functioning of delegation in France, I want to dispel two arguments in the political economy literature reviewed in chapter 1. The first is the notion that the political left is necessarily irresponsible on budget issues. Readers who know some of the literature on the effects of partisanship might think that François Mitterrand pushed up the budget deficit significantly and that he reined it in only when "world capital" punished him sufficiently. The second is that minority governments are necessarily paralyzed in making economic policy. In chapter 6 I will refute this notion with case studies of Denmark and Sweden, but a brief look at the successive minority governments during the period 1988–93 indicates that the particular institutional rules in place in France significantly strengthen the government. It should have been an easy job for a center-right government to control the budget in time to join the euro. In 1993, the government controlled 82% of the seats in the National Assembly and should have been able to pass any budget cuts or tax increases it wanted. The "strong government" thesis did not hold because of dissension within the coalition government. France did manage to qualify for Stage Three of EMU based on its 1997 figures, but with a budget deficit that was only 0.05% of GDP below the 3% limit.

François Mitterrand's presidential election victory in 1981 was a political earthquake in the French system. It was the first time that a Socialist candidate had gained the Élyssée since the Fifth Republic was established in 1958. His government immediately set out a series of leftist economic and social reforms. On the economic front, the reforms included nationalization of some sectors such as telecommunications, electronics, and energy. The retirement age was lowered to sixty, and workers received a fifth week of annual vacation. These measures were all expensive, and they pushed up the deficit from what had been budget balance in 1980 to 2.7% in 1982 (European Commission 1999a). Yet, sensing the effects of the growing budget deficit, the government under the guidance of Minister of Economy and Finance Jacques Delors instituted an austerity plan in June 1982 that cut FF 20 billion in spending. It also stated a goal that the deficit should not grow to be more than 3% of GDP. In March 1983, the government introduced a second austerity plan that cut spending by FF 24 billion and raised taxes FF 40 billion, with especially deep cuts in government investment (Hall 1985, 86–87; Muet and Fonteneau 1990, 266). Even under the farthest left government France had seen in the Fifth Republic, it was possible for the finance minister to rein in spending. The budget deficit exceeded 3% only in 1983 at 3.1%, and even then these were figures for a period when France was in recession. The cyclically adjusted deficit was 2.6% in 1983 (European Commission 1999a).

The second episode illustrates the functioning of delegation under a minority government in France. After Mitterrand was reelected in 1988, he dissolved the National Assembly and called new elections. The Socialists failed to win an absolute majority, and they chose to form a one-party minority government under Prime Minister Michel Rocard. As I argued in chapter 2, and demonstrate in chapter 6, countries with consistent minority governments can develop a mixed form of fiscal governance. The finance minister centralizes the budget process, but some form of fiscal contract with one or more opposition parties is needed to pass the annual budget. As Huber (1996, chap. 6) describes, the first year of the French minority government's negotiations over the budget resembled the type of secret budget negotiations between the finance ministry and opposition parties that regularly occur in Denmark. Prior to passage of the 1989 budget, the government struck deals with both the small Center Union party and the Communist Party. Before the debate on the 1990 budget, however, the government did not reach an agreement with either opposition party, and it resorted to the use of Article 49.3, under which a government's bill becomes law unless a majority of the parliament censures the government, to pass the 1990 budget (Huber 1996). This type of censure is treated as a vote of confidence, and in the early 1990s the Communist Party refused to vote for a censure motion that would bring down a Socialist government. Resort to Article 49.3 then became a regular practice of the government; either part of the budget, as under Rocard in November 1990, or the entire budget, as under Prime Minister Edith Cresson in November 1991 and under Prime Minister Pierre Bérégovoy in November 1992, passed using this mechanism.

A minority government, therefore, could pass its budget largely unchanged. The minister of Finance and of the Economy until he became prime minister, Bérégovoy was able to centralize the budget process without much fear that parties in the Assembly would be able to overturn the results of his negotiations with cabinet ministers. Moreover, the minister had some success in maintaining fiscal discipline. The budget deficit stayed at or below 2% of GDP through 1991.

The economic recession that began in 1992 coincided with a preelection year. Polls predicted a devastating loss for the left, and the government seemed paralyzed to take any measures to keep the budget in order. The deficit rose to 4.2% of GDP in 1992 and to 6% in 1993 (European Commission 1999a). When France signed the Treaty of Maastricht in 1991, it appeared that it would have to take no action to qualify for the common currency. Just two years later, however, the country had a deficit twice the allowable level.

In the 1993 elections, the center-right won four out of five seats in the National Assembly. Scholars who focus on the size of the government's majority to predict the success of policy would anticipate that the new government would have little problem making changes to the budget to get the deficit back under control. There were, however, some complications. Eduard Balladur became prime minister in 1993, and soon after assuming power he became popular with French voters. The presidential election was scheduled for 1995, and a rivalry broke out between Balladur and the heir apparent, Jacques Chirac. Most of the UDF and some cabinet ministers from the RPR openly sided with Balladur. Chirac, however, managed to hold most of the RPR together. Both candidates ran in the 1995 elections, and the electoral rules dictated that the two candidates who received the most votes would face each other in the final poll. Chirac finished second to the Socialist Party candidate, Lionel Jospin, thus knocking Balladur out of the race. Chirac then triumphed over Jospin.

When he appointed a new government, it was clear that Chirac would not choose Balladur to be prime minister; the president replaced him with Alain Juppé. Few former supporters of Balladur remained in the cabinet. Alain Madelin, a previous cabinet member and a neoliberal who had been one of the few prominent members of the UDF to support Chirac's presidential candidacy, became the minister of Economics and Finance. Madelin's time in government was to be short. Only three months after his appointment, he left government "as in a divorce—by mutual consent." He had wanted to push through quick, and deep, cuts in social spending as well as a reform of the pension system. Such rapid change was unpopular within the coalition, and Juppé refused to back Madelin. Upon Madelin's resignation, his prime minister stated that "France does not want a change with brutality but with harmony" (*Les Echos,* August 28, 1995, my translation of both quotes).

Yet it was unclear whether "change with harmony" was possible. The new minister of the Economy and Finance, Jean Arthuis, faced a tough situation. The budget deficit for 1995 would hit 5.5%, still well over Maastricht's allowed 3%. The initial budget negotiations did not seem to go well, and there was a more general sense of policy drift. In November, only three months after Madelin's resignation, Chirac dismissed much of the cabinet. The French press, which kept track of who supported which presidential candidate, noted with some satisfaction the return of some previous supporters of Balladur (*Le Monde,* November 8, 1995).

Yet the return of some Balladur supporters did not seem to unite the right. Later that month, during debates in the National Assembly about how to reform social security, the government proposed an additional 0.5% increase in the income tax to fund the social security deficit. Social security deficits counted against the government's general budget deficit, and Juppé's goal was to bring the social security account into balance by the critical year of 1997. The government also announced an increase in the value-added tax; a reform of SNCF (the national railroad), which would cut state spending; and a freeze on public sector wages. Balladur was harshly critical of the government's plans to raise taxes for social security, and he called for expenditure cuts instead, arguing that tax increases should be used only to reduce the budget deficit. Criticism was even more forthcoming outside the right. Unions criticized the reform plan as too harsh, and they organized massive strikes in November and December that paralyzed much of the country. As the *Economist* commented at the time, "Strikers by the millions riot in the street; the *évènements* in France . . . make the country look like a banana republic in which an isolated government is battling to impose IMF austerity on a hostile population" (December 9, 1995).

The strikes, combined with continued dissension on the political right about the nature and size of spending cuts, made it difficult to push through additional austerity measures. The goal in the social security area became to reduce the deficit to FF 30 billion by 1997 rather than to eliminate it entirely, as had been the case in 1995. Additional revenues or cuts in spending would need to be found elsewhere. A onetime measure that Eurostat allowed to count against the general budget deficit helped to get the deficit down to exactly 3% of GDP. The government agreed with France Telecom to a transfer of money in 1997 amounting to 0.5% of GDP in exchange for the government's assumption of the company's pension liabilities.

Each of these episodes illustrates the strengths and weaknesses of France's use of delegation. Socialist finance ministers from Jacques Delors to Pierre Bérégovoy were successful in maintaining fiscal discipline. A minority government had little effect on the budget because the government possessed institutional means to push legislation through parliament without the formal approval of a majority of parliamentarians. Yet dissension among the ruling right parties, together with large protests in the streets against government policy, slowed the consolidation of public finances in the mid-1990s.

When considering the effects of Maastricht on budget performance, there is an irony about the need for Maastricht to clean up the budget in the first place. Prior to 1991, France did not have a problem keeping deficits below 3% of GDP. It certainly did not expect to have to do anything to qualify for Stage Three of Economic and Monetary Union. Deficits became a problem exactly when one would think pressures from Maastricht would bring them under control. Yet the effects of Maastricht mirror those in Germany. There was a concerted effort to bring the deficit below 3% of GDP for the critical year of 1997. Juppé's finance ministers, Madelin and then Arthuis, scrambled for additional funds every bit as much as their German counterparts, Theo Waigel. Yet Maastricht did not lead to any obvious fiscal reforms or changes in the way French governments made and executed budgets.

Greek Politics and Greek Fiscal Institutions

Greece returned to democracy after the domination of "the Colonels" ended in 1975. It wasted little time in applying for European Community membership, and it became a member in 1981. Given its fiscal track record, which included regular budget deficits around 15% in the mid-1980s, few observers thought that Greece had any hope of qualifying for Stage Three of EMU. Although the observers were technically correct—Greece was the only country left out of EMU in 1997 because of its macroeconomic performance— the country did succeed in getting its deficit problem under control.

The actors that set fiscal policy were generally in the cabinet. The Bank of Greece was not a critical independent factor. It was truly the government's banker, and it was often the only actor that had a clear understanding of the entire budget. Yet it was not politically independent from the government until the 1990s. The parliament was a sometime participant, at least in the 1980s. Parliamentary votes were supposed to be secret, and amendments to government budget bills were allowed. Yet the frequency with which parliament could undermine the government on important votes was limited. Contrary to the law, PASOK, the Socialist Party, required its legislators to vote with colored ballots on some votes so that it could monitor its parliamentarians (Alivizatos 1990).

Unlike in France, which has multiple political cleavages, the main political cleavage in Greece is a simple left-right divide. Even given this simple cleavage structure, which would likely lead to a two-party system, the electoral system ensures that one party wins a majority of seats in parliament. Although there have been some minor changes from election to election, the country uses what is called "reinforced proportional representation," which provides a bonus of seats to the party that finishes first in the balloting even if that party does not win an absolute majority of the votes (Lijphart 1994, 1999). The party system usually has one party with a majority of seats in parliament, a second opposition party, and the small Greek Communist Party. There are therefore regular one-party governments. During the time that Greece has been a member of the European Union, PASOK has been the government in power every year from 1981 to 2002 except for 1991–93. The exceptional period occurred when the conservatives (the New Democracy Party) entered a coalition with the Communists. The two parties had wide policy differences, and they were able to coalesce into one government only as a temporary alliance to drive the Socialists out. The coalition did not last, and after 1993 the Socialist Party returned to power.

Given the party system, which encourages regular one-party majority government, one would expect a delegation form of fiscal governance in Greece. Indeed, the use of delegation is an important part of the story that explains why Greece qualified for Stage Three of Economic and Monetary Union and joined the common currency in 2001. Yet fiefdom was clearly the rule in government through the mid-1990s, and the prevalence of this form of fiscal governance explains why fiscal performance was so poor in Greece during this period.

From Fiefdom to Delegation

The balance of power within the cabinet under the first Andreas Papandreou government (1981–89) represents a classic case of fiefdom. Ministries made proposals for their budget figures. The strong ministers in government all represented the big spending ministries, such as defense, education, and health. The full cabinet made decisions on public spending, and the cabinet votes were public votes to the participants. This made it easier for cabinet ministers to support one another's pet spending programs. Yet one should not focus only on the expenditure side of the budget ledger. Fiefdom Greek-style relied as much on the tax side. Different clienteles of the Socialist Party simply did not have to pay taxes that were on the books, and this practice was especially prominent in election years.

There was a finance minister in the cabinet, but he was generally considered the tenth or eleventh most powerful minister in government. An illustration of the weak position of the finance minister comes from May 1982.

His ministry had already begun collecting tax forms for a new tax. While driving home from work, he heard Prime Minister Papandreou announce on the radio that the government was canceling the tax. The decision had been taken without any consultation with the finance ministry, and the finance minister promptly resigned (author interview, Bank of Greece, September 2000).

A particular problem also concerned the hiring of public servants. The prime minister's office, known as the Ministry to the Presidency of Government, was responsible for public hiring (OECD 1992). There was usually a rash of new hires in October of each year, which was a time chosen so that the full budgetary impact of the hiring decisions would not be clear until the following year (interview, Bank of Greece, October 2000).

The Greek budget deficit was consistently in double figures through much of the 1990s (fig. 4.3). Fiscal policy was especially disastrous under the short-lived conservative-Communist coalition. The total debt burden at the time of the signing of the Maastricht treaty was relatively manageable at 82.3% of GDP. Just two short years later, however, in another election year, the debt ratio had gained more than 25 percentage points of GDP to finish at 110.2% (European Central Bank 2000, 30).

The climate for greater fiscal discipline improved in 1993. Both major parties considered the state of public finances a political issue, and both committed themselves in the elections to clean them up. The Socialists won the 1993 elections and formed the next government, once again under Andreas Papandreou. The prime minister was chronically ill, however, and the needed centralization of the budget process did not occur until Kostas Simitis replaced Papandreou as the leader of the party and of government.

Under Simitis in 1996, PASOK pledged to meet the Maastricht criteria, and the new prime minister took this pledge seriously. Institutionally, he merged the responsibility of the ministries of Economy and Finance under one person, Yannos Papantoniou. Unlike previous ministers of finance, Papantoniou was "fully responsible for the fiscal policy of the government and, at the same time, fully trusted by the Prime Minister" (correspondence with Greek financial journalist, September 29, 2000). The finance minister now had the final word on all ministry budgets and could make cuts in spending where necessary. To control personnel spending, he began with the public wage bill. In 1997, he instituted a public wage freeze, and he introduced a rule that five people would have to leave a ministry before one new person was hired (interview with civil servant, Ministry of the National Economy, Athens, September 2000). He also cut some subsidies to public agencies, and he set out to close the legal loopholes that allowed individual ministries to overspend their assigned budgets (*Financial Times*, November 25, 1997).

Perhaps most important, however, taxes that had been on the books were finally enforced. Withholding of taxes at their sources became more widespread. Tax police investigated cases and prosecuted people who were not

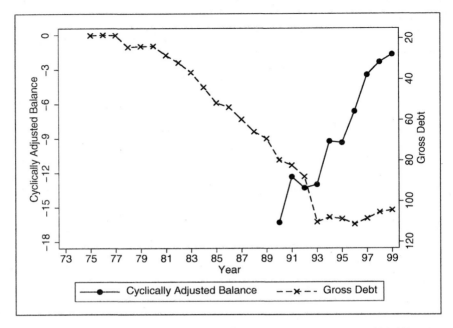

Fig. 4.3. Cyclically adjusted budget balance (1975–99) and gross debt level (1990–99) in Greece. There are no comparable figures for Greek deficits reported by the European Commission prior to 1990. Source: European Commission 1999a.

paying their taxes. As a result of these and other minor changes, revenue from personal income taxation increased 27% in 1997 and another 20% in 1998. Similarly, corporate income tax revenue jumped 23% in 1997 and an astounding 57% in 1998 (Bank of Greece 1999, 172, 174).

The effects of these measures on the budget were dramatic. The budget deficit, which had been at –10.1% of GDP in 1995, moved up to –4.0% of GDP in 1997, only 1% away from Maastricht's target, and by 1998 it was comfortably below the Maastricht deficit criterion.

In the Greek case, there is certainly a "Maastricht effect." It is hard to imagine a concerted effort to get the budget in order in the late 1990s without the promise of EMU membership. Yet it is important to understand how Maastricht interacted with domestic factors. First, nonparticipation became a political issue in domestic politics. This occurred at a time when the party system was becoming more competitive. An incumbent government that did not get public finances in order was likely to be in political trouble. The April 2000 election, for example, was quite close. PASOK's margin of victory was less than 1% of the vote, 43.8% to New Democracy's 42.9%. Greece's reinforced proportional representation system gave the party almost 55% of the seats in parliament and a comfortable majority to rule, but the closeness of the election indicated that the results could well have been different had Greece not improved its economic statistics for the year before and thus missed Economic and Monetary Union.

The second factor to consider is *how* Greece qualified. In chapter 2 I predicted that states with one-party governments would delegate powers over the budget to a finance minister. This is exactly what the Greek government did. The budget process within the cabinet changed. Papantoniou became the joint minister for both ministries involved in the economy. He negotiated bilaterally with spending ministers on the budget, and he became the primary agenda-setter (Hallerberg, Strauch, and von Hagen 2001). His prime minister also backed him in cabinet debates. Finally, although I did not find much evidence that parliamentary amendments led to big increases in spending when deficits were high, parliamentary rules were changed so that the parliament could not make any amendments to the government's budget but could only approve or disapprove the entire package. This makes it impossible for a spending minister who loses an issue in the cabinet to ask a parliamentarian to add the money back in when parliament debates the budget.

Conclusion

In this chapter I have reviewed four cases in the European Union where one would expect a delegation form of fiscal governance to develop. Such states have party systems that lead to regular governments with either one-party majority governments or governments with coalition partners that are close to one another ideologically. The most developed form of delegation is found in the United Kingdom. A chancellor of the exchequer was playing some sort of delegation role a century ago. This system evolved, and today's budget process preserves the power of the chancellor while including some limited two-year expenditure targets that he sets. Germany, in contrast, tests the limits of delegation. It has regular coalition governments, and coalition partners do not delegate much power to the finance minister when their spending preferences diverge. There are also additional checks on the power of the finance minister that can limit his control over the budget. France is a case that is in between the two. Its coalition governments tend to be more united, yet the finance minister cannot centralize the budget process effectively when coalition partners do not cooperate. Finally, Greece illustrates the importance of competitive elections. When elections are not competitive and when fiscal discipline is not a priority for voters, budget deficits will be large. In the 1990s, joining EMU became a campaign issue, and the Socialists probably would have lost the elections without a concerted move to bring the budget near balance. Maastricht is clearly more relevant for Greece than for the other three countries in this chapter. It encouraged only short-term budgetary adjustments in France and Germany, and the charge that these countries used tricks to qualify for EMU has a ring of truth.

Yet one should not ignore the broader lesson of this chapter. Delegation has been generally successful in maintaining fiscal discipline. When one examines the fiscal histories of the three countries that had delegation in place already, one sees that the budgetary difficulties of the mid-1990s are aberrations. The "trick" involves bringing countries back in line with their previous fiscal performance.

5

The Commitment Form of Fiscal Governance

T he fiscal rules required by a commitment form of governance have evolved in the Netherlands, Belgium, and Finland. The first two states are original members of the European Union, while Finland did not join until 1995. All three sought to join Stage Three of Economic and Monetary Union as part the first round of countries to introduce the euro in 1999, and all three qualified under the Maastricht treaty's fiscal criteria.

Each country has had its fiscal troubles. For the Netherlands the troubles came in the early 1980s after the second oil crisis, but the country staged a fiscal recovery that it has maintained since then. Belgium similarly had problems adjusting to the two oil crises in the 1970s, but, unlike in the Netherlands, the entire 1980s became a fiscal nightmare. Deficits were chronically high, and the debt burden expanded until it was well over 100% of GDP. In Finland, the real shock came in the early 1990s following the collapse of its trade with the former Soviet bloc and the near-collapse of its banking sector.

To get out of these difficulties, each country made reforms that fall under the commitment form of fiscal governance discussed in chapter 2. Commitment is the optimal form of fiscal governance to address the common pool resource problem in countries with regular multiparty majority coalition governments. Coalition partners sign what amount to fiscal contracts, which are explicit budget targets that are included in their coalition agreements. Portfolio distribution includes a decision about which party will manage which ministry. Because the spending targets are decided in coalition negotiations, ministers have little say about actual spending levels for those ministries. Violations of the targets constitute violations of the coalition agreement. If there is little competition among political parties for coalition spots, then the threat to exclude a defecting party is not credible.

The Netherlands fits this model most closely. It first adopted a form of fiscal contracts during a deep recession in 1982. The initial contracts, while they controlled spending, represented more general targets on the budget deficit. After another recession in the early 1990s, where the targets did not prevent some additional spending above what the parties themselves wanted, the new coalition partners in 1994 agreed to much more specific targets for every ministry as well as detailed rules on how to adjust the contract during unforeseen economic shocks.

Its neighbor to the south, Belgium, suffered from fiefdom fiscal governance. As in the Netherlands, coalition partners did agree to a type of fiscal contract that set spending targets for the government. Yet, unlike the Netherlands after 1982, these targets simply were not credible. The country's deep ethnic cleavage meant that no coalition could be composed exclusively of Flemish parties or of Walloon parties. In 1988 and 1993, steps to federalize the country reduced the tension between the regions, and fiscal contracts that an outside body, the High Council of Finance, wrote for the national and regional governments became credible. Although not as institutionally developed as the Netherlands, Belgium does approximate the commitment form of fiscal governance.

Finland has been the most pro–European Union, and most pro–Economic and Monetary Union, of the Scandinavian countries. In 1994, its referendum to join the European Union passed by 14%, a larger majority than in Sweden (in Norway, a majority of voters rejected EU membership). Finland was also the only Scandinavian country to begin Stage Three of EMU with the first wave of countries in 1999.

Finland differs from the other Scandinavian countries also in terms of its type of government. Instead of the minority governments that are common in Denmark, Norway, and Sweden, as a rule Finland has regular multiparty majority coalitions. Moreover, these coalitions have been oversized, that is, they have included more political parties than are needed to reach a majority in parliament. In this country, the move was from an informal form of commitment to a more rigid one during the economic depression the country suffered in the early 1990s. Compared to the Netherlands, there is scope for change that would institutionalize further a commitment form of governance.

Netherlands: The Ideal Case of Commitment in Practice

Political Background

The Netherlands is in many ways a land of political contradictions. It is one of the most open states in Europe economically, culturally, and socially. During its golden age in the seventeenth century, the country was the premier trading state in the world. Although its status declined over the centuries because of its small size relative to competitors with larger populations, trade remains a defining feature of the Dutch economy. Rotterdam today does more business than any other port in the world. Philips stereos, Royal Dutch Shell gasoline, and agricultural goods like tomatoes and tulips are sold all over the world. Dutch capital flows readily across borders, and, after Ahold's takeover of Giant Supermarkets in 1999, Dutch investors became second only to the British, surpassing the Japanese, as foreign owners of American assets (*Financial Times,* July 21, 1999). Culturally, the Netherlands encourages exchanges with other countries in ways rarely seen elsewhere. Playwrights, dancers, and singers in the annual monthlong Holland Festival in Amsterdam are overwhelmingly non-Dutch. The National Dance Company, the Nederlands Dans Theater, rarely has Dutch dancers. One can get a sense that there it is an appreciation of the non-Dutch that defines the Dutch. The Dutch are also known for their tolerance of alternative lifestyles. Marijuana possession, although technically illegal, is not prosecuted.

Yet, in this country the size of a small American state (or twice the area of Massachusetts) and with a remarkable amount of diversity, these examples are deceiving. Some agricultural goods are produced for the local market, and rural areas of the country can seem as provincial as other rural areas in Europe. The reputed tolerance of the Dutch arose in a country where a majority of the population professed a particularly conservative form of Protestantism that was anything but tolerant. In the seventeenth century, the church even forbade singing and silenced church organs. Although Calvinism has since modernized, a significant portion of the population remain firm believers. Moreover, the Catholic south culturally feels almost like another country. The religious-nonreligious cleavage remains important today. While the buildings of Maastricht may not be all that different from those in Gröningen, accents and attitudes do differ. Anyone who has attended a soccer game involving the national squad would see in the rabid sea of orange that nationalism has not died away.

The Netherlands has been and remains a complex country. This complexity has led to what political scientists characterize as multidimensionality in the cleavage structure of society. Lijphart (1999, 80–81) documents clear divisions in society on three dimensions: economics, religion, and postmaterialism (Lijphart 1999, 80–81).[1]

In terms of the political institutions that structure the interaction among the various cleavages, the Netherlands has maintained the most proportional

1. Lijphart defines postmaterialism as "the two issues of participatory democracy and environmentalism" (1999, 86), with the Radicals and D66 the postmaterialist parties in the Netherlands. In his earlier work, Lijphart (1975) describes an institutional framework to moderate the various factions in Dutch society, which he termed "the politics of accommodation." He traces the breakdown of the "politics" to the election of 1968, a period before that covered in this book. See also Jones 1995 for a discussion of the decline of consensus-style democracy in the Netherlands (as well as in Belgium).

electoral system in Europe. The parliament has 150 members who are selected through proportional representation. There is only one national district, which means that a party has to receive only 0.7% of the national vote to gain entry to parliament. As one would expect in a country with a low electoral threshold and with multidimensionality in its cleavage structure, traditionally several political parties vie for office and receive parliamentary seats. The three traditional parties are—from left to right on a socioeconomic dimension—the PvdA (Partij van de Arbeid), or social democrats; the CDA, or Christian Democrats; and the VVD (Volkspartij voor Vrijheid en Democratie), or liberals. The religious cleavage separates the CDA from the other two parties, and especially from the PvdA. The low electoral threshold has encouraged new parties to form, and several small parties have gained entry into parliament and served in the government, including D66, a reform party organized in the 1960s, and, more recently, the Pim Fortyn List, organized around the controversial former sociology professor who was murdered on the campaign trail in May 2002.

No party has received an absolute majority of seats in parliament in the postwar period. Majority coalition governments are the norm. Moreover, in the postwar period through 1994, every one of the coalition governments included the Christian Democrats.[2] The inability of other parties to punish the Christian Democrats by excluding them from office may have contributed to the disastrous fiscal performance of the country in the middle and late 1970s. The party system became more competitive in the early 1980s, and the Christian Democrats were excluded from government between 1994 and 2002. Moreover, it became the rule that any party was a potential coalition partner of any other. As a reporter for the *Financial Times* put it before the 1982 elections, "Coalition, as practiced here, is an ever-changing pattern, in which role-reversal is the norm. The enemies of today are the trusted colleagues of tomorrow" (September 8, 1982). Through the early 1980s the pattern was that the centrist Christian Democrats would ally either with the liberals or the social democrats. In 1994 the PvdA and VVD formed a coalition for the first time.

The regularity of multiparty coalition governments would suggest that a commitment form of fiscal governance would develop in the Netherlands. Indeed, the negotiation of the coalition agreement has become a key institutional feature of the building, and the functioning, of consensus. In the 1970s the country found itself in a deepening fiscal crisis. There were some attempts to centralize the budget process around a finance minister, but these efforts failed when coalition partners balked at delegating such power to a central figure. The coalition agreement reached in 1982 under

2. In 1977 three religious parties merged to form the CDA. Before 1977, it is more accurate to speak of KVP, or the Catholic People's Party, which was one of the three religious parties to form the CDA, as the central party (Timmermans and Andeweg 2000, 358 n. 1).

Prime Minister Ruud Lubbers proved to be a watershed. The parties nego- tiated budget targets for the life of the coalition, and they stuck to these tar- gets during the execution of the budget. The coalition government then won the 1986 elections, and this method of setting the budget in advance became institutionalized. More recent reforms have fine-tuned the model, extend- ing the targets to every ministry, and creating provisions for what the gov- ernment should do in the case of unforeseen economic shocks. This fiscal institutional development occurred at the same time that the party system became more competitive. A party that violated a coalition agreement could legitimately be threatened with replacement. The Netherlands now serves as the model for a commitment form of fiscal governance.

Fiscal Policy and Fiscal Actors

In the Netherlands the debt level grew at an almost exponential rate from 1976 to 1982 (fig. 5.1). It then flattened out, and it remained stable at around 77% of GDP through the mid-1990s. The cyclically adjusted budget balance has remained negative throughout the period. It worsened noticeably from 1976 to 1980, overlapping the deterioration of gross debt, moved below −3% of GDP in the early 1980s, then deteriorated again in the late 1980s. After bottoming out in 1990, it improved through most of the 1990s, with some fluctuation, and, by the end of the 1990s, it approached balance. The budget balance clearly declines in most preelection years. Election years include 1977, 1981, 1982, 1986, 1989, and 1994, and cyclically adjusted budget balances were at local lows each preceding year. The only time this pattern was clearly broken was in 1998. Not coincidentally, the budget figures for 1997 were the basis for determining what countries would join Stage Three of EMU.

As in other European countries, the principal decision makers on the budget appear in the government. Yet, unlike the delegation states France and the United Kingdom, there are three other political bodies that have some role in the budget process. First, the Central Planning Bureau, or, as it is called now, the Bureau for Economic Policy Analysis (regardless of official name, the abbreviation has remained the same—CPB), is an agency independent from government. Its mandate is to produce politically unbi- ased economic forecasts, which include economic growth and budget esti- mates.[3] It also provides information on the state of current public finances. It therefore serves a watchdog function. A second actor is De Nederlandsche Bank, the Dutch central bank. Like the German Bundesbank, the Dutch cen- tral bank had (and has) a staff that monitors fiscal policy developments. It does not, however, usually challenge the CPB's budget figures. Instead, the

3. Although there is a broad consensus in government circles that the CPB is independ- ent of government, the CPB does receive its financing from the government and is formally under the Ministry of Economic Affairs.

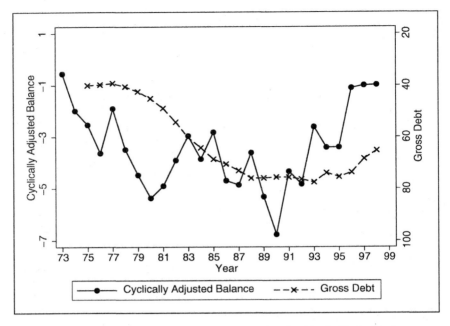

Fig. 5.1. Cyclically adjusted budget balance and gross debt level in the Netherlands, 1973–98. Source: European Commission 1999a.

governor of the bank will, on occasion, remind the government to get, and keep, its finances in order. These warnings were especially frequent, and especially pointed, in the late 1970s (Messing 1988, 551–55, as cited in Visser and Hemerijck 1997, 99). Like the CPB, the bank is also largely independent from the government.[4]

A final actor is relatively unknown in scholarly circles.[5] It is known as the Studiegroep Begrotingsruimte, or, in English, the Study Group of the Budget Margin, and it has played, and continues to play, a critical role in the design of fiscal institutions in the Netherlands. Senior civil servants from the main ministries and agencies that deal with the economy compose this arcanely named body (referred to in the remainder of the text simply as the Study Group). Members include the head of the CPB, the governor of the central bank, and several senior servants from the Finance ministry. The Study Group writes a report on the state of fiscal affairs in the year before an election. It focuses on future challenges to the soundness of Dutch fiscal policy. It also makes recommendations on how the future government can improve the

4. Measures of central bank independence in the literature consistently place the Dutch bank only slightly below the Bundesbank in its level of independence. See, for example, Cukierman and Bernhard 1998.

5. I have found no academic literature on the Studiegroep in either English or Dutch.

formulation and execution of fiscal policy. The intent is to create a nonpartisan document that, in theory, any future government could use to improve policy. The seniority of the writers of the report is meant to lend it credibility. As a central banker remarked to me, "The report is a joint statement of the highest civil servants of the most important departments" (Amsterdam, July 2000). The Dutch press publicizes the group's report when it is published.

The Study Group, therefore, traditionally provides a set of guidelines, and the politicians have the choice of following them or not. The Study Group's work has been useful from the early 1980s on, when governments resolved to maintain fiscal discipline. In the 1970s, however, the politicians generally ignored the Study Group's advice.

1973–82

As it did in other industrialized countries, the first oil crisis hurt the economy of the Netherlands. At first, the government was not too concerned about the budgetary implications of the shock. Policy makers (as elsewhere) assumed that the economic impact would be temporary, and there was little concern about spending more than originally budgeted (Study Group of the Budget Margin 1988). Unlike the situation for most OECD countries, the increase in world energy prices was not necessarily bad from a Dutch point of view. Revenues from gas receipts equaled 0.5% of Net National Income in 1970, but they had increased to 5% by 1983 (Goudswaard 1990, 273). Some of the increase in welfare payments that were a result of the economic recession could be paid for without increasing the overall tax burden.[6]

A final, more political, factor has to do with the Dutch system of budgeting at the time. Coalition agreements were vague documents, and they did not commit the coalition partners to specific spending targets. Even in aggregate, there was little consideration of overall figures for the budget. If the budget deficit increased or spending increased in different sectors, there was no prescribed procedure for correcting the budgetary outcome. Social spending under this framework was particularly problematic. There were no general targets for spending in this category each year. Instead, the institutional setup encouraged large increases in spending. Beginning in 1974 the minimum wage and social security benefits were indexed to the average private sector wage. Public retirement benefits had been indexed to the minimum wage since 1960. And the key variable in all of this, private sector wages, was in practice indexed to the inflation rate. The oil crisis therefore hit the budget twice, once when it pushed up inflation and a second time when unemployment increased.

6. These additional gas receipts were not an unqualified benefit for the Dutch economy. In what has become termed "Dutch disease," the jump in the sale of natural resources led to an overvalued currency that hurt manufacturing exports on world markets. For a theoretical discussion see Bruno and Sachs 1982.

As spending pressure grew in the mid-1970s, the government's initial reaction was to attempt to centralize the budget process around the finance minister. If successful, this centralization would have been a delegation form of fiscal governance. At the time of the oil crisis, none other than the future first president of the European Central Bank, Willem Duisenberg, was one of the principal social democrats in the coalition government of his party and the Christian Democrats. He served as finance minister from 1973 to 1977. As a share of GDP, expenditures grew dramatically during his first two years of office, from 43.8% of GDP in 1973 to 50.5% in 1975. In an attempt to control the budget, he pledged in 1977 to impose a limit on expenditure growth of 1% of GDP (Snels 1999). If the rule had been followed, overall expenditures would have increased only from 51% of GDP in 1977, to, say, 54% by 1980. Although this rule seems not to be that binding (the rule implies that the economy would eventually be entirely nationalized), it was considered a serious attempt to stem the growth of public spending. It was controversial, especially in Duisenberg's own party. A cabinet member noted that Duisenberg's stance "was considered quite courageous at the time" (author interview with former cabinet member, summer 2000). The rule was not followed, in any event. Duisenberg and his party entered the opposition ranks later that year, and overall public spending increased to almost 57% of GDP by 1980.

The coalition between the Christian Democrats and social democrats ended after the 1977 elections. The liberals entered government with the Christian Democrats under the Christian Democratic Prime Minister Andreas Van Agt. Once again, a politician with a future career at the European Union level, Frans Andriessen, attempted to become a strong finance minister.[7] He sought to limit public spending on wages, and this stance put him in confrontation with Minister of Social Affairs Willem Albeda, who, like Andriessen, was a member of the CDA. Prime Minister Van Agt did not support Andriessen in the budget battle, and Andriessen resigned. In the 1981 elections the social democrats lost nine seats, but the new coalition brought the social democrats as well as D66 into government with the CDA. The finance minister, Fons van der Stee (CDA), once again tried to impose expenditure cuts. Not only did he face opposition from the minister of Social Affairs and Employment, Johannes Marten Den Uyl (CDA), but the social democrats refused to tolerate any of van der Stee's proposed cuts. They left the government soon after it was formed over social spending reductions, and a minority government composed of just the CDA and D66 lasted until new elections in September 1982 (Snels 1999). From 1977 until 1982, a series of governments with a series of finance ministers tried to rein in spending, but they had little success. A change was in the offing.

7. Frans Andriessen served as commissioner for Competition Policy, 1981–84; vice-president of the European Commission responsible for agriculture, 1985–88; and vice-president of the European Commission responsible for external relations and trade, 1989–93.

1983–2002

The state of public finances was a major campaign issue in the September 1982 elections. All parties, including the social democrats, pledged to make budget cuts and to end wage indexing tied to inflation (*Financial Times,* September 8, 1982). The coalition that emerged from the 1982 elections brought together the liberals (VVD) and the Christian Democrats (CDA) under a Christian Democratic prime minister, Ruud Lubbers. The parties agreed, for the first time, to have budget targets for the life of the coalition. These targets focused on the size of the budget deficit. The coalition partners pledged to lower the central government deficit to 7.4% of Net National Income, which would represent a reduction of the deficit by approximately 3% of GDP (Goudswaard 1990, 272–73). They also negotiated detailed policy agreements with the different ministries. One of the spending cuts was a reduction in unemployment benefits from 80% of an unemployed person's last income to 70%, which came into effect between 1984 and 1986 (Thomson 2001, 181).

H. Onno Ruding left private banking to become the new finance minister. One of his first acts was a comprehensive review of spending in all government departments. He also became known popularly as an aggressive cutter of the budget. Yet his role in the Dutch government differed from that of his counterparts in France and the United Kingdom. Although he proposed changes in the spending levels of different ministries, his principal job was to keep the government to the deficit targets in the coalition agreement. Similarly, the finance minister had the power to review any spending proposals that were to be debated within the cabinet, but, again, the task was to check whether the proposals were consistent with the coalition agreement. If the finance minister judged that a proposal was not, the full cabinet would not see it (author interview with former civil servant in the finance ministry, August 2000). The overriding importance of the coalition agreement led to parodies of it in the Dutch press—cabinet meetings were portrayed as meetings where ministers each quoted from different parts of the "Bible" to make their points.[8]

This method of setting targets in the coalition agreement and having a finance minister keep the ministers to the agreed deficit targets was judged a success on two counts. First, government spending as a percentage of GDP declined for the first time in a decade, with the share dropping from 60.8% in 1983 to 58.0% in 1985. The overall budget deficit during the same period also declined from 5.8% to 3.6% of GDP (European Commission 1999a). The increased centralization of the budget process was certainly one cause of the economic success. It was not, however, the only one. The agreement between unions, employers, and the government in a suburb of The Hague,

8. One parody noted the substance of a debate as taking the form of "We open the Holy Agreement and read Part III, Verse 1" (Timmermans and Andeweg 2000, 380).

known as the Agreement of Wassenaar, also affected the health of the budget. The unions agreed to the end of automatic wage indexation in exchange for a reduction in work hours. Also important for the budget, Wassenaar marked the end of a direct connection between public and private wages.

Voters considered the government's efforts to rein in the budget a success. In the 1986 elections, the Christian Democrats won nine additional seats in the 150-member parliament, while the liberals lost nine. The liberals' loss was due at least in part to a scandal that involved the award of public grants to a private company in Rotterdam. Hence, despite concerns that a party that cut spending would lose votes, the coalition emerged from the elections at the same strength. The leadership of the CDA, in particular, considered their victory a vindication of the coalition's approach to fiscal policy (author interview with cabinet member from the 1980s, August 2000). From 1986 on, the budget accord became the framework for the complete cabinet program. As a person who was a civil servant in the Finance Ministry in 1986 told me, the budget accord became the "engine block" of the car that was the coalition agreement. The partners first agreed on the budget, then on the remainder of the agreement (author interview, August 2000).

Other changes were also introduced in the 1986 coalition agreement. The parties agreed to the so-called rules for budget discipline, which made ministers responsible for overspending in their own ministries. If the overspending was serious, a guilty minister was expected to resign. Spending targets as a percentage of Net National Income were also added to the deficit targets that had been present in the first agreement.

The second coalition agreement, although more developed than the first one, was a mixed success in fiscal terms. During the attenuated lifetime of the coalition, which lasted only through 1989, the deficit dropped from 5.1% in 1986 to 4.7% in 1989, but, after taking into account economic growth's effects on the budget balance, the cyclically adjusted deficit worsened, from 4.7% to 5.3%. One reason for the mediocre performance was a drop in revenues from the natural gas sector, which decreased from 5% of Net National Income to 2.5% in only one year (1987), when gas prices dropped precipitously. Although this reduction was unforeseen, the Study Group, in its document written before the 1989 elections, placed the blame for the mediocre fiscal performance squarely on the design and execution of the coalition agreement. The agreement had two types of targets, budget balance and expenditure targets in nominal terms, but it did not provide guidance concerning which target should be followed when they diverged. In the late 1980s, the economy grew more than expected, which should have more than compensated for the drop in natural gas revenues. In practice, however, the increased economic growth meant that ministries could spend in nominal terms more money than they first thought without violating the deficit targets (Study Group of the Budget Margin 1988, chap. 6).

In 1989, a new government formed that brought the PvdA and the Christian Democrats into coalition. The social democratic leader, Wim Kok, replaced Onno Ruding as finance minister. Once again, the parties agreed to a fiscal contract on the budget before agreeing on the distribution of portfolios. As in previous contracts, however, the budget agreement was not explicit about what the government was to do in the case of unforeseen shocks. This proved problematic at the beginning of the 1990s when the Netherlands experienced an unexpected increase in the number of applicants for disability benefits. A political crisis over the issue almost brought down the coalition. The government eventually agreed on a reform package that required employers to assume more of the burden of paying disability benefits and to take additional measures to reintegrate their employees who had become unfit for work (Thomson 2001).

While the budget deficit improved somewhat, from 3.9% of GDP in 1992 to 3.2% in 1993, there was general dissatisfaction in policy circles with how budgets had been made under the CDA-PvdA coalition. This displeasure led to a set of recommendations from the Study Group in 1993 that focused on how the design of the coalition could account for different types of shocks to the budget. The future finance minister, Gerrit Zalm, was at the time the director of the CPB, and he participated fully in the Study Group's deliberations. The Study Group suggested that the country adopt trend-based budgeting. It added that, in the coalition agreement, the parties should focus on spending targets only per ministry, not on a budget deficit target. Moreover, the targets should be in real terms so that unforeseen increases in inflation would not push up spending. It also suggested that the government include intentionally conservative economic forecasts.

The 1994 elections hit the incumbent government hard, especially the Christian Democrats, who lost twenty of their fifty-four seats in parliament. Afterward the liberals, social democrats, and D66 formed what was known as the purple cabinet, which excluded the Christian Democrats from office for the first time since the end of World War II. This result, as well as the relative stability of the coalition during the years that it was in power, marked the end of the "strong" party of the center that could not be excluded from office. The new government also promised to reduce the budget deficit. The means to reach this goal appeared in the coalition agreement, where the parties included most of the significant suggestions in the Study Group report. It introduced trend-based budgeting. The government intentionally implemented a cautious growth scenario of a little over 2% of GDP in all budgetary planning. The goal was to make it more likely the government would have to deal with positive shocks instead of negative ones. Also, expenditure and revenue decisions were deliberately separated. The government established final expenditure totals (based on the coalition agreement) in the spring of each year and made any revenue decisions in the fall. Ministers could no longer justify additional spending because an unexpected positive shock meant that they were meeting their deficit targets. Finally, the government agreed to fixed numerical ceilings for social security, health care, and the central government budget. Any expenditure overruns were to lead to cuts in spending in the same category. This additional set of targets was included to address possible overruns in social security and health benefits.

In practice, this coalition agreement led to a successful fiscal policy. The overall budget deficit was at 1.1% of GDP in 1997, comfortably below Maastricht's 3%. The economy also performed well; growth averaged 3.25% of GDP from 1994 to 1998, a full percentage point higher than the government's budget forecasts. The public approved. Although D66's representation in parliament dropped from twenty-four to fourteen, the government gained five seats because of increased support for the liberals and the social democrats (Irwin 1999). The coalition agreement for the second purple government closely followed the 1994 agreement, with detailed budgetary targets and explicit rules for dealing with economic shocks.

Reasons for the Success of Dutch Fiscal Policy

The form of fiscal governance in the Netherlands evolved over time. In the mid-1970s, the country had a clear fiefdom form of fiscal governance. Coalition agreements were vague documents, and government ministers essentially set their own budgets. When the deficit worsened, the government's initial reaction was to centralize the process around the finance minister. This strategy failed, however, as coalition partners, and ministers within the finance minister's own party, refused to accept the finance minister's budget cuts. In 1982, the coalition partners reached a detailed coalition agreement that included, for the first time, explicit budget targets for the life of the coalition. In 1994, these targets extended to every ministry for the life of the coalition, and detailed rules as to what to do in the face of economic shocks (both positive and negative) were also included in the coalition agreement.

It is difficult to argue that EMU, and international pressure more generally, "forced" the Netherlands to get its budget situation under control. The initial reforms of the fiscal system were introduced in 1982, almost a decade before the signing of the Maastricht treaty. One could argue that another economic factor at the Community level affected the level of budget discipline, namely the European Monetary System. The EMS represented a largely successful attempt by a group of Community members to fix their exchange rates with each other. The Netherlands was a core member of the group that successfully kept its rate close to the German rate. Continued loose fiscal policy might have undermined the ability of the Dutch to continue to successfully shadow the German mark.

Although loose policy could have had a negative impact on the functioning of the EMS, the relevant question is whether the EMS served as a proper disciplinarian. This is difficult to answer for one country alone. One way to assess the relative weight of the EMS is to contrast the Dutch fiscal performance with another country that had a similar level of reliance on world markets and that also participated in the EMS. An ideal candidate country is Belgium, which had an open economy and saw itself as having one of the "hard" currencies in the EMS. As the next section will illustrate, unlike the Dutch, the Belgians did not successfully introduce similar reforms in the 1980s. Moreover, budget deficits remained high and the debt burden bloomed. Reforms began only in the early 1990s. This outcome strongly suggests that the EMS did not serve as an external constraint on the fiscal policies that Dutch coalitions pursued.

Belgium

Political Background

Belgium is a divided country. Belgians in the north of the country live in Flanders and speak Flemish, a dialect of Dutch. In the south, Belgians live in Wallonia and speak French. The dividing line between the two regions is essentially the furthest reach of the Roman Empire, a measure of how long the two regions have been divided. As is often the case, economic divisions have largely paralleled the ethnic and linguistic divisions. After the founding of the relatively young Belgian state in 1830, an economically prosperous Wallonia complained about its backward countrymen in the north. In the mid-twentieth century, as services in Flanders replaced the heavy industry and coal fields of Wallonia as the principal economic engine of the country, the economic disparities reversed. Flanders is now the wealthier part of Belgium. To complicate matters further, the capital city, Brussels, is bilingual, while a section of eastern Belgium consists of land that was part of Germany before World War I, and it is German-speaking.

These cleavages have had an important impact on Belgian politics and fiscal policy. As Neto and Cox (1997) explain, the country's use of a proportional representation electoral system, when combined with the multiple cleavages in society, has resulted in several viable political parties. Until 1965, there were three main parties—Christian Democrats, Liberals, and Socialists. Between 1968 and 1978, these parties then split into separate Flemish and Walloon parties as the salience of regional and linguistic cleavages increased. Furthermore, the development of nationalist parties as well as Green parties meant that fourteen parties received representation in parliament in 1981 (De Winter and Dumont 2004). Majority coalition governments with between four and six parties have been the norm since the 1970s. Despite the development of regionally based parties, parties of the same ideological family from each region have always participated together either in government or in opposition. Until 1999, the coalition always consisted of the Christian Democrats together with a collection of additional parties. These parties expect to run against each other in future elections. The theory I presented in chapter 2 suggests that commitment to fiscal contracts should be the form of fiscal governance that addresses the common pool resource problem in Belgium.

Fiscal Policy and Fiscal Actors

One of the more striking features of Belgian public finance is that in the period from the end of Bretton Woods to the beginning of Stage Three of Economic and Monetary Union the cyclically adjusted budget deficits were always negative (fig. 5.2). Moreover, during 1979–92, the period when Belgium was firmly rooted in the Exchange Rate Mechanism, the cyclically adjusted budget balance never was better than –6% of GDP. As a consequence, the overall debt burden in Belgium doubled from close to 60% of GDP in 1973 to almost 135% by 1993. This figure strongly suggests that EMS could not have been much of a fiscal disciplinarian. Although the debt burden reached an all-time high in 1993, the trend of high deficits then reversed. From 1993 through 1998 the cyclically adjusted deficit progressively narrowed while the overall debt burden moved beyond stabilization to improvement.

In terms of the relevant actors involved in fiscal policy, through 1995 both houses of parliament, the National Assembly and the Senate, had virtually the same competencies. In 1995, the Senate lost the power to dissolve government, pass the budget, and conduct interpellations of the government (De Winter and Dumont 2004). Even in the pre-1995 period, the similarity in the electoral system for each chamber meant that the chambers' compositions were virtually the same. A government that could pass a budget in the National Assembly did not (as a rule) have problems passing legislation in the Senate.

In terms of additional participants in the budget process outside the government, there are several parallels with the Netherlands. First, an independent agency, the Federal Planning Bureau, parallels the Dutch CPB. This bureau has existed since 1959, and it makes economic forecasts that the government uses in its public planning. It also publishes the public accounts twice a year. Second, there is a sort of "committee of experts," the High Council of Finance. This body was originally formed in 1936. In contrast to the Dutch Study Group of the Budget Margin, which makes recommendations about the structure of Dutch fiscal rules prior to elections, today's Belgian High Council of Finance takes a direct role in the budget process by writing

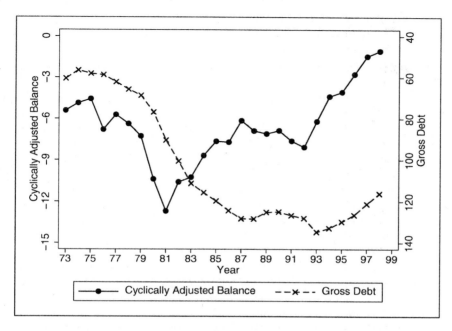

Fig. 5.2. Cyclically adjusted budget balance and gross debt level in Belgium, 1973–98.
Source: European Commission 1999a.

the budget targets that governments, both at the central and regional levels, are expected to respect. A third actor, the Belgian National Bank, was not as independent from government until the mid-1990s, and the bank's governor did not make similarly influential public pronunciations on the budget to the public as the Dutch or German governor did. Instead, the bank exerted its influence on the High Council of Finance, where it held three of the ten seats on the High Council of Finance's subcommittee that dealt with budget issues. The increasing prominence of the High Council of Finance, together with the devolution of many budget competencies to the regions, largely explains the success of a commitment form of fiscal governance in the 1990s.

Public Finance, 1973–89

Belgian fiscal policy resembled a classic case of the fiefdom approach in the 1970s and 1980s. Successive governments attempted to set spending targets, as indeed one would expect with coalition governments, but these targets failed.

The oil crisis in 1973 hit Belgium particularly hard. Unlike its northern neighbor, it did not have natural gas reserves to insulate it from the negative shock. At first, the government simply spent more and collected more in taxes. General government spending shot up 9 percentage points in just five years, from 41.5% of GDP in 1970 to 50.5% in 1975. Taxes at first increased at almost the same rate, so that the overall budget deficit increased only to 5% of GDP in 1975 from 2.2% in 1970. The budget situation then worsened, and it did not improve with the minor economic recovery in the mid-1970s. Deficits averaged over 6% of GDP from 1976 to 1979. The Leo Tindemans cabinet attempted to introduce some initial budgetary reforms in 1976, but these efforts failed (Jones 1995, 202).

The situation was especially dire following the second oil crisis, 1981–83, when the debt level doubled and interest payments increased from 10% to 17% of the total budget (Smits 1985). Belgian cabinets tried to introduce budgetary targets, as one would expect under a multiparty coalition government. The governments in power in the early 1980s took two steps. First, they asked for, and received, from the parliament in successive years "special powers," which allowed them to pass decrees on budget and other economically important areas without approval from parliament. Second, they agreed to different budgetary targets in an effort to get their deficits under control.

The situation that faced the newly elected (although not new) prime minister, Wilfried Martens, in 1985 was emblematic of the problems facing any attempt to cut expenditures. During the coalition negotiations after the fall elections, the future prime minister first tried to write budget cuts of BF 70 billion into the coalition agreement (BF 34.6 = $1). Yet the future coalition partners could not agree on this amount. The reports of the sitting Budget and Finance ministers stated that the amount was BF 20 billion too little because of a shortfall in income, while the likely minister of Economic Affairs wanted to spend more money on the coal sector in Wallonia and Flanders. Moreover, during the negotiations, the sitting ministers of Education were still awarding building contracts for schools even though there was a moratorium on new school construction emerging in the formation agreement. At first Martens simply dropped any reference to cuts in the coalition agreement, but the deal that emerged in the final document was to cut BF 200 billion without any details about how these cuts would be enforced.

During the negotiations on the budget the next year, it appeared that this pledge would be kept. The cabinet agreed to reduce spending by BF 195 billion in May 1985, which, the prime minister asserted, meant that the government had met its goal. Yet even within that year the targets did not hold up. The Francophone education minister refused to make the serious cuts allocated to him, asserting, without providing proof, that the number of students was increasing. The government also weakened, and in some cases abandoned entirely, several planned cuts, including in unemployment compensation and pension funding. Individual spending ministers did not take seriously getting parliamentary approval for their budgets, and by the end of 1986 not a single fiscal-year 1986 budget of any ministry had been approved, even though, in theory, they were supposed to have been passed before the end of 1985. Ivan Couttenier summed up the sentiment directed toward the new government that had promised real spending reductions: "Not only the opposition parties, but also spokesmen for the majority parties expressed their dissatisfaction with the little care the Government was showing about budget orthodoxy" (Couttenier 1987, 373). In the end, the government missed its budget target for 1986 by 2.9% of GNP.

A further problem was the inability of regional groups to exclude one another from any special help from the federal government. The cleavage between Flemish-speaking Flanders and French-speaking Wallonia complicated (and continues to complicate) enormously the conduct of politics in the country, and, by extension, fiscal policy. A classic case comes from the federal government's bailout of four municipalities in the early 1980s. Liège in Wallonia had more or less fallen into default, and the federal government felt obligated to bail out the city. It assumed the city's debts on condition that the city pay it back over thirty years and agree to a restructuring plan. Luckily for the politics of the issue, a corresponding city in Flanders, Antwerp, had similar fiscal problems, and the federal government concluded a similar agreement with it. Yet the debt levels still did not match. To assure that the federal government was not favoring one region over the other, it "bailed out" two additional cities, Ghent and Charleroi, whose finances were nowhere near as troubled. The result was a significant increase in the debt burden on the federal government (interview at the Ministerie van de Vlaamse Gemeenschap, July 9, 1998).

The first of two reasons why a commitment form of fiscal governance failed to take root was the lack of ministerial-level fiscal targets. This made it difficult to reach any broad promise on the size of the budget deficit. The late passage of budget bills in parliament compounded this problem. As De Winter and Dumont (2004, 267) note, "Departmental budget bills (indicating planned expenditures for the coming year) were usually submitted quite late—after the budget year had already begun. Thus, most of the money was spent before the final budget was approved!"

Second, how were intransigent ministers and parties to be punished if they spent more than they were allocated? The theoretical discussion in chapter 3 predicts that the punishment mechanism would probably be lacking if the fiscal contracts were agreed to but not honored, and indeed the most significant problem in the 1980s was the inability of coalition partners to punish "defectors" who overspent their targets—in the few cases in which targets were explicit. It is striking how similar Belgium is to the Italian case I will discuss in chapter 7. As with the Italians, it was virtually impossible for Belgian coalition governments to exclude the Christian Democrats from power. From 1958 until 1999 every coalition government included this centrist party.[9] Moreover, every coalition had to have representatives from

9. Indeed, it took the dioxin scandal in summer 1999 to finally chase the Christian Democrats from power.

both Flanders and Wallonia. To the extent that fiscal issues centered on this ethnic divide, the punishment mechanism was again absent. When I asked a member of the Flemish Christian Democrats what happened in cases of overspending he replied that there was simply no expectation of punishment (Brussels, April 2001).

The institutional form of the ministries further encouraged ministers to care about specific party constituencies. Unlike in many countries where the ministerial staff is explicitly nonpartisan, in Belgium a minister's staff is tied directly to the minister's party. Indeed, "the ministerial cabinet, especially the lower-levels staff, is responsible for running the clientelist machinery, especially in the minister's electoral constituency. Dozens of ministers' staff members also work directly and exclusively for the party, and hardly ever show up at the offices of the minister's personal cabinet" (De Winter and Dumont 2004, 265). This institutional feature suggests that the common pool resource problem will be especially severe. Without a centralization of the budget process to establish spending targets for the ministries, staff members will propose spending to their ministers that targets member constituencies. To the extent that civil servants in ministries are employed to work for a particular party, ministerial employment budgets will also be bloated.

A partial solution to the problem of a lack of a credible punishment for overspending ministers resulting from the regional conflict between the Flemings and the Walloons was to decentralize the country. After elections in 1988 it was initially not possible for parties from the two regions to form a new coalition government. The future Christian Democratic prime minister, Jean-Luc Dehaene, agreed to accept King Baudouin's offer to attempt to form a new government, but only if he could negotiate what amounted to changes in the organization of the state itself.

For two weeks fifteen men representing five political parties bargained with one another and established a new constitutional order.[10] What was most important for fiscal policy was the transfer of powers to the regions. From 1989 on, the three regions assumed responsibility over all so-called territorial policies, such as public infrastructure, special employment practices, public works, agriculture, and the like. The three communities assumed

10. The bargaining would be a fascinating topic for a dissertation on public choice. One of the fifteen persons in the room related the following story to the author. All negotiations were conducted with the use of spreadsheets that set out the implications of different proposals. At first Jean-Luc Dehaene wanted to negotiate in n dimensions, but this was not possible because the negotiators could not understand what it was that they were gaining or giving up, so they refused at first to support any change at all. Dehaene then broke down the negotiations into two to three dimensional spaces. This allowed compromises to be struck. After all of the dimensional spaces were finished, everything already agreed to was put into one package. I would guess that this is the only time where people writing a new constitutional order literally compared different spreadsheets, not just documents.

responsibility over the big-ticket item of education.[11] These bodies received half their funding from a fixed share of national taxes and some minor taxes they imposed themselves and half from federal government grants. Overnight the share of public budget devoted to the regions increased from 8.4% to 33% (Hooghe 1991). A 1993 law further devolved the competencies of international relations, foreign trade, the environment, agriculture, and scientific policy (Bogaert and Père 2000).

This transfer of competencies did not solve the problems the two nationalities had with each another, but it did reduce their demands on the federal government. The funding structure guaranteed that the regions always got the money promised them, even during economic recessions, meaning that the federal budget would bear the full effects of any revenue shortfalls. The full debt burden also remained with the federal government. Yet this change did not resolve the problems within the national government, and there were temptations for the regional governments to create excessive deficits of their own. Clearly more institutional change was needed to prevent this reform from exacerbating Belgium's fiscal problems.

1990–98

There was a strong consensus among political parties in Belgium that the country had to be be part of the first wave of EMU. Yet it was unclear *how* Belgium would manage to get in. Indeed, as late as 1995 the German finance minister, Theo Waigel, put Belgium and the other states with weak deficit records on notice that there would be no exceptions for countries that did not meet the criteria (Jones 1998). The road to fiscal discipline was driven by credible fiscal contracts at the national level. Fiscal contracts between the national and subnational levels of government also played a critical role. The major innovation was the strengthening of one institution, the High Council of Finance, which wrote and monitored the execution of the yearly fiscal contracts.

The High Council of Finance had existed since 1936, but it had been only an advisory body to the Ministry of Finance and had little practical importance. The High Council of Finance that was newly constituted in 1992 remains in the same form today; it has thirty members in full council, including representatives from the regions, the Ministries of Finance and of Budget, four other federal ministries, outside experts in tax and fiscal matters, and officials

---

11. To keep the levels of government straight, the regions are based on territory and there are now three: Flanders, Wallonia, and Brussels (the last with somewhat reduced powers in comparison with the other two regions). The three Communities, on the other hand, are based on language—Flemish, French, and German. One nuance that is relevant in budget policy is that the Flemish Community and the Flanders region are one, while this is not the case for the French Community and Wallonia. The exact overlap for the Flemish gives them somewhat more flexibility in budgeting. Flemish universities, for example, are generally better funded than Walloon universities.

at the central bank. The High Council of Finance has three sections, and it is the section for fiscal policy that is most critical here. It has only ten members: one representative from the Ministry of Finance, six representatives from the three regions, and, perhaps most important, the top three officials from the Belgian National Bank—the governor, vice-governor, and senior director.[12] The fiscal policy section at its own initiative can recommend to the Minister of Finance that the borrowing capacity of any level of government be curtailed. It also establishes fiscal targets for each level of government. This small group is, by design, composed of "representatives of fiscal orthodoxy."[13]

The High Council of Finance assumed a pivotal role after Maastricht, although it required more autonomy in order to carry out its new functions. In June 1992, parliament assigned the council the role of monitoring the compliance of each level of government to the Convergence Programme of Belgium. The stated goal was for the general government debt burden to be reduced progressively to 3% by 1996, one year before the year that the Council of Ministers would use to decide participation in EMU. The High Council of Finance also became the forum where the responsibilities of each level of government for reducing the overall debt level were decided. Indeed, because the regions received most of their money from federally collected taxes, the regions were especially concerned with how the convergence program targets were to be met. The agreement was that the real expenditure pattern of the regions should follow real regional growth rates and a target figure for the real growth rate of regional debts through the year 2000.

The execution of the agreement immediately proved problematic. In 1992 the country headed into recession, which affected the regions unequally. The High Council of Finance, based on the guidelines that new spending should largely follow economic growth, apportioned Flanders 1.25% more spending, Brussels only 0.45% more, and Wallonia a *cut* in spending of 0.64%. Politically this was unacceptable; Wallonia, already experiencing a sharper hit from the recession, resented the increased spending in Flanders, and, not surprisingly, the Walloon regional government exceeded its spending target. Flanders followed suit, knowing that Wallonia was not sticking to its target, and the federal government overran its spending limit in what was an election year. Hence, *no* level of government met its target, and the general government deficit was 6.9%, 1.2% over the convergence program's target (Stienlet 2000, 25).

This initial failure to rein in spending alarmed the economic elites in the parties and in government. Representatives of different levels of government agreed to reinforce the High Council of Finance. They required the council to write a report every March on all levels of government, which detailed

12. It is noteworthy that the council did not include any representatives from parliament.
13. In interviews in April 2001 in Brussels, staff members at the Federal Bureau of Planning noted that the director of the bureau only has observer status in the council. The reason they gave for this is that the director in the early 1990s was perceived as too "Keynesian."

whether they had reached the targets of the previous year. If a body had not, this notification was expected to be early enough to allow the offender to pass a supplementary budget that reduced its deficit. All levels of government were also expected to abide by the accounting rules of the High Council of Finance, which were stricter than the ESA rules that the European Commission used. Reaching the High Council of Finance targets would therefore automatically get Belgium under Maastricht's reference level of 3%.[14] The council drew up new targets with the same stated aim of reaching the 3% level in 1996. Most of the burden was placed on the federal government, which was expected to make two-thirds of the reduction in the general government deficit level.

From this point on the targets stuck. Indeed, the federal government was forced to pass repeated supplementary measures—which together represented over 6% of GDP—to meet the targets every year from 1992 to 1996 (OECD 1999). The final targets were set in 1996 for 1997. The High Council of Finance proposed 2.8%, and, for the first time, one of the levels of government disagreed with the council's target. The federal government demanded a deficit of exactly 3%, but even the compromise amount of 2.9% was overly pessimistic. Because of stronger-than-expected economic growth, Belgium coasted under the 3% reference level with a deficit of only 1.9%, a full percentage point below the target (Conseil Superieur des Finances 1999).

Unlike in previous periods, when such targets were not credible, the political party elites believed that violating budget targets would lead to high political cost at the polls. The coalition governments in 1995 and 1999 pledged in their coalition agreements to reach whatever targets the High Council of Finance proposed. Moreover, formal rules such as the Golden Hamster provided a framework for what the country should do with additional revenues when the economy performed better than expected.[15] These measures together removed the budget from political contention; as a staff member at the National Assembly commented to the author in October 2000, "Parliament isn't interested anymore in the budget."

Why Did Belgium Reform?

It is useful to take a step back and consider the role of the High Council of Finance more broadly within the theoretical context presented here. The High Council of Finance generally wrote the guidelines for the budget and

14. In particular, several public institutions are considered "enterprises" under ESA rules and hence do not count toward deficit and debt levels, while they do count under HCF rules (Stienlet 2000).

15. The Golden Hamster requires that all excess revenues beyond what was budgeted must be spent on reducing the overall debt limit. Because the government intentionally adopts pessimistic economic forecasts, there is usually a larger than "expected" revenue collection. For further details, as well as for a comparison of such rules to deal with economic shocks across the European Union, see Hallerberg, Strauch, and von Hagen 2001.

set the deficit targets for all levels of government during the critical four years before 1997. In theory the targets were "recommendations," but in practice all levels of government adopted them unchanged except in 1996, and even then the differences in targets were minor (interview at the Belgian Ministry of Finance, July 1999). One should not forget, of course, that representatives from the federal and regional governments sat in the key section of the council and participated in the decision making, but this development still represented a change from decision making pre-1993. The cabinet and, for that matter, the parliament were both by-passed in the decision-making process. Indeed, based on interviews I had with officials at the regional, federal, and European Commission level in Brussels, all sides considered the (nonelected) representatives from the Belgian National Bank to be the key participants. The federal and regional representatives believed the bankers to be impartial brokers between the two levels of government, and the bankers' suggestions were often incorporated into the council's recommendations.[16] The perceived credibility of the bankers also carried over to the credibility of the council's recommendations. The only doubts about the targets arose in 1992–93 during Belgium's recession, and even then all parties quickly agreed to revise them.

The clear "stick" in the process was that no one level of government or political party wanted to be accused of being responsible for the exclusion of Belgium from the first wave of EMU. Once again this was a change from the situation in the 1980s, when each of Belgium's regional parties refused to back down in the name of "budget discipline." The episode in 1992–93 illustrates that these regional cleavages still mattered, but all sides had a clear incentive to ensure that the defections did not happen again. Moreover, unlike in Italy, a failure to qualify for EMU might have signaled the end of the country itself. Regional leaders had been clamoring for more and more competencies at their level, and a failure by the national government could have provided new ammunition for regional extremists who would have liked nothing better than to see the federal government collapse (Jones 1998).

The European Union role in Belgium is less obvious but still significant. By simply establishing the stick of exclusion from EMU, the European Union placed pressure especially on the federal government to abide by the targets. Moreover, meetings of the Council of Economic and Finance Ministers to discuss progress toward meeting the Maastricht criteria served as a constant reminder to the minister of finance from his peers in other EU countries that the Belgian effort in the early years was not on target. The Union's designation of Belgium as an "excessive deficit" country was a public statement that Belgium had not done enough. The establishment of a certain target of

16. The central bank also holds an informational advantage over the other participants in the council. Contrary to the practices of other European countries, the central bank prepares the national economic statistics on which the debates are based.

3% of GDP by 1997 was also a clear benchmark that had not existed before. Although there was already pressure inside the country to do something about the high deficits, it is doubtful that Belgium would have made cuts in spending and raised taxes as quickly and as deeply without the 3% target.[17] Because the target was for "general" rather than simply "central" government debt, it was imperative that the state find a solution to its budget troubles that included all levels of government, and, as one official in the Flemish regional government put it, the High Council of Finance became "the natural institution to use" once Maastricht was agreed on (interview at the Ministerie van de Vlaamse Gemeenschap, July 9, 1998).

Yet, it is reasonable to conclude that it was the High Council of Finance, rather than the monitoring that the European Commission provided, that was most important to the success of the fiscal contracts in Belgium. The participants monitored one another through this forum and laid the path toward meeting the magical 3% threshold. The Union's role was to set the ultimate target at the end of the period and to provide the stick if one or more levels of government failed to keep its target set in the High Council of Finance.

Finland

Political Background

Although located geographically in the area often thought of as Scandinavia, Finland's political profile does not fit what one would think of as a "typical" Scandinavian state. The country does have a developed welfare state, with public expenditures representing 47% of GDP in 1990, but this figure is closer to Britain (at 42%) than to Sweden (at 62%) for the same year. Finland rarely has had Danish- or Swedish-style minority governments. Instead, oversized multiparty coalition governments with four or five parties that can represent up to 80% of the seats in parliament are common.

One reason for oversized coalitions comes from an important parliamentary rule. Until 1992, one-third of the parliament could vote to delay a bill's final adoption until after the next elections, which could leave the bill in abeyance for up to four years. This rule meant that it was often better to include parties in the government in the first place than to risk the possibility that opposition parties would vote as a bloc to delay key parts of the government's program.[18] As we shall see in more detail below, the rule also

17. An official at the federal Finance ministry made this argument to me (July 28, 1999).

18. Some Finnish political scientists do not believe this rule was the only reason for oversized coalitions. As Nousiainen (2000) points out, such coalitions have remained the rule since the parliamentary procedure was phased out. A second reason he gives for the large coalitions is the need to create an ideological balance among different coalition partners that often are quite different from one another ideologically.

affected the making of state budgets. As Meklin et al. (2000, 4), explain, "The leaving of a bill in abeyance was often directed at laws making expenditure cuts introduced in connection with the budget proposal."

There are traditionally three main parties in Finnish politics, and two of them, together with an appropriate weighting of smaller parties, usually form governments. On a left-right dimension, the Social Democratic Party anchors the center-left, the Center Party, naturally, the center, and the National Coalition Party, or Conservative Party, the center-right. A second dimension, an urban-rural one, is also relevant. The Center Party descends directly from the Agrarian Party, which renamed itself the Rural Party in 1965. While the party has broadened its appeal beyond independent farmers (Arter 1999), it still maintains its core support in the less populated regions of central and northern Finland. The Social Democrats and the Conservatives, in contrast, are strong in the cities. Through 1987 it was difficult to include the Conservative Party in government because of an implicit veto from Finland's large neighbor to the east, the Soviet Union.[19] This situation changed in 1987 when the Conservatives and the Social Democrats jointly formed a coalition with the Swedish People's Party (a Finnish party of the Swedish national minority). The coalitions that followed provide a sense of the diverse coalitions possible—after the 1991 elections the coalition included the Center Party, the Christian League of Finland, the Conservative Party, and the Swedish People's Party, while the "rainbow" coalition formed after the 1995 elections included the Left Wing Alliance, the Green Party, the Social Democratic Party, the Swedish People's Party, and the Conservatives.

Finland is one of only three European Union states (the others are France and Portugal) where the president has some policy-making power.[20] Dating back to the Constitution of 1919, the president has maintained responsibility for foreign affairs and for defense. The constitution dictates that most internal policies be the domain of the cabinet. A president can, however, influence internal policy through his role in the appointment of governments—the president names a party leader after elections to lead negotiations on possible government coalitions (Nousiainen 2001). One president in particular, Urho Kekkonen, also played a more informal, yet also influential, role in framing the domestic political debate during his long term in office (from 1956 through 1981), but no president before or since has been as prominent. More generally, because the president has never been one of the principal actors in the budget arena, the focus here will be on the policies of successive coalition governments.[21]

19. The country bordered the Soviet Union, and it had fought against the Soviets in World War II. The geopolitical reality in the postwar period was that Finland was expected to be neutral.

20. For this reason, Duverger (1980) considers Finland to be "semi-presidential."

21. A recent constitutional reform has weakened the position of the president still further. Since March 2000, the parliament elects the prime minister after discussions among

The regularity of majority coalition governments would suggest that a commitment form of fiscal governance would be most appropriate to address the common pool resource problem.

Budget Policy

Until the early 1990s, a characteristic of Finnish budget policy was its stability. Unlike most other European states, the country maintained regular cyclically adjusted budget surpluses, and its overall debt burden remained below 20% of GDP (fig. 5.3). When compared with Belgium or even the Netherlands, its budgetary performance through the 1980s was remarkable. Indeed, the overall performance of the Finnish economy was impressive. Unlike other Western European countries, Finland did not suffer from a recession in the late 1970s to early 1980s. Economic growth did decrease from 5.1% in 1979 to 2.1% in 1980, but growth never dipped below this low and averaged a healthy 3.6% for the 1980s.[22]

This streak came to an abrupt end. The sharp drop in trade with a disintegrating Soviet Union, the collapse of an asset bubble that had developed in the late 1980s, and an overinflated currency all deepened a recession that hit all of Western Europe. Brisk economic growth of more than 5% in 1989 reversed direction to become a decline in growth of 7% in 1991. The general government budget deficit worsened even more than one would expect given the economic shock. Cyclically adjusted deficits became negative in 1991, and they returned to surplus only in 1997. The changes in the overall debt burden were even more dramatic. The general government debt burden, which had been only 14% in 1990, ballooned to 57% in three short years. Even these figures understate the dire situation at the central government level—among the three components of general government according to EU definitions, the social security account maintained regular surpluses of around 4% of GDP through the early 1990s; subnational governments had smaller, though consistent, surpluses; and central government deficits, in contrast, amounted to over 11% of GDP in 1993 and 1994 (International Monetary Fund 1997).

A political economy explanation for this performance focuses on the institutions in place to deal with the budget. Indeed, in the 1970s and 1980s Finland had an informal version of commitment. Spending ministers had little

party leaders, and the president merely confirms parliament's choice. The president's foreign policy role has also declined in recent years because of Finland's accession to the European Union. One of the most important foreign policy areas today, Finland's relationship with the European Union, is the responsibility of the cabinet. Ironically, the legitimacy of the president has increased. Through 1988, an electoral college informally determined the president. Martti Ahtisaari became the first directly elected president in February 1994 (Nousiainen 2001).

22. Figures provided by a staff member of the Finnish Ministry of Finance, December 4, 2002.

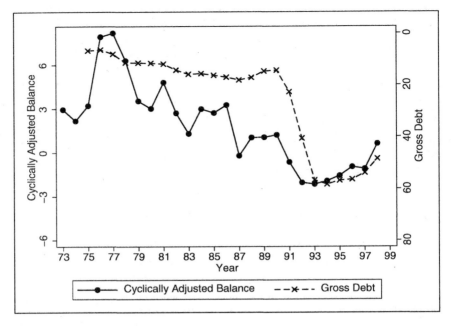

Fig. 5.3. Cyclically adjusted budget balance and gross debt level in Finland, 1973–98.
Source: European Commission 1999a.

direct autonomy over their ministries. As chapter 2 illustrated, this autonomy is the main source of the common pool resource problem as it arises in
cabinets. There were some institutional checks to monitor the coalition partners. Moreover, the nature of the coalition governments, which usually
included more parties than were needed to form a majority, meant that, in
some cases, a party that violated the fiscal contract could be excluded from
the government without bringing down the government.

This informal version of commitment functioned well enough during normal times. The system broke down during the sharp economic shock that
hit Finland in the early 1990s. Since then, the country has adopted some formal rules that find parallels especially in Belgium.

1980s

The goal of commitment is to assure that all political parties consider the full
tax burden of their decisions. The common pool resource problem grows
when decision makers consider only part of the tax burden when making
spending decisions. In cabinet situations, this becomes problematic when
ministers are autonomous in making decisions for their ministries. In the
Dutch case, cabinet ministers were constrained through explicit expenditure

targets that political parties wrote into coalition agreements, which in practice constituted a fiscal contract. The Belgians used the High Council of Finance to write the fiscal contracts, which the government then executed at the beginning of the 1990s.

The Finnish parties did not agree to an explicit fiscal contract in the 1980s, nor did they have an outside committee write a contract for them. They did, however, greatly restrict the relative autonomy of spending ministers. The most important institutional constraint was the practice that no single party could control key ministries. Each key ministry usually received two ministers to run them who came from different political parties. Except for the Esko Aho government from 1991 to 1995, even the finance ministry was divided from 1980 until 2002. In the coalition government that formed in 1999, for example, a Conservative, Sauli Niinistö, was formally finance minister, but Suvi-Anne Siimes from the Left Alliance held the position of minister at the Ministry of Finance. Hence a member of the party the furthest to the left politically in Finland checks a finance minister from the right. The same is true for the Ministry of Social Affairs, with, in 2002, the Conservative Maija Perho sharing the ministry with the Swedish People's Party's Eva Biaudet.[23] These dual heads of ministries allow the parties to check each other; as Nousiainen (2000, 283) notes, "[The two ministers] are of course able to watch each other very carefully and to report the doings of their colleague to the party and to the coalition leadership."

A second factor concerned the decision-making process within the cabinet. A cabinet-level finance committee that met weekly considered all important matters related to the budget. The prime minister chaired it, all ministers were invited, and, on average, half regularly attended. Through 1977 the committee discussed any measure that was to have a financial impact. This mandate became too much work, however, and some matters were delegated to a political economy committee, while minor financial matters came under the purview of the finance ministry alone. Important financial decisions remained, however, within the Finance Committee. As Arter (1987, 146) explains, "A government ministry cannot proceed with a measure which exceeds the estimates laid down by the Finance Committee, and the latter thus exercises a powerful veto right over departmental spending." The committee made it easier for parties to monitor one another even when they did not have a minister of their own in a given ministry.

There was an additional forum where ministers could discuss the budget, namely the prime minister's "evening school." The tradition dates back to a

23. Other ministries that commonly receive two ministers include Interior, Trade and Industry, Foreign Affairs, Environment, and Education. While there are multiple ministers in several ministries, these ministers do have clear responsibilities; for a list of the responsibilities of the ministers in the current government see http://www.valtioneuvosto.fi/vn/liston/base.lsp?r=695&k=en.

1937–39 coalition between the Social Democrats and the Agrarians when the prime minister held informal evening meetings at his residence. Ministers would arrive first for a joint sauna. They would then discuss matters over drinks, at first in the prime minister's residence, then later before a large fireplace. The frequency of the meetings decreased from every week to every other week by the 1980s (Arter 1987) as ministers became increasingly pressed for time, and these days the "evening school" is held monthly (Peters 2000).

This style allowed the prime minister to lead discussions of proposals in a more informal setting; but in general the prime minister did not have many formal tools at his disposal to get his way. The exception was his ability to call a vote of no confidence. In 1986, for example, Prime Minister Kalevi Sorsa used this power when the Rural Party insisted that the government spend more on agriculture, and the Rural Party dropped its position (Arter 1987, 137). This power aside, the prime minister's principal job was to build a consensus among political parties.

All of these factors contribute to a general sense of collective decision making, and the autonomy and responsibility of each individual minister has been, in international comparison, minimal. The principle of collective decision making, so deeply rooted in Finnish central administration, has meant that no coalition party needs to be afraid of what is happening outside the policy fields it directly controls (Nousiainen 2000, 270).

In a comparative sense, Finland managed to contain the common pool resource problem at the cabinet level in the 1980s, and it did so without the formal rules that work so effectively in the Netherlands. Unlike Belgium during the same time period, it was not routine for spending ministers to overspend their targets, and, if they did so, there was the cabinet Finance Committee to insist that the limits be respected. Moreover, as an incident in 1982–83 with the Communist Party demonstrated, the surplus coalition structure allowed parties in government to expel a "defecting" party from the coalition. The Center–Social Democratic coalition dropped the Communist Party from government when the Communists refused to honor the norm of collective responsibility.

At the same time, those limits were not settled in a coalition agreement. Ministries did establish medium-term spending plans, but these plans had little weight in government, and, importantly, the coalition parties made no political commitments to them (author interview, June 2001, Ministry of Finance, Helsinki). There was also a clear fiscal political business cycle present. If one looks at figure 5.3, one can easily tell the years of national elections by the dips in the cyclically adjusted balance. Spending increased noticeably in 1979, 1983, and 1987. This cycle did not do too much damage to the health of the budget in good times but was a potential source of trouble when the economy turned bad. Moreover, the cabinet rules, combined with the ability of one-third of parliamentarians to delay laws for two to four years, made the system rigid. Indeed, these political institutional factors all contributed to a worsening of the budgetary situation during Finland's sharp economic downturn at the beginning of the 1990s.

1990s

Finland entered the 1990s with an economy that, if anything, was performing too well. In August 1989 the Organisation for Economic Cooperation and Development complained that the grand coalition composed of Social Democrats and Conservatives was doing little to cool an overheated economy growing at over 5% of GDP. There was a large credit expansion that followed the government's financial market liberalization. The situation seemed especially severe in the labor market, with wages averaging yearly increases of nearly 10% while the unemployment rate remained low at around 2.5%. The budget was in surplus with a balance of 1.5% of GDP (Honkapohja and Koskela 1999, 404; *Financial Times,* August 16, 1989).

This bright economic picture darkened quickly. By fall 1990 the economy had slowed to almost zero growth, and unemployment grew 2.5%. In 1991, the economy contracted 7 percentage points of GDP. By June 1992, the unemployment rate had increased to 12.7%, and a year later the *Financial Times* predicted that the rate would remain above 10% for the remainder of the decade (October 11, 1993). The most obvious cause of Finland's economic difficulties was the collapse of the Soviet Union. The 1948 Soviet-Finnish Treaty of Friendship, Cooperation, and Mutual Assistance stipulated that the Soviet Union would ship Finland oil and gas in exchange for Finnish consumer goods. This arrangement cushioned Finland from the vagaries of world energy markets. It also provided a ready market for Finnish goods— as recently as 1985, 21.5% of Finnish exports went to the Soviet Union. By 1990, that has diminished to 10%, and it was to drop further as the decade progressed (*Financial Times,* November 15, 1990). Other external factors contributing to a decline in economic growth included recessions in two important trading partners, Sweden and the United Kingdom. Within Finland, the country experienced a financial crisis, and the banking system virtually collapsed.[24]

In this climate, the government reacted slowly to the worsening economy. It initially seemed to ignore the implications of the economic difficulties for the budget, and what action it did take did not appear credible. Budget policy was usually set by agreement among cabinet ministers without an overarching target. For the first time, the Finnish government set an overall spending target for the budget when, in October 1990, it proposed that real

24. Honkapohja and Koskela (1999) emphasize the financial system problems over the external shocks Finland experienced in the early 1990s.

expenditure growth increase only 4% for 1991. Yet the government would be expected to meet this target only if it remained in office after upcoming spring elections, and even members of the finance ministry at the time did not believe that the target was credible (author interviews with Finnish Ministry of Finance officials, Helsinki, June 2001). The reaction of the financial markets was swift—expressing doubt that this target could be achieved, the credit rating agency, Moody's, cut Finland's credit rating from the highest possible score of AAA to AAI, which "reflect[ed] the gathering gloom among forecasters about the country's immediate economic prospects" (*Financial Times,* November 15, 1990).

Doubts about the budget's targets were justified. Spending increased 8.5 percentage points of GDP in general government terms in 1991. The greatest increase was in transfers to households, which grew 19.3% over the previous year, while compensation to public employees increased more than 11% (AMECO 1999). Certainly, the recession contributed to expenditure growth. Yet it was not the only factor. Elections were held in spring 1991, and there was pressure within the government, for electoral purposes, to increase spending above previous levels in areas such as old-age pensions, home care for the sick and elderly, and rural post offices (*Financial Times,* November 15, 1990). Indeed, the election results led to the end of the grand coalition and the formation of a Center-Conservative coalition.

The goal of the new government was damage control, and there was a continuing sense that the government was always one step behind economic developments. When it became clear how serious the budget situation had become, the new government proposed a series of measures that focused on the expenditure side of the budget. Once again, a government established an overall expenditure target at the beginning of the budget process for the upcoming year—its 1992 budget promised to increase expenditures in real terms only by 1% over 1991 levels. To meet this target, the government planned to freeze all social service spending. Because unemployment levels were still rising, the only way to reach an overall freeze was to cut existing benefits, and the government proposed to cut the amount of unemployment compensation, to cancel the indexing of public pensions for a year, and to increase the early retirement age from fifty-five to sixty. To spread the pain, the government wanted to lay off seven hundred thousand civil servants for two weeks. It also intended to introduce a tax on all travel abroad. According to the *Financial Times,* one group that was spared significant cuts was one of the Center Party's main backers, farmers, who faced a budget cut of only FM 300 million while receiving FM 1.5 billion in export subsidies (FM 5.1 = $1) (*Financial Times,* October 4, 1991).

The ultimate fate of these changes, however, was initially uncertain. Although the government had a majority in parliament, its supporters did not add up to two-thirds of members of parliament, which was the ratio needed to assure passage of legislation.[25] The government also sought to convince unions to freeze wages for 1992, something it could not simply legislate. Unions agreed to a freeze at the end of November only after a markka devaluation of 12.3% against the ecu (European Currency Unit) on November 12. The government had fixed its currency unilaterally to the ecu in May 1991. Previously, it had maintained a fixed but adjustable peg versus a currency basket. By fixing to the ecu and adopting a harder "fix" than the country had had before, the government hoped to add credibility to its policies. It also sent a signal that it might want to join the European Monetary System in the future.

A package of cuts did eventually pass the legislature, but conditions continued to worsen both in the economy and in the budget. In frustration, the governor of the Bank of Finland, Rolf Kullberg, publicly attacked Prime Minister Aho and his government's conduct of fiscal policy. Adding to the sense that the government was adrift, the day after Kullberg's comments, an IMF report was made public that criticized the government for not taking necessary steps to rein in public spending. Panic hit the markets, with FM 10 billion leaving the country on that fateful Friday alone. Kullberg announced his resignation two days later (*Süddeutsche Zeitung*, April 6, 1992).

Government ministers seemingly stumbled from one crisis meeting to another, and on the weekend following Kullberg's comments, the government proposed deep cuts once again, including cuts across the board totaling FM 10 billion, which represented roughly 2% of GDP. The package again targeted social programs such as public pensions, unemployment compensation, and education, as well as agricultural support programs; markets at first reacted positively to the package (Bank of Finland 1992, 16; *Financial Times*, April 7, 1992; *Times* (London) April 7, 1992). Although a somewhat reduced package worth FM 7 billion passed in June, the budget situation did not improve. Hoping that an early announcement of plans for the 1993 budget would increase its credibility, in June the government proposed another package that would reduce overall government spending 2 percentage points of GDP. Yet the situation deteriorated further, and in August it brought up the timing of the expenditure reductions focused especially on social programs (Bank of Finland 1992; *Financial Times*, August 21, 1992).

Markets were again not calmed. Moreover, trouble was brewing throughout the European Monetary System. While Italy's and the United Kingdom's decisions to end their participation in the EMS received the most attention, Finland was the first country to abandon the system, in September 1992. The Finnish markka quickly depreciated 30%. The government introduced yet another round of budget cuts a month later (*Financial Times*, December 6, 1992).

25. As the Bank of Finland's annual report went to press in late fall 1991, it could only comment that "the passing of the 'savings laws' aimed at halting the growth of government spending was considered uncertain" (5).

Not all of the news from 1992 was bad. One institutional change that made budgetary reform more likely was the end of the abeyance law. After June 1992 it was no longer possible for just one-third of the members of parliament to delay the passage of a bill. Although this change emerged from a parliamentary commission to study constitutional reform, established during the boom years of the late 1980s, the budget situation made its passage urgent, and the abeyance provision was rescinded for most items (European Commission 1999b). The government formed in 1991 had 115 members, or only 57.5% of the seats (Nousiainen 2001, 266–67). Also, on March 18, 1992, Finland formally applied for European Union membership.[26]

Finland hit bottom in budgetary policy in 1993. The government vowed in its 1993 budget proposal to return spending in real terms to 1991 levels, repeating a pattern of setting overall spending targets one year ahead. A growing problem in the private sector, however, forced it to renege on this pledge. The banking sector was in the midst of a crisis of its own. The problems hit banks in Sweden and Norway as well, but they were most severe in Finland. After financial deregulation in the late 1980s, asset prices soared and the private sector went on a borrowing binge, with domestic bank lending increasing more than 80% from 1987 through 1990 (European Commission 1998b, 6). This classic bubble burst in 1990–91, leading to rapid reverses in asset prices and a wave of corporate bankruptcies that put severe pressure on Finnish banks. The government felt forced to intervene to prevent a complete collapse. Already in September 1991, the Bank of Finland had taken control of Skopbank, which was regarded as the "central bank" of the savings bank system. In early 1992 the government issued preferred capital certificates and established a government guarantee fund to support the banks (Honkapohja and Koskela 1999). These measures did not have a direct impact on the budget because they amounted to the government assuming substantial amounts of private debts. They did, however, balloon the government's debt burden by 10 percentage points of GDP, and, with it, increase interest payments that came out of the central government budget (European Commission 1998, 2). More public money went into the fund's capital in early 1993, and the government was able to end its support of the banking sector only in 1994.

Matters improved only in 1995. Indeed, 1995 was a pivotal year for several reasons. The fiscal history of Finland in 1993 and 1994 mirrored that of 1991 and 1992; the budgetary situation continued to worsen with central government deficits at around 11% of GDP for both years. And the government responded with supplementary budgets to cut spending. Even with these cuts, the budgetary situation remained precarious. At the beginning of 1995, the Ministry of Finance issued a report arguing that if policies remained the same, the overall debt burden would increase 30 percentage points to over 90%

26. What, if any, effect this application had on public finances in Finland will be discussed later in the chapter.

of GDP. The year 1995 was also an election year, and, given the tone of the campaign, a "no change in policy" policy was unlikely. In comparison with years past, all major parties argued for deep cuts in spending before the election. Prime Minister Aho's Center Party called for FM 15–20 billion in cuts, and the Social Democrats set a public target of FM 20 billion in cuts, with cuts especially targeted on agriculture subsidies. An article from the *Deutsche Presse-Agentur* noted that "a leftist politician said recently the discussion about public savings reminded him of a poker game where the participants dare each other to come forth with the highest stakes in savings" (March 2, 1995). Indeed, the party that emerged from the elections with the most seats in parliament, the Social Democrats, also promised the largest savings.

An important institutional change in the budget process introduced during the coalition negotiations brought Finland closer to the form of fiscal governance in place in the Netherlands. The parties that formed the new coalition, which was known as the "rainbow" coalition because it included parties from the full spectrum—from the Conservatives to the Greens—agreed on overall spending targets for the life of the coalition, not just for the upcoming year, as had been the practice under the previous government. In aggregate, the new coalition adopted the Social Democratic proposal that spending be reduced FM 20 billion (*Frankfurter Allgemeine Zeitung*, April 24, 1995). For the first time, the parties also negotiated the level of spending cuts per ministry in a document meant to last the expected term of the new government, or four years. Only after the ministerial budgets had been set did the parties decide the allocation of ministerial portfolios (author interviews, Finnish Ministry of Finance, Helsinki, June 2001).

Before returning to fiscal policy developments, it is important to note that 1995 was also pivotal because it was the year Finland joined the European Union. Although there had been some initial skepticism in the press and among members of the Finnish parliament that voters would support accession, the final vote was 57% in favor and only 43% against. If Finland were to qualify for Economic and Monetary Union, it would need to get its general government deficit, which had been at 6.2% of GDP in 1994, below 3% of GDP by 1997.

Indeed, the government's program was followed as promised in the coalition agreement. One-half of the savings came from social transfers to households, one-fourth from reductions in transfers from national to local governments, and one-fourth through miscellaneous savings. Moreover, real economic growth returned to a healthy 4.5% in 1994, and it remained positive through the rest of the 1990s. Total central government spending, when expressed as a percent of GDP, dropped from a high of 36.5% in 1993 to 30.6% in 1997, almost 6 percentage points. Over the same period, the tax take increased 3 percentage points of GDP, due especially to increases in the income tax take (European Commission 1998). As a result of these developments, Finland successfully reduced its general government balance to –1.6%, comfortably above the –3% level, while its overall debt level according to Maastricht definitions was 54% (European Commission 1999a.) Commenting on Finland's turnaround, the IMF concluded in a 1999 press release that "the conduct of macroeconomic policies in Finland since the early 1990s has been impressive by any standard . . . a decade that began with the steepest recession among the advanced economies is ending with the public finances in balance, activity strong, and founder membership of the euro zone secured" (1).

Voters, too, credited the government with turning the economy around, and it remained in office after the 1999 elections. While the Social Democrats lost some support, they continued to constitute the largest party in parliament, and their main coalition partners, the Conservatives, gained seats. As in 1995, one of the main campaign issues again concerned the need for expenditure cuts. Also as in 1995, the coalition negotiations followed the ideal one expects under a commitment form of fiscal governance. The parties again negotiated budgets by ministry for the life of the coalition. Those agreements are explicit, and they are freely available to the public.[27]

Reasons for the Success of Finnish Fiscal Policy in the mid-1990s

There are at least three possible explanations for why Finland turned around its fiscal performance. The first is that international pressure made Finland do it. The second is that EMU, and the Maastricht process more generally, made Finland do it. The third is that the domestic institutional framework changed. The first and third explanations are most persuasive, and they probably interacted with each other.

The connection between EMU and the turnaround in fiscal policy would seem at first to be compelling. Finland has performed well fiscally since joining the European Union in 1995, and it became one of the founding members of the euro just four years later. The government, unlike its Swedish counterpart, argued that participation in EMU would be beneficial to the Finnish economy.[28] Yet the government consciously decoupled its fiscal reforms from EMU in public debates. There was concern that identifying possibly unpopular cuts in spending with EMU would make it more difficult to adopt the common currency. Moreover, the sense among Finnish policy makers was that the EMU framework was a rather weak constraint on

27. English readers can download the agreements in English at http://www.valtioneuvosto.fi/vn/liston/base.lsp?r=696&k=en.

28. The comparison of Finland and Sweden is interesting here. Both countries established expert commissions to study the costs and benefits of EMU participation. One would think that two small Scandinavian economies would receive equivalent recommendations based on economic criteria. Yet the Finnish commission tilted toward participation, while the Swedish committee recommended that Sweden stay out.

fiscal policy. The goal the government set was to move the country to regular fiscal surpluses, which were judged to be needed to meet future pension obligations. Policy makers certainly wanted to get the general government accounts in order by 1997, but keeping the budget balance above −3% was not a great concern (interviews at the Finnish Ministry of Finance, Bank of Finland, and at academic think tanks, Helsinki, June 2001.)

Concerning economic openness, there is an undoubted connection between international shocks and the course of Finnish fiscal policy. The end of capital controls at the end of the 1980s, together with the abolition of restrictions on bank lending rates, led to a flood of capital into the country. The liberalization turned out to have a downside as well, as capital flowed out of the country just as freely when the economy weakened. New packages of budget cuts often followed panicked days on the markets in the early 1990s. Moreover, to keep capital in the country, interest rates were often high, and often volatile, which contributed to the economic malaise and increased the cost of government debt.

Nevertheless, the impact of the international economy is not a sufficient explanation on its own. The government did not act quickly to stem growing deficits, and, when it did act, one-third of the members of parliament could block expenditure cuts. Even when this institutional barrier in parliament was eliminated, the government was slow to respond. As the *Financial Times* noted in 1991, "Criticism is now leveled at the excessive growth in public spending . . . and the general unwillingness by the authorities to recognise that the brake should have been applied earlier. Rather belatedly, the new government is trying to remedy the country's economic ills" (October 4). The title of an article written by two Finnish economists who analyzed Finland's economic performance at the beginning of the 1990s accurately conveys the interaction between the world economy and domestic decisions—"Finland's Depression: A Tale of Bad Luck and Bad Policies" (Honkapohja and Koskela 1999).

The reform of the budget process must, therefore, receive some credit for Finland's fiscal recovery. Budget goals are set in multiyear programs, and since 1995 political parties make political commitments to keeping those targets. The conditions for changing the fiscal institutional framework parallel those in the Netherlands. An economic crisis made the need for better institutions more acute. These institutions were adopted after voters supported political parties that were best able to implement them.

Conclusion

All three of the countries that developed commitment forms of governance experienced economic shocks, with Belgium and the Netherlands experiencing the same difficulties during two oil crises. The Netherlands began to reform its fiscal institutions in 1982 by setting fiscal targets in the government's coalition agreement. It then deepened these institutions, first in 1986 and again in 1994. Belgian governments similarly attempted to set fiscal targets, but these targets failed. There was little accountability for ministers who overspent, and what fiscal successes there were were short-lived. Credible fiscal targets came after the country federalized and after the High Council of Finance assumed a more prominent role. Finland had an informal form of commitment in place through the early 1990s. Although the system performed well enough during good economic times, it broke down during the recession of the early 1990s. Finland, too, revised its institutions more in accordance with what one would expect under a commitment form of fiscal governance.

There are several important lessons for policy makers in states with multiparty majority governments where the parties expect to run against each other. First, cuts in expenditures that are written into fiscal contracts seem most effective when they are scheduled for the beginning of the coalition. This is especially clear in the Dutch and Finnish cases. It is difficult for parties to initiate potentially painful cuts on the eve of elections.

A second important point concerns the role of outside bodies or commissions. In places with multiparty governments, such commissions may be able to solve coordination problems that exist when no one party wants to bear the potential electoral scorn for a given decision or reform. In the Netherlands, the Study Group of the Budget Margin produces a set of recommendations before the elections take place. In Belgium, a similar commission writes the overall targets that appear in the fiscal contract. The role for this outside body is, therefore, more direct. There is no equivalent body of outside experts in many of the delegation states discussed in the previous chapter (Hallerberg, Strauch, and von Hagen 2001).

6

Why Minority Governments Are Different: The Mixed Systems of Fiscal Governance in Sweden and Denmark

Sweden and Denmark are quite similar in many ways. Cultural classifications of European Union member states would usually put them together. Politically, each has a tradition of strong social democratic parties, long periods of Social Democratic Party governments (although Swedish Social Democratic rule has been more consistent than Danish), and proportional representation systems that make one-party majority governments rare. They also have the most developed welfare states in the world: in share of public revenues as a percent of GDP, Sweden and Denmark ranked first (60%) and second (55%) in the industrialized world in 1990 (OECD 2001). Indeed, social benefits and the size of the public sector go hand in hand.

These northern European countries also share a skeptical view of Economic and Monetary Union. Denmark negotiated an opt-out clause from EMU participation, and the loss of a popular referendum on the issue in 2000 reinforced the determination of a majority of Danes to stay out. The euro has been unpopular in Sweden, and, largely because of splits within the Social Democratic Party—which has been in power since 1994—the government has made no formal attempts to move forward.[1] Unlike Denmark, Sweden does not have an opt-out from EMU, but the country has not qualified: its central bank does not fit the guidelines for independence because the Swedish kronor is not a member of the Exchange Rate Mechanism.[2] These countries

1. This skeptical attitude seemed to be changing. A majority of Swedes expressed support for joining EMU in the first year after the introduction of euro bills and coins on January 1, 2002. Sentiment changed, however, and voters rejected the common currency in a September 2003 referendum by 56 to 42%.

2. Because of the absence of the opt-out clause for Sweden, according to Article 122(2) of the treaty every two years the European Commission must review whether Sweden has satisfied the formal criteria to join Stage Three of EMU. In practice, the Swedish government made clear in the early 1990s that it did not consider membership in the European Union as requiring membership in EMU. The Swedish government issued a declaration just prior to joining the European Union in 1995 that Sweden would make a decision on EMU at a later time.

joined the European Union at different times, with Denmark participating in 1973 in the first wave of Community enlargement and Sweden in 1995 in the last wave before enlargement to the east; but the longer time within the Union has not led to greater public support for EMU in Denmark.

Most important for the purposes of this chapter, Sweden and Denmark traditionally have minority governments, which affects the type of fiscal governance that can be put in place to address the common pool resource problem that all governments face. In the last two decades, Sweden had majority coalitions only during 1979–81 (Bergman 2000, 196). Denmark similarly had majority coalition governments for only two years, 1993 and 1994 (Damgaard 2000, 234–35). In both instances the majority coalitions were made up of "bourgeois" parties that did not last an entire period between elections before they disintegrated into minority governments. The two countries, therefore, provide ideal test cases for the mixed model of fiscal governance discussed in chapter 2. Mixed cases are likely to be institutionalized in countries where minority governments are generally the rule. They are mixed because they take on predictable elements of delegation and commitment. Within the government, a finance minister can centralize the decision-making process. Elements of delegation to a strong finance minister appear at the governmental stage of the budget process. Yet, because the government cannot pass its budget on its own, it needs to bring in partners from the opposition. In its ideal form, which addresses the underlying common pool resource problem directly, the budget process includes a stage in which the cooperating parties write fiscal contracts that clarify the budget agreement between the parties.

Denmark made the move from the fiefdom to the mixed model of decision making during the economic crisis it faced in the early 1980s. With some minor differences, it has relied on this framework since then. Sweden did not make major changes to its budget process in the early 1980s, even though it suffered a similar economic crisis. One reason is that Social Democratic minority governments through the mid-1980s could approximate a delegation style of governance. Social Democrats could count on the Communist Party of Sweden for almost unconditional support, so real bargaining with the opposition was not necessary. Once the Communist support waned, the previous institutional setup that relied on a strong finance minister to coordinate the system no longer worked. During the economic crisis in the early 1990s that followed the collapse of the Soviet Union, the government initiated a series of far-reaching fiscal reforms. The new Swedish system epitomizes the mixed form of governance.

The cases of Denmark and Sweden also illustrate the limits of European Union, and EMU, pressure as an explanation for fiscal reform. Both states made significant reforms, yet one state made the reform before EMU and the other consciously decoupled the reform from EMU in public debates.

The public position on EMU—in this case, a lack of support—did not lead politicians to change their behavior. Moreover, EMU and European Union pressure on the states played at best a marginal role in budgetary reforms.

A more interesting question concerns the *timing* of the reforms. Reforms occurred during significant fiscal crises, yet a crisis alone did not always lead to reform of budget institutions. Political incentives were also necessary. Governments thought they needed to appeal to voters by "doing something" to get their fiscal houses in order during tough times. The political system had to be competitive so that the government anticipated that it would lose office if it did nothing, and public finances had to be a clear worry for the voters. Moreover, the shape the reform took depended on the type of government. In the minority governments of Sweden and Denmark, the institutional path moved from fiefdom to mixed. Centralization of decision making took place within the government around the finance ministry, but the minority government needed to reach agreements with opposition parties to get its budget passed. Finally, electorates rewarded the reformers, which encouraged the institutionalization of the budgetary reforms. Both countries retain the institutions introduced in crisis periods.

Sweden

Political Background

Sweden is the social welfare state par excellence. It has not always been this way, however. In the 1930s, when the Social Democratic Party first came to power, Sweden was a laggard in Europe on social protection (Esping-Andersen 1990). Since the end of the 1930s the Social Democrats have been in government for all but two periods: 1976–82 and 1991–94. Yet with two exceptions (after the wartime election of 1940 and after the election of 1968, when they won 50.1%) they have held power as a minority government, and, with the exception of the coalition government with the Center Party from 1951 to 1957, they have held office alone. The Social Democrats could maintain stable minority governments over a long period of time because of the support they received from the Communist Party or, as of 1990, from its successor, the Left Party. After World War II the Communist Party committed itself to not causing the fall of a Social Democratic government, a commitment that lasted through the early 1980s (Bergman 2000). This gave the Social Democratic Party a relatively free hand to implement its policies. The opposition has traditionally consisted of three parties—the Center Party, the Conservative Party, and the Liberal Party—with a fourth, the Christian Democratic Party, entering the scene in 1991. These parties have often been more at odds with one another than with the Social Democratic Party. The Center

Party has been willing to act as a partner to the Social Democrats from time to time, and in recent years the Social Democrats have preferred to work with the Center Party rather than with the Left Party when the Center Party's votes have sufficed to reach a majority in parliament.

This lack of one-party majority governments is partly a consequence of Sweden's proportional representation system, which is extremely proportional. First, 310 seats are distributed across twenty-eight multimember constituencies. Once the first-tier seats are distributed, thirty-nine seats are used to fill in party seats so that the percentage of seats won more closely approximates the national percentage of votes. A party must receive at least 4% of the vote nationwide or 12% in one constituency to qualify for participation in the distribution of seats.

The regularity of minority governments suggests that a mixed model of governance would be appropriate for Sweden. However, in the early period, because of the Communist Party's almost unconditional support, Sweden followed a delegation model. This changed in the 1980s as Communist support became increasingly conditional and internal conflicts within the Social Democratic Party undermined the finance minister. Sweden's decision-making process on the budget has fit the mixed model most closely since 1998 when the Social Democrats cooperated with the Green Party and the Left Party. Reforms in the mid-1990s also strengthened the position of minority governments in the budget process and made it sometimes unnecessary for the government to enter formal agreements with the opposition, as the theory would expect.

Budget Policy

It is useful to begin with an overview of Sweden's fiscal performance in the last two decades. The structurally adjusted budget balance was above zero through 1977 (fig. 6.1). It then deteriorated and remained around –4 percentage points of GDP in the early 1980s. An initial recovery began in 1983, which coincided with the return of the Social Democrats to power, and the budget remained in surplus from 1987 to 1990. The structurally adjusted budget balance once again declined but with more severity: from 1992 to 1995 it averaged less than –7 percentage points of GDP. The balance then recovered, and it reached a positive balance of nearly 3.5 percentage points of GDP in 1998. What can explain the wild ride that fiscal policy has taken since 1973?

Although *Domestic Budgets* is limited to the period after the collapse of the Bretton Woods system, a few words about Sweden's political, and budgetary, organization over a longer term will help put the institutional changes in perspective. Until 1976 Sweden had regular one-party minority governments. Their prime ministers could count on the often unconditional support of

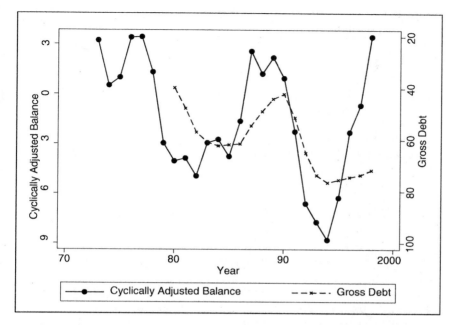

Fig. 6.1. Cyclically adjusted budget balance (1973–98) and gross debt (1980–98) level in Sweden. Source: European Commission 1999a.

the Communist Party to get legislation, especially important budget bills, through the Riksdag. The Communist Party pledged not to cause the downfall of a Social Democratic government, and budget bills were often potential areas of conflict where the government put its survival on the line.[3]

Based on the theoretical arguments made in chapter 2, Sweden was a good candidate for delegation to a strong finance minister. There was only one party in government, and little, if anything, needed to be negotiated with the political opposition. The finance minister could, therefore, serve in a centralizing capacity to keep the common pool resource problem low. Indeed, such legendary Social Democratic finance ministers as Ernst Wigforss and Gunnar Strang were economic pragmatists who reined in the excesses of their spending ministers. Ministers appealed to specific constituencies, such as the trade union organization, and the finance minister would centralize the budget process.

This arrangement broke down in the mid-1970s. Like other OECD states, Sweden was hit hard by the oil crises. The economic conditions, together with the party's handling of the nuclear power issue, led to the Social Democrats'

3. On minor bills the government did, however, sometimes accept amendments to guarantee the bill's passage (author correspondence with parliamentary official, May 2002).

exit from power after the 1976 elections. A center-right government came into office with cabinet posts split among three parties. The finance ministry was split in two, with the Conservatives getting the newly formed economics ministry and the Liberals what remained of the finance ministry (Bergman 2000, 217). The institutional split conforms to the predictions of the theory elaborated in chapter 2. When political parties with different policy preferences form a coalition, they are unlikely to delegate decision-making power on the budget to one central actor, such as the finance minister. The distrust among the political parties suggests a move to the alternative governance model, commitment to fiscal contracts. Such contracts can succeed only under formal rules and formal targets. As the cases of the Netherlands and Finland showed, the parties should negotiate fiscal contracts that stipulate spending levels for all ministries in the coalition agreements. In this way, the parties can internalize the tax externality of their spending in ministries and reduce the common pool resource problem within their governments. Moreover, there must be institutions that monitor the budget's implementation as well as implicit or explicit punishments for failing to stick to the agreement.

The center-right government that took office in 1976 did not make many of the necessary adjustments. One positive development, according to the theory, was the placement of junior ministers from other parties in the most important ministries. This allowed the parties to monitor what the others were doing with their portfolios (Bergman 2000, 211–12). Yet the government did not use explicit spending targets for the ministries, and without clear targets there is nothing to monitor. Such agreements (even when they exist) are difficult to enforce without stability within the government, and this was also missing—there were four center-right governments of various party combinations from 1976 to 1982, and one coalition fell in 1981 over fiscal policy issues after the Conservative Party went into opposition because of disagreements over taxation. The deteriorating economy exacerbated problems for the governments of the period. GDP did not grow at all in 1981, and it grew a paltry 1% in 1982. Partly as a consequence, the unemployment rate rose to 3.5%, which was high by Swedish standards and more than double the rate when the government came to power in 1976 (OECD 2002). As a consequence, deficits rose to 13% of GDP by 1982, and the overall debt level increased 18% from 1980 to 1982.[4]

The 1982 victory of the Social Democrats under Olof Palme should have restored the pre-1976 equilibrium. One of the new government's first acts was to reunify the finance ministry under one minister, Kjell-Olof Feldt, a step toward greater centralization of the budget process. Feldt made some expenditure cuts and kept spending more or less in line so that additional revenues from an improving economy were used to reduce the budget deficit.

4. More generally, the overall debt level as a percentage of GDP more than doubled from 27% when the coalition government took office in 1976 to 59% in 1982.

Rising prices, which followed the devaluation of the kronor after the 1982 election, also helped. Sweden had progressive income tax rates, and the inflation pushed taxpayers into higher tax brackets, which topped out at a marginal rate of 82% (author interview, Stockholm, June 2001). The aggregate fiscal position then stabilized, with budget deficits under Feldt dropping from 13% of GDP to the first budget surplus in twenty-seven years in 1989. Feldt was also widely credited with introducing a series of financial reforms, the most important of which were the deregulation of foreign capital markets and the abolition of currency regulations. In short, he played the role of business's favorite Social Democrat, something one would expect from a successful finance minister in a one-party Social Democratic government.

Yet this discussion masks growing problems in the 1980s of not keeping the common pool resource problem in check—not considering the full effects of one's spending decisions on the full budget. The power of the finance minister eroded on two fronts—within the cabinet and within the Riksdag. Under a delegation form of governance the finance minister negotiates one-on-one with the spending ministers, and the system works best when the resolution of any disagreements between the two ministers is likely to favor the finance minister.[5] Although the finance minister held such meetings with spending ministers and would try to cut spending where possible, as one finance ministry official noted, these meetings usually "meant we had to put in extra money." It became increasingly "impossible for the minister of finance to say 'no' to his government colleagues" (author interview, Stockholm, June 2001). One ministry staffer remarked only half-jokingly that the finance minister knew the size of the budget only on the day all budget bills had passed in parliament (author interview, Stockholm, June 2001). In his memoirs, Feldt complains about the lack of support from Prime Minister Ingvar Carlsson in his battles with other ministries (Feldt 1991).

Why did the power of the finance minister erode? The simple answer is that this erosion served useful political ends. The Social Democrats were no longer a shoo-in to win the next elections as they had been for decades before. In the 1988 election, for example, the Social Democrats promised a series of spending increases, including an increase from nine to eighteen months in paid parental leave, increasing statutory vacations from five to six weeks, and a program to improve the environment. Feldt was forced to deny the obvious—that taxes would have to be raised to pay for his party's promises (*Financial Times,* June 18, 1988). Finance ministry officials complained that ministers could get around finance ministry objections by appealing directly to the

5. Chapter 4 showed at least two ways the finance minister can be favored in practice. In the United Kingdom, a committee of ministers without portfolios resolves the issue. These ministers should have no political stake in the decision, and the expected ruling favors the chancellor of the exchequer. In France, the finance minister's power comes from support from the prime minister.

voters during the campaign. A promise to increase spending was difficult to renege on after the election simply because the finance minister objected (author interview, Ministry of Finance, Stockholm, 2001). There was a sense in the population, and within the Social Democratic Party, that the provision of particularistic goods won votes. Indeed, the election result seemingly confirmed this sense: in the 1988 elections, the "bourgeois" opposition suffered its worst collective defeat since 1944 (*Financial Times,* September 20, 1988).

Pressure came from within the party as well. As new revenues piled in and the budget situation improved in the mid-1980s, several core supporters of the Social Democratic Party demanded that they share in the spoils of the growth. Feldt aimed in 1988, for example, to keep wage increases below 4% and warned that increases of 7% would be "catastrophic," yet this is the approximate amount that average wages increased that year (*Financial Times,* April 14, 1988). Despite Feldt's objection, the increase in wages was higher in 1989, at 10% on average, with even larger increases in the public sector, including an astounding 25% wage increase for teachers and police officers (Benner and Bundgaard Vad 2000, 424–25). Feldt became increasingly disillusioned, and in his memoirs he blamed the unions for many of the fiscal problems Sweden experienced (Feldt 1991).

Another problem for the finance minister was implementation of the budget. The government did not set a clear budget target, and overspending, when it occurred, did not require adjustments in the offending ministry or in other ministries. Moreover, there were no limits to open-ended expenditures, which rested at the heart of the Swedish welfare state. Expenditures on items such as unemployment benefits and social security are, of course, difficult to enforce, but there seemed to be few concerns about how higher-than-expected spending in these areas would affect the total budget. The spending limits that did exist covered such budget items as administration costs.

A third problem for the functioning of the delegation form of governance concerns parliament. No matter how much the finance minister centralizes the process within the government, this can all come to naught if parliamentarians add their favorite spending proposals to the government's bill before it can pass. The parliamentary budgetary process was decentralized, with upward of six hundred spending bills in some years (finance ministry, author interview, Stockholm, June 2001). Political parties in government and in the opposition repeatedly introduced amendments and new spending programs, and the government could introduce proposals for additional spending at any time of the year. Moreover, the minority government generally did not negotiate with opposition parties before it presented its budget to parliament. In the 1980s, when negotiations became more necessary for the Social Democrats to pass legislation, deals to garner majority support usually were made in the parliamentary committees that handled different parts of the bill. Negotiations among party leaders were quite unusual (Mattson

1996, 149). This meant that there was no overarching view of the total budget. The common pool resource problem became more severe as a result of the Riksdag negotiations as well as the breakdown in the disciplinary abilities of the finance minister.

Of course, so long as the government usually got what it wanted through parliament the decentralization was not too problematic. Unconditional support from the Communist Party had meant only minor changes to the Social Democrats' budget bills. Yet the Communist Party's support became increasingly conditional in the 1980s, especially when the economic situation deteriorated in the late 1980s. Feldt introduced an austerity package in 1989 that included tax increases both to improve the fiscal situation and to improve an overheating economy, but he failed to get most of his package through parliament. Instead, the Social Democrats had to cut a deal with the Center Party and, as the *Financial Times* reported, "the agreed measures bear little resemblance to the proposals revealed just over three weeks ago by Sweden's finance minister" (May 24, 1989). Tax increases included an environmental tax and a property investment tax in the Stockholm-Uppsala area, but the impact on the economy, and on the budget balance through new revenues, was nowhere near what Feldt had expected from his proposal to tax employment and to raise indirect taxation 2%. In 1990 the economic situation worsened, and Feldt wanted to propose a starker austerity package. He lost the battles within the cabinet, and, on the day he presented the budget, he resigned. The scaled-back austerity package the government brought to the Riksdag, which included a ban on strikes and a wage and a price freeze, failed to get a parliamentary majority, and the government resigned (*Financial Times,* February 16, 1990). Although the Social Democrats were able to form a new government and to pass a crisis package with the help of the Liberals (Mattson 1996), their credibility had been undermined. A new center-right minority government assumed power after the 1991 elections.

These examples illustrate the component of a fiefdom model of governance that is particular to minority governments. Even when the ruling party makes decisions that lead to lower levels of spending, it must still come to an agreement with one or more opposition parties to get the budget passed. Without an electoral incentive to support budget cuts, it is more likely that the opposition party will expect "favors" in the form of higher spending in areas it cares about in exchange for support of the budget.

External Sources of Crisis

When the economic situation deteriorated in the early 1990s, Sweden's fiscal situation seemed to get worse and worse. The scale of the problems the incoming government faced in 1991 was clearly not expected. A strong push toward reform came from outside Sweden. The government attempted to pursue several goals at once, including the stabilization of the economy and, through the central bank, the defense of a fixed currency. The Social Democrats had fixed the kronor to a basket of currencies before leaving office, and the incoming government pledged to uphold this decision. The hope was that the fixed currency would help control inflation.

There was another external effect on the economy that, in the end, mattered as well. The liberalization of capital markets in the late 1980s under Feldt had what may have been an unintended effect on the ability of the Swedish state to borrow money. The end of capital controls meant that it was initially easier for the state to get money on world markets when it needed to borrow large amounts at the beginning of the 1990s. Indeed, as one finance ministry official put it, "there was no problem to borrow. I *wish* we had had problems to borrow" (author interview, June, 2001). The interest rate on bonds in foreign currencies was low, although the problems in fiscal policy did affect kronor-denominated debt. The solution was to go to world markets for financing.

This situation could not last. In November 1992 the markets finally reacted. The central government budget deficit was at 10% of GDP and was accelerating to what would be 15% of GDP in 1993, while the general government debt burden had ballooned to 69% of GDP in 1992 from just 47% three years earlier (IMF 1998; OECD 2001). With no clear prospects of reform or of a change in fiscal course in sight, Sweden's debt position became precarious. Market pressure grew on the kronor both because of the fiscal problems and because of a domestic banking crisis. In response, the central bank at first pledged to raise overnight interest rates as high as 500% to defend the currency. Yet after increasing the longer-term interest rate to 20% without much tangible effect, Sweden was forced to abandon its peg and let the currency float (*Financial Times*, November 13 and November 20, 1992). The central bank then replaced its currency peg with an inflation target.

This crisis occurred on the eve of the first meeting of a parliamentary commission to consider reform of the budget process. It was clear that Sweden's budget policies had been one of the causes of the economic difficulties the country now faced. As I was told in virtually every interview I conducted in Stockholm, the economic crisis opened a "window of opportunity" for reform. There was little disagreement among policy makers, and increasingly among the population itself, that something had to be done. Yet a similar window arguably opened in the early 1980s and no tangible reforms occurred. Would the 1990s be different?

Budgetary Reforms, 1992–95

The parliamentary commission's mandate was to consider changes to the budget process in the Riksdag only. The commission identified several of the issues mentioned above. There were few incentives to think of the budget as a whole when considering expenditure proposals; moreover, there were no concrete spending objectives, that is, no clear spending caps.

And, perhaps most important, there was a sense that the government should have a fair opportunity to get its budget passed, even if it were a minority government. The Social Democrats were still smarting from their compromises with the Center Party in 1989–90 and did not want to see this situation repeated when they were back in power (author interview with Social Democratic parliamentarian, Stockholm, June 2001). The minority center-right government was similarly learning the same thing through its dealings with the populist New Democracy Party. This party, which was first elected to parliament in 1991, had both an antitax and an anti-immigrant platform, and its anti-immigrant positions meant that the party was not *hoffähig* (coalitionable). Nevertheless, the minority coalition had to rely on it to pass legislation, and New Democracy was even less cooperative than the Center Party had been with the Social Democrats. In one famous incident, New Democracy changed its public pledge to support a government-sponsored bill based on the bill's merits and sided with the Social Democrats simply to embarrass the government and force it to the negotiating table (author interview, Riksdag staff member, June 2001).

The ultimate shape the reform took was influenced by what the game theory literature would call an "entrepreneur," someone willing to take the lead on a given issue and to bear the costs of promoting a policy. A finance ministry official, Per Molander, had been working on fiscal policy issues before the parliamentary commission was created. He had read a report from a German economist then at the University of Mannheim, Jürgen von Hagen, that compared budget institutions across the then twelve members of the European Community (von Hagen 1991). Von Hagen created a budget institution index based on four parts of the budget process: the preparatory, parliamentary, and implementation phases, and, more generally, the level of transparency, and had aggregated the parts to rank the countries. Molander used the von Hagen framework to create an index for Sweden. He found that Sweden had the second worst institutions among the EC-12, below Greece and slightly above Italy. Molander presented these figures to the parliamentary commission (Molander 1992).

It is hard to determine how important this comparison was in the debate, but at least among policy elites it seemed to focus the debate. In interviews at the finance ministry one person noted that "von Hagen's document cannot be overestimated. It had an enormous impact on thinking here." Another individual at the Performance Management Unit, when asked why it was necessary to reform fiscal institutions in Sweden, replied unprompted that "we had almost an Italian budget discipline." Similarly, a staff member of the parliament commented that it was embarrassing to be in the "Spaghetti League" (author interviews, Stockholm, June 2001). The report therefore had some impact on the overriding sense that something had to be done.

The commission published its reform proposals in 1993 and 1994, and, because they were regarded as changes to the constitution, they were required to pass in two successive parliaments. They passed overwhelmingly, both before and after the 1994 elections.[6]

The shape the reform took fits well into the theoretical framework presented in this book. One of the first priorities was to strengthen the government's position in the budget process. There were to be two debates within parliament on the budget each year, one in the spring (by April 15) to set general fiscal policy guidelines and one in the fall (by September 20). The spring bill divides spending into twenty-seven policy "frames," or categories, that sum up to the total budget, and explicit spending caps are established for each frame for a three-year period. There are frames for policy areas such as "Justice" (frame #4), "Health Care, Medical Care, Social Services" (frame #9), "Education and University Research" (frame #16), and the like.

Under the new process, the opposition can propose changes to the frames, but it must present a complete alternative to the entire government budget proposal. The opposition can no longer simply choose one expenditure area on which it can garner a majority and pass it. In the fall, the debate centers on the specific spending items within the various frames; spending in a given frame cannot exceed the frame cap agreed to in the spring. At least in theory, debates in the spring focus on setting the level of spending three years into the future. Next year's frames for the budget should have already been decided by a previous vote in the Riksdag two years before. At no other point should budgetary bills be introduced.[7]

Of course, a natural question concerns *where* debates on the size of the frames take place. If every parliamentary committee got to debate the frame for its area of specialization, this would likely exacerbate rather than reduce the common pool resource problem in parliament.[8] The designers of the reform foresaw this potential problem. Under the new system only the Finance Committee deliberates on the frame proposals. The votes begin with the most extreme proposals against the government's position. Parliamentarians typically abstain from voting for a bill they have not supported. In the end, the proposal that receives the most positive votes is the one that passes—usually the government's original bill (Molander 2001).

6. The Greens, who had not participated in the commission, voted against some parts of the reform after the elections. The Left Party similarly voted against some parts of the reform after the elections, although its member on the commission supported the reform without reservation. The remaining parties voted for the reform.

7. A good summary of the budget procedure in parliament is found in Swedish Riksdag 1999.

8. In the American context see Weingast 1979; Weingast and Marshall 1988.

There was also an accounting change that affected the final shape of the frames. So-called open-ended expenditures, such as payments for unemployment or social security, would no longer exist. Instead, they became "flexible" expenditures. They allowed both borrowing and conditional carryovers of funds of 3% for administrative expenditures and 5% for transfers (Molander 2000, 204). If Sweden's economy worsened, payments would no longer automatically increase. Any such borrowing would have to come out of the frame's own funds and have to be paid back.

In addition, the reform moved the period covered by the budget from the fiscal to the calendar year. This made it easier to match economic data published annually with budgetary planning. To encourage longer-term planning within the government, the reform also moved the electoral calendar from a three-year to a four-year cycle beginning after the 1994 election.

The new system forced the parliamentarians to think about the entire budget for the first time. The root of the common pool resource problem is the ability of decision makers to focus only on the spending and the taxation effects of an expenditure increase on their own constituencies, and the introduction of frames at least forced the parliamentarians to consider the wider picture. Just as important, the new procedures made it harder for the opposition to defeat the government's budget proposal. As one Social Democratic parliamentarian told me, "Unholy alliances of the left and the right over the center are now more difficult than in the past" (author interview, Stockholm, June 2001). The new system also eliminated the many small spending bills from political parties that used to be common under the old system.[9]

Strengthening the position of a government vis-à-vis parliament is only one part of resolving the common pool resource problem in minority governments. The governmental stage also required changes. The center-right government did not attempt any notable reforms at this level. It did, however, function more like a fiscal contract state than the previous coalitions during the 1976–82 period. The total number of words devoted to the coalition agreement exceeded fifty thousand, ten times more than in previous agreements. The parties also agreed to one central staff under the prime minister to coordinate issues (Bergman 2000, 212–15). The coalition was too short-lived, however, and too preoccupied with the economic crisis of the early 1990s to institutionalize these arrangements in the organization of ministries.

The government-level reform, instead, was initiated under the Social Democrats. In the 1994 election, the party asked the voters for a mandate to address the country's fiscal problems. This received a great deal of press coverage, and the party believed that its election victory gave it a free hand to further the institutional reforms (author interview, Social Democratic parliamentarian, Stockholm, June 2001). Finance Minister Göran Persson took

---

9. Private members may still introduce bills on their own, but they have little chance of passage under Sweden's parliamentary system.

office under a one-party minority government, and he had a personal interest both in the reform and in instituting tighter fiscal discipline. In meetings in New York and London with the financial community to arrange more financing of Sweden's debts, he was berated by "25–30 year old sneering financial yuppies," and swore when he returned home that Sweden would "never more" find itself in such a situation (Persson 1997, 100; author interviews, Stockholm, June 2001).

The theoretical framework developed here suggests another reason for Persson's impetus toward reform, namely the need for a finance ministry in a one-party government to have more power in centralizing the decision-making process within the cabinet. The main component of the common pool resource problem at the cabinet level exists because ministers have no incentive to think about how their expenditure decisions affect the total budget. There are at least two important components to this reform that bear emphasis here. First, the government proposed that a total spending cap be decided in the spring of every year for the budget three years into the future.[10] The twenty-seven different spending caps were required to sum up to this cap, and parliament was to determine the total cap for the third year out. Second, following Norway's example, there was to be a two-day meeting of the cabinet every March to consider budget issues. Cabinet ministers were to discuss the long-term development of the budget, including an agreement on the total expenditure cap based on a finance ministry proposal. The three-year delay between the total cap and its use was meant to discourage politicians from building additional spending into the cap for their ministries. Parliament would then approve the total cap together with spending caps on the twenty-seven frames as part of the annual spring budget bill. The total expenditure cap foresaw the need for corresponding cuts in other areas to assure that the cap would be kept.

If they became law, these reforms would strengthen the position of the finance minister in governmental debates. The group meeting in March would encourage the ministers to consider the entire budget and its corresponding tax burden. Moreover, any spending minister who proposed additional spending for her frame(s) would have to propose corresponding cuts in another frame. When planning for the following year's budget began, the finance minister could use the overall target to put pressure on individual ministers to stick to the agreed-upon targets. It would be more difficult for the spending ministers to overrule the finance minister, as happened in the late 1980s.

10. There is some uncertainty about who first proposed a total spending cap as a reform. Some people insist that the Center Party first floated the idea, while others who were directly involved in the reform insist that, while the Center Party did ultimately support a total cap, it was not the originator of the idea (interviews with current and former members of the Finance Ministry, June 2001). In any case, the government ultimately proposed the reform in parliament.

Officials within the finance ministry once again took the lead in proposing the reforms. They expected to meet some resistance within the government from the largest ministries, welfare and health and employment. Welfare and health turned out to be sympathetic to the reform, but the labor minister remained critical. At the crucial cabinet vote in spring 1995, however, the labor minister did not attend and the cabinet passed it. Parliament soon voted for the total expenditure ceiling, and the remaining parts of the reform packages passed within a year (author interviews, Stockholm, June 2001).

Functioning of the New Budget Process

This new budgetary framework was first used for the 1997 budget. The government set a target of a general government deficit of 3% of GDP for 1997 and budget balance for the following year (Ministry of Finance 1996). Because of the reforms and a general economic upturn, Sweden exceeded both goals, with a budget balance of –1.6% of GDP in 1997 and a surplus of 2.1% in 1998 (Ministry of Finance 2001). The government has since set a budget surplus of 2% over the business cycle as its broad target because of concerns about future pension system liabilities. A point of pride among finance ministry officials is that there have been no overruns of the expenditure target since their 1997 introduction. There have, however, been some criticisms, especially from the left, of the reforms.

Politically, the reinforcement of the power of the finance minister within the cabinet as well as the strengthening of a minority government's position in parliament seems to have had some effect. After taking office in 1994, the Social Democrats at first thought that they had an agreement with the Left Party for support in parliament. Soon thereafter the sides disputed what they ultimately had agreed to, and the Social Democrats turned to the Center Party for support. There is no "paper trail" that provides details about the informal agreement, but it is clear that the Center gained some concessions for farmers.

There has, however, been a change in the level of negotiations since the 1998 elections when the Social Democrats and the Center Party both lost seats. They could no longer muster a parliamentary majority, and the Social Democrats turned to the Left Party and, for the first time, the Green Party. Mattson (1996) noted in his comparison of the Danish and Swedish budget processes that the negotiations in Sweden were less formal and less detailed. The procedure now resembles to a greater extent the process in Denmark. Each of the three parties sends four representatives to negotiations at least twice a year, once before the spring fiscal policy bill (usually in March) and once before the fall budget debate (usually in August). The Social Democrats send their most prominent people on budget issues, such as the minister of finance, the minister for industry and labor markets, the undersecretary of finance, and the chairman of the Riksdag's Finance Committee. The

Greens send four parliamentarians. The Left Party, too, sends parliamentarians, but they consciously have different people represent them each year in the negotiations. This procedure, while it prevents the Left Party representative from becoming too "cozy" with the government, also may make it difficult for the Left Party to get as much from the annual discussions. One person familiar with the negotiations commented that there is no chance to build on any trust established in previous negotiations (author interview, Stockholm, June 2001). Once the negotiations are concluded, there is a press conference where the parties discuss their agreement. The bill that is then presented to the Riksdag states in its text that the Social Democrats, the Left Party, and the Green Party have all agreed to the following bill. The bill itself then becomes the public document that establishes the agreement.

Although the new system gets generally high marks, fatigue appears to be setting in with some of the procedures. In their March meetings, some officials pointed out that ministers would rather talk about reforms and proposals today than budget targets three years out. Similarly, many parliamentarians complained that too much time was spent on budget issues. The spring fiscal policy bill had grown into a full debate about spending priorities within frames instead of simply a debate about the level of spending for the frames themselves. Based on these concerns, the Riksdag decided in June 2001 to move the decision on the caps on total spending and on the individual frames to the fall, when the content of the frames was also considered. In theory, the discussions of the caps should be for the third year out, with the more detailed budget discussions of what should be included in next year's a separate issue. There are concerns within the finance ministry, however, that this shift will represent a move away from top-down to bottom-up decision making. Officials agree that the process had become too detailed in the spring, but their proposed solution was to go back to discussion of the general caps only, as was originally intended. Another concern is about the electoral cycle. There will now be no debate about the frames and the total expenditure cap before the fall elections. Without the spring debate, the parties may be tempted to propose more "irresponsible" platforms just before the election to win votes.[11]

The Role of Europe and Reasons for Budgetary Reform in Sweden

It is worth summarizing why the budgetary reforms happened. It is clear that the international environment mattered. The costs for Sweden of continuing "politics as usual" in the early 1990s were high. Although Sweden could have

11. A staff member at the Riksdag noted, however, that the 1998 experience indicates that the spring debates were not a real constraint on party behavior anyway. The Social Democrats proposed new spending on kindergartens in their electoral platform without any mention of this proposal in the government's spring fiscal policy bill (author interview, Stockholm, June 2001).

continued borrowing from international capital markets, it would have cost more to borrow because of much higher interest rates.

These higher costs alone, however, cannot explain why the reform occurred. Sweden found itself in much the same position in the early 1980s yet did not make institutional changes. There was also a clear political impetus. Political parties believed they could win votes by cleaning up public finances, and, as a consequence, all mainstream parties agreed that something had to be done. Social Democrats who came to power in 1994 emphasized again and again in the popular debate that sound public finances, and by implication sound budgetary institutions, were necessary for the preservation of the welfare state. This impetus was missing in the early 1980s when the major worry among the population and in the political parties was unemployment.

It is equally clear that the European Union played at best a secondary role. Based strictly on a timeline of events one could argue that there is a connection between EU membership and budgetary reform. The major reforms began, after all, only a year after the Treaty of Maastricht and were completed in 1995, the same year Sweden joined the European Union. It also is not accidental that the 1997 deficit target of 3% is the same maximum value allowed under the Maastricht criteria. Indeed, policy makers insisted in their planning for the 1997 budget—the budget the European Council would use to decide whom to support for entry into Stage Three of EMU—that Sweden have the choice either to join or not to join, and parliamentarians took the rationale for this deficit target seriously (finance ministry 1996; author interview, Stockholm 2001).

Yet, even if the European Union can explain one deficit target for one year, it cannot explain the budgetary reforms. The changes at the parliamentary level occurred in 1992–93 and were a direct response to Sweden's economic crisis, not to a Maastricht treaty that Sweden had not signed. Sweden was not yet a member of the European Union, and it was by no means a sure thing that it would join. Indeed, the vote on the referendum to join the European Union in fall 1994 was also tight at 52.7% for and 47.3% against, and EMU has not to date received much support in the population. Attaching the reforms to the cause of EMU would have made the reforms more unpopular rather than less. The government therefore made a conscious effort politically to distance the domestic reforms from the debate on Europe (author interviews, Stockholm, June 2001).

Given the improvement in public finances, it is not surprising that both the government's and the Riksdag's published evaluations of the new budgetary system have generally been positive.[12] Sweden has had budget surpluses every year since 1998. This is quite a turnaround from double-digit deficits at the beginning of the 1990s.

---

12. See, for example, Finansdepartementet 2000.

It is important to stress how this reform changed the nature of debates on the budget, and the nature of debates in *politics* more generally. Since 1996, opposition parties have published alternative budget proposals with figures for every frame in the government's budget. Parties now have difficulty proclaiming that they want to raise spending on a host of popular programs while at the same time cutting taxes. Recent debates on the ceilings for 2003 show, for example, that the Conservatives and the Christian Democrats wanted lower expenditure ceilings.

One should also think through the effectiveness of the different reforms possible under different types of governments. The reforms had two main effects based on the theoretical lens applied here. First, they strengthened the position of the finance minister in the budget formulation stage. Second, they made it more likely that the government would get its budget passed by the Riksdag. The latter effect—the strengthening of minority governments in the budget process—should remain the same regardless of who wins future elections. Whether the strengthening of the finance minister will last, however, is an open question. When they defeat the Social Democrats, the bourgeois parties generally enter government as a coalition. It is unlikely that one political party from the bourgeois bloc will assume the same dominant position that the Social Democrats have maintained on the left. Moreover, the parties compete intensely among one another for votes on the right, which makes delegation to a strong finance minister problematic.

Denmark

Political Background

Before 1973 one could divide Danish politics neatly into two opposing blocs of parties.[13] The Social Democratic Party has been the largest party in parliament since 1924. After World War II it also participated in all governments through 1973 except for 1950–53 and 1968–71. Moreover, when the party formed a minority government it always did so as a one-party minority government; the exceptions were majority coalition governments in fact (or in practice) from 1957 to 1964 either with the Radical Liberals and the Justice Party or with the Radical Liberals alone.[14] The main opposition parties were the Danish Liberal Party and the Danish Conservative Party. They formed

13. The only exception to this statement was the small Radical Liberal Party, which tried to position itself between the two blocs.
14. Damgaard (2000, 239) states that the minority governments of 1960 and 1962 were in practice majority governments because one nonparty member of parliament from Greenland was appointed minister for Greenland while two nonparty members of parliament abstained on government votes, thus handing the government a majority.

coalition governments from 1950 to 1953 and, together with the Radical Liberals, a coalition government from 1968 to 1971.

Yet the traditional left-right divide began to close in the 1960s. The Danish Socialist People's Party (SF), whose leader had been expelled from the Communist Party, was established to fight NATO membership in 1960. Foreign policy issues meant that a formal alliance between the Social Democrats and the SF would be difficult, and when one was attempted after 1966 the SF soon split and the coalition's "Red cabinet" dissolved (Esping-Andersen 1985, 94). European Economic Community membership similarly united the ends of the political spectrum against membership and against the center, and, while the referendum on membership received a majority in 1972, it split the Social Democrats and its traditional leftist allies. Finally, two economic issues, housing and taxes, led to the creation of two parties at the beginning of the 1970s—one in the political center (Danish Center Democratic Party) and a second on the right (Progress Party).

These challenges to the traditional party blocs of the left and the right culminated in the 1973 election. Scholars have called it variously the "landslide" (Green-Pedersen 2001), "earthquake" (Elklit 1999), and "catastrophe" (Esping-Andersen 1985, 97) election. It changed the political landscape in Denmark and played an important role in the inability of the government to respond to a series of budgetary crises through the early 1980s. The political support for the parties already in parliament declined, and five parties that had not been in the previous session of the Folgeting gained seats (Elklit 1999, 67). The Danish Center and the Progress Party were able to enter parliament with 8% and 16% of the vote, respectively (Esping-Andersen 1985, 96–98). Indeed, the electoral system encouraged new party entry and facilitated the relatively quick change in the number of parties. Denmark had (and has) a proportional representation system with an electoral threshold of 2%, which means that a party needs to gain just 2% of the national vote to win seats in parliament.[15]

After 1973 it was difficult for either the left or the right to pass legislation. No one wanted to cooperate with the Progress Party because of its punitive positions on immigration, and without its votes or without cross-bloc defections, nothing could get through parliament. After a Liberal minority government that lasted less than fourteen months, the Social Democrats returned to power and continued to field one-party minority governments through 1982 except for a brief coalition with the Liberals during 1977 and 1978. A bourgeois minority government replaced the Social Democrats in 1982 and remained in office with combinations of two to four parties through 1993. Following a short-lived majority coalition government in 1993–94, the Social

15. In Lijphart's (1994) study, in which he calculates a figure for the "effective threshold," that is, the percentage a party needs to gain to win seats, among current EU members only the Netherlands has a lower effective threshold.

Democrats returned to office in minority governments in coalition either with the Center Democrats and Radical Liberals or with the Radical Liberals alone. Partisan differences did not translate into differences in fiscal performance. Rather, it was the move from a fiefdom to a mixed style of fiscal governance in 1982–83, which has been in place since, that led to the dramatic improvement in Denmark's fiscal position.

Budget Policy

The regularity of minority governments suggests that a mixed model of governance would be the most likely institutional solution to the common pool resource problem. The presence of two clear opposing blocs of parties (as in France) suggests that some elements of a delegation form of decision making would also have been present. Although minority governments were the rule, it was a foregone conclusion which political parties would support the government's budget in most years. Some centralization of the budget process around a finance minister, especially under the one-party Social Democratic minority governments that predominated before 1973, would be expected.

There was an important institutional change in the coalition structure after 1973 that affected budgetary institutions. The inability of first a minority Liberal government and then a succession of Social Democratic governments to find regular opposition partners after the "earthquake" election seriously eroded the government's capacity to set the budget debate. Budget making became increasingly more decentralized, which, as one finance minister stated before he resigned in 1977, put the country on the "brink of the abyss" (as cited in Green-Pedersen 2001, 1). The difficulty in getting budgets through parliament illustrates the importance of both stages in the formulation of the budget under minority governments. The government must be coherent enough to have a budget to propose to parliament that solves the underlying common pool resource problem. And the government must be able to negotiate encompassing budget contracts with opposition parties. Paralysis on budget issues occurred when governments had to cave in on key elements of their efforts to decrease the deficit, such as sensitive expenditure cuts or painful tax increases.

An overview of Denmark's budget performance in the 1970s and 1980s is revealing. Public expenditure exploded in Denmark, moving from 41% of GDP in 1973 to 60% in 1983 (AMECO 1999). The general government budget balance began the period in surplus, and, indeed, in 1973 Denmark had a healthy 5.2% budget surplus. The surplus first turned into a deficit in 1975 with the budget balance at –1.4%, and it remained in deficit until reaching its lowest level at –9.1% in 1982. Cyclically adjusted budgets, which take into account the economic cycle, parallel the deterioration of the actual budget

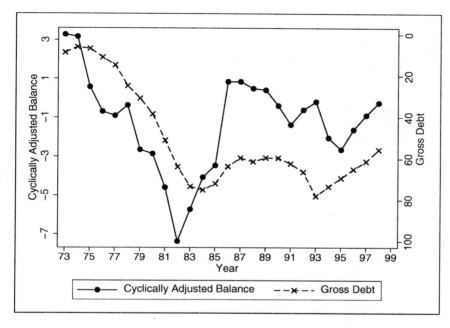

Fig. 6.2. Cyclically adjusted budget balance and gross debt level in Denmark, 1973–1998. Source: European Commission 1999a.

figures (fig. 6.2). Denmark began the period running surpluses even with its economic difficulties. These surpluses disappeared by 1976, but the country managed to keep its balance near zero for three years. There is, then, a steep decline in the balance, reaching a low of –7.4% in 1982. The balance then improves. What is notable is that after a few years of surpluses, the balance does not experience the swings from the mid-1980s on that it had experienced in the previous period.

These figures are for the general government, of course, and, before discussing reform at the central government level, a few comments about subnational governments are necessary. Reforms in the 1970s devolved ultimate responsibility for some budget items such as social security, primary education, and infrastructure improvements to the subnational level, and these governments spend up to 45% of the general government budget (Blom-Hansen, 2000, 5–6). Yet, in practice, local governments adhere to a Golden Rule in spending that dictates that they maintain balanced budgets except for some capital expenditures. Moreover, the subnational governments negotiate directly with the finance ministry on what they spend every June before the actual budget year. Although the agreements amount to "nonbinding coordination," subnational governments have not overspent appreciably (author interview, Ministry of Finance, Copenhagen, April 2000; Blom-Hansen

2001). The swings in the general government budget balance are therefore attributable mostly to actions at the central government level.

In an institutional political economy explanation for the budget difficulties, the "earthquake" election of 1973 affected the ability of the central government to set macroeconomic policy. By increasing the number of parties in parliament, the number of parties required to pass the budget increased. All else being equal, this increased the costs of negotiating budgets. Yet not all else was equal—the election also meant that a bloc of seats would oppose *any* budget, which decreased the room for negotiations. On paper, the political right won a majority in parliament in 1973. In practice, however, any bourgeois legislative coalition would have needed the newly elected Progress Party, which seemingly came from nowhere to emerge as the second strongest party in parliament after the Social Democrats. The mainstream right considered the Progress Party not to be *hoffähig* because of its punitive positions on immigration, while the Progress Party considered itself a "self-styled parliamentary outcast" (Esping-Andersen 1985, 98). An outright coalition including all right-wing parties was consequently out of the question in the 1970s. With the Social Democrats unable to form a working coalition of their own, there were several elections but no resolution of the problem. Neither the left nor the right could form consistent majorities to pass budgets through parliament.

After the 1973 election, the Liberals formed a feeble government with just 22 of 179 seats in parliament (12.3%) under the prime ministership of Poul Hartling. This weak government managed to pass some expenditure *and* tax cuts in 1974 with the support of other bourgeois parties and the center parties, but it still had difficulty enacting crisis legislation to deal with the worsening budget situation and economic climate. The government called new elections in 1975 in the hope of improving its bargaining position. Although the Liberals did in fact almost double their seats in parliament, those seats came at the expense of the parties' allies. The Social Democrats picked up some seats as well, and they formed the next minority government (Elklit 1999). Like the Liberals, however, the Social Democrats could not form a firm bloc of opposition votes to support their legislation.

In an attempt to break the deadlock, the Social Democrats moved across the traditional divide and invited the Liberals into what had been a one-party minority government in August 1978. Two changes occurred to the internal organization of the government. First, an internal cabinet committee, the Planning Committee, was set up to coordinate policies, including budget issues, within the government. Second, the government created so-called contract ministers. Each minister was paired with a minister from the other party, and any decision a minister took had to be cleared by his contract minister (Christensen 1985). In theory, both of these arrangements should have led to greater coordination and greater centralization of the budget.

Even in coalition, however, the parties failed to settle their differences, and the fall of the coalition a year later led to new elections. The Social Democrats returned to power alone in a minority government, but "still without any real chance of finding support for an effective crisis policy" (Esping-Andersen 1985, 98–99). Indeed, a deadlock on economic reforms led to yet another election in fall 1981, after the Social Democrats failed to gain the needed support in parliament. The new elections once again did not end the deadlock between the two blocs. The Social Democrats, consequently, remained in office with Radical and SF support in the opposition, but the SF pledged not to allow any cuts in welfare benefits. The deficit continued to worsen, with initial forecasts that deficits would approach 11.5% of GDP. One union leader warned that the budget deficit could lead to a state of bankruptcy (*New York Times,* January 21, 1981). The government responded to the continuing deficit problems with a three-point plan that included spending cuts for large-ticket items such as unemployment and social welfare benefits, tax increases on pension fund incomes, and wage moderation. The finance minister, Knud Heinesen, pleaded for his package before parliament and before his party, but to little avail. In frustration, he resigned with the comment that "Denmark is riding towards an economic free fall on a first class ticket" (*Politiken,* August 17, 1982).

Heinesen's resignation and the general inability of the government to pass its legislation represent important examples of the limits of the "strong finance minister" model. As discussed in chapter 2, some scholars argue that a strong finance minister can, as a general rule, improve budget discipline (Inter-American Development Bank 1997). The Danish case shows that a finance minister cannot centralize the process if he does not have internal political support. The government decided to retreat from Heinesen's pledges to cut social spending because of strong internal party opposition. Heinesen's difficulties were mirrored in the demise of the Planning Committee, which was used under the Social Democrat–Liberal coalition. After the Liberals left the government, the Planning Committee initially remained. The finance minister tried to use this forum to impose much-needed spending discipline. The Social Democratic environmental and labor ministers strongly objected to this practice under their one-party government, however, and the Planning Committee fell into disuse (Christensen 1985, 136–37).

This episode also illustrates the importance of coordination with partners in the political opposition. All non–Social Democratic parties opposed tax increases on pensions, and, without some defectors from their camp, the tax increases could not pass. As Green-Pedersen (2001, 12) writes, the complicated party relationships in parliament meant that "these governments were in a difficult situation. Their only possibility of building a majority was to gain support from several of the right-wing parties. In other words, cross-bloc cooperation was needed." The government, therefore, experienced breakdowns both within the government and within negotiations with the opposition. Without changes at both stages of the formulation of the budget, reform was not possible.

Budget Reforms after 1982 and the Mixed Form of Fiscal Governance

The so-called four-leaf clover government replaced the Social Democrats in September 1982 when it became clear that the Social Democratic Party would not be able to muster a majority in parliament for its budget (Mattson 1996). The Conservatives, Liberals, Center Democrats, and Christian People's Party comprised the new coalition under Prime Minister Poul Schlüter. When it first came into office, the coalition seemed to have little chance of reversing the country's general economic slide. These parties had just 66 of 179 seats in parliament. The leader of the Progress Party, Mogens Glistrup, told the press that while he would not want to see his party join the government, he would of course make himself available as finance minister in the new government. As outlandish as this episode seemed, it also illustrated the weakness of the new government. With the Progress Party, the Social Democrats, and the two parties to the left of the Social Democrats firmly in the opposition, the only alternative to cooperation with the Progress Party remained cross-bloc negotiations with the Social Democrats.

In October the four-leaf clover government presented its budget proposal. It addressed the deficit problem with expenditure reductions and no tax increases. Areas cut included sick pay and unemployment benefits, both sacred cows under the previous government. To the further chagrin of the political left, the government also proposed suspending wage indexation until at least 1985. Finally, and most important for this analysis, the bill included concrete spending targets for total expenditure, which mandated that spending should fall by 6%. The bill also imposed a 4% ceiling on the growth of public sector wages over the following two years.

As expected, parliament did not pass everything the government wanted. Yet, after the defection of three members of the Progress Party including Glistrup, the government did manage to suspend the automatic index-linked increases of wages, salaries, and welfare payments; end the linkage of public sector wages to private sector ones; and institute a five-month wage freeze. The spending targets also were passed, even if the unemployment benefit reductions did not survive.

Although these measures certainly helped, they did not by themselves lend immediate credibility to the government's plans to stabilize the debt burden. The budget balance was –9.1% in 1982, and, as a consequence, in January 1983 Standard and Poor's downgraded Danish credit from AAA to AA+ (*Politiken,* January 13, 1983). Yet by April 1983 there was a general sense that the government was about to turn the corner. Bond prices made a recovery, and inflation was expected to fall from 10% to under 4% due largely to the end of wage indexation (*Politiken,* April 23, 1983). In May the government announced plans to reduce public expenditures for the following year by 3% in real terms, half of what it had proposed in the previous year. The only real growth in total spending would be increased interest costs on the burgeoning debt burden (*Politiken,* May 19, 1983).

Initially the government appeared to have support for its budget bill. It hammered out an agreement with the Radical Liberals and the Progress Party that reduced its proposed spending cuts from DKr 10 billion to DKr 8.7 billion (DKr 6.40 = $1). Yet, once the government presented the bill before parliament, the Progress Party pulled out of the agreement, and the government lost its vote on the budget as socialist parties refused to support benefit cuts, while the Progress Party demanded tax cuts. Schlüter then called new elections.

The new elections were favorable for the government. The coalition partners won twelve additional seats, and, just as important, the Progress Party lost ten of its sixteen parliamentarians. The government could then get legislation through parliament with just Radical Liberal support. It also considered the election results a mandate from the voters to stay on its austerity course. The government continued what the press referred to as its "potato diet" until the 1987 election, and budget balances improved from –7.2% of GDP in 1983 to a surplus of 3.2% by 1986.

The election results were not the principal reason why the budget situation improved. The analysis presented here indicates that one should look at the institutional makeup at both the governmental and the parliamentary levels of government. The changes in procedures at the parliamentary stage are clear. Similar changes occurred at the cabinet level, although the *timing* of the changes is less obvious. At the parliamentary stage, Mattson (1996) argues convincingly that the Social Democratic and Progress vote against the 1984 budget had a profound impact on the way budgets are negotiated in Denmark at the parliamentary stage. Before 1983, the government usually formulated its budget and then presented it to parliament. This process made tactical retreats and arm twisting necessary to get the budget through. Of course, this way of dealing with parliament led to an ad hoc, and decentralized, treatment of the budget. Opposition parties could provide nonnegotiable stands on specific parts of the budget, and there was little incentive for them to consider the full implications of their requests on the entire budget. As we saw in chapter 2, this form of decentralization increases the common pool resource problem and the size of budget deficits. The Social Liberals, for example, often focused only on the level of social benefits and prepared to vote against any budget bill that tried to cut them. In practice, there were plenty of last-minute bargains to

get the budget through parliament (see Mattson 1996, 103–26, for details).
When last-minute deals did not work, the government had to either
resign or call new elections.

The new process introduced in 1983—which has remained mostly
unchanged since then—brought selected opposition parties together with
the government to hammer out a comprehensive budget agreement before
parliament receives the government's budget bill. The government first formulates its budget internally. The finance ministry proposes overall spending controls to the cabinet's Economics Committee in January. The Economics Committee discusses the overall spending level and approves an amount.
The government usually agrees to an across-the-budget cut in all ministry
budgets of 1–2%, which is meant to represent "efficiency" savings. This cut
makes the initial allocations "fair" to all ministries, and, by extension, to all
coalition partners when there is a coalition government. The spending total
for each ministry then represents the fiscal contract, and ministers begin
work on budget proposals for their ministries based on these spending
ceilings. Ministries also formulate new initiatives, with funding for new
programs to come only out of the efficiency savings.

The finance minister also plays an important role. There are usually bilateral negotiations between the finance minister and the spending ministers, and, in June, the Economics Committee agrees to a full budget proposal
(Jensen 2000, 23–24), which includes projects the government would like to
fund based on the ministry proposals. The budget proposal includes explicit
spending limits for each ministry, which are further subdivided into explicit
limits on consumption, income transfers, and salaries (Finansministeriet
1999, 4). At the same time, the finance minister also negotiates with local
governments to set the level of the block grants from the national to the subnational level. The finance minister is also a critical part of the negotiations
with opposition parties in parliament. In August, the parliamentary phase
of the budget officially begins when the government introduces the budget
bill to the Folgeting. The parliament's Finance Committee has the exclusive
right to discuss the budget, and all discussions take place behind closed doors.
Yet the real action occurs in the finance ministry. The government invites
certain parties to the ministry for negotiations on the budget.[16] In practice, the number two people from the parties involved in the budget come
to the ministry. During the negotiations, the finance minister consults with
the opposition parties and with coalition colleagues to determine what changes
are, and are not, acceptable. In November, with reporters camped outside
the ministry and negotiations into the night, the parties agree to a detailed
budget agreement. Within twenty-four hours the Ministry of Finance
prints the agreement in full. The agreement covers the budget as well as

16. Until 1990, the negotiations took place on a bilateral basis with specific parties rather
than on a joint basis with all parties included in the same room (Mattson 1996, 141).

some nonbudget items, and it indicates what amendments to the government's bill the parties will approve within the parliament's Finance Committee. Parties that are included in the final agreement are expected to vote with the government on the budget and to abstain from introducing any amendments. In practice, the opposition parties have kept their promises on budget issues (author interview, finance ministry, Copenhagen, April 2000). Finally, the finance ministry monitors the spending ministers during the execution of the budget to determine whether they are sticking to the spending targets (Finansministeriet 1999).

This change in the parliamentary stage had two notable effects. First, the negotiations in the finance ministry significantly diminished the importance of the debates within parliament and shifted the decision-making arena on budget issues from parliament to the finance ministry. Second, the agreement meant that opposition parties discussed the entire budget with the government. Last-minute deals focused on dismantling key parts of the government's austerity measures that infringed on a constituency would no longer be the rule.

Yet, before moving on, the limits of this institutional approach to solving budget issues should be noted. This procedure relies on the presence of viable opposition partners. It has made it more difficult for minor parties to demand large concessions at the last minute in exchange for supporting the government's budget. The passage of the 1987 budget indicates that this procedure does *not* assure fiscal discipline when cross-bloc voting is necessary to pass the budget. After the 1987 election, the bourgeois government once again could not pass a budget without the support of either the Social Democrats or the Progress Party. The Social Democrats demanded DKr 100 million in extra spending (Mattson 1996). The deal the government ultimately struck with the Social Democrats came "at a very high price. The result was an agreement implying significant improvements to most social security benefits and thus contributing to the wavering fiscal policy" (Green-Pedersen 2001, 13). This problem was short-lived. Based on the negotiating procedure discussed above, the government was able to bring the Progress Party into the fold on budget issues after an inconclusive election in 1988.[17]

Similar changes in budgetary procedures occurred at the governmental stage. The four-leaf clover government established a new permanent committee to coordinate government policies. After the elections in 1984, the committee became much more like the Planning Committee under the Socialist-Liberal coalition, which focused on budget issues (Christensen 1985, 130). Cabinet-level committees also played an explicit centralizing role under the Social Democratic–dominated governments that came to power in 1993. Jensen (2000) discusses in detail the Economics Committee, which met weekly

17. There was some reshuffling of the parties, with the Center Democrats and the Christian People's Party leaving and the Radical Liberals officially entering the government.

to discuss budget issues. Under the governments from 1993 to 1998, the Social Democratic minister of finance chaired the meeting. Other participants included both the party leader of the Social Liberals, who doubled as the minister of economic affairs, and when the Center Democrats were in the coalition, their leader, who served as the minister of industry. The prime minister's secretary was the secretary for the meeting (Jensen 2000, 22). This committee clearly existed to coordinate budget policy across political *parties*, not across ministries, and was necessary because of the multiparty nature of the minority government. Moreover, the role of the finance minister also fits the theoretical framework presented here—the finance minister centralized the budget process primarily for her own party, the Social Democrats. Jensen (2000) interviewed some of the key actors in the budget process in 1997, and his findings are revealing. The Social Liberal leader at the time, Marianne Jelved, considered the finance minister "responsible for keeping all the Social Democrat spending ministers in line. It could lead to conflicts within the coalition government if she, as the smaller coalition partner, had to keep all spending ministers in line" (22). More generally, if there are coalition disagreements, those agreements generally go to the cabinet's Coordination Committee, which adds the prime minister and the foreign minister to the Economic Committee (Jensen 2000, 23). Notably, the discussion did not take place before the full cabinet that includes all of the spending ministers. This discussion therefore provides some evidence that the budget process was coordinated at the governmental stage of the budget process.

These changes to the budget process led to better fiscal performance in Denmark. In the first year of the four-leaf clover government, spending in real terms increased only 0.6% of GDP, leading to a comment in the Danish paper *Politiken* that Henning Christophersen had earned a place in financial history for being the first finance minister in thirty years to stem the growth of the public sector (June 21, 1984). More generally, fiscal policy has become more predictable and more stable. Since 1984 the structurally adjusted budget deficit has never exceeded 3% of GDP (see fig. 6.1). Just as important, the variance in the structurally adjusted balance has decreased.

Assessing the Change in Budget Institutions in Denmark

Denmark moved from a decentralized system of negotiating budgets under minority governments to a more centralized system in the early 1980s. Why did the Danes undertake this reform, and why in the early 1980s rather than the 1990s, as the Swedes did?

Clearly, Economic and Monetary Union did not contribute to the reforms in the early 1980s. It makes little sense to attribute the exemplary fiscal performance of Denmark, which had more surplus years than deficit years from 1986 to 2000 and which never exceeded the Maastricht treaty's 3% of

GDP reference level for budget deficits in any year after 1984, to a "Maastricht effect." Denmark set an institutional course before there was any European Union–level pressure to get deficits and debt levels under control.[18]

International pressure was certainly present in the early 1980s. The drop in Denmark's credit rating at the beginning of 1983 increased the costs of borrowing abroad. Yet the drop increased the cost of capital only marginally. Moreover, with an AA+ rating there was no threat of credit rationing from abroad in the near term. The question was whether the country would be willing to pay the somewhat higher interest rates.

One can speculate that a monetary policy issue, rather than a fiscal one, may have played a role. Denmark was a member of EMS at the time, and a desire to remain in EMS may have made Danish policy makers more concerned about what currency markets thought about the credibility of fiscal policies. But tight fiscal policy was *not* a prerequisite for EMS participation. In the 1980s Belgium and Italy ran sizeable budget deficits, and deficits larger than any in Denmark since 1973, yet they maintained their currencies in EMS.

The crucial factor, again, was electoral support for real reform. The Schlüter government perceived that reforming the budget system was a winner. Indeed, the domestic press lauded the government's attempts to rein in spending.[19] The government ran on its budget plan after its failure to pass the budget for 1984, and it won, enabling it to pass legislation without the support of either the Social Democrats or the Progress Party. As Iversen (1999, 141) notes, "The government's policies enjoyed broad support in the electorate, which could not help but notice the improvements of the economy and the image of 'standing at the edge of an abyss' in fresh memory." Although external factors contributed to the tone of the debate in Denmark, internal pressure drove the pace of the reforms.

Conclusion

In this chapter I have examined two European Union states that adopted mixed forms of fiscal governance, combining elements of the more pure forms of delegation to a strong finance minister with commitment to fiscal contracts. This form is appropriate in countries where minority governments are the rule. To function properly, it requires that the finance minister play a centralizing role within the government and that the government sign what amount to fiscal contracts with one or more parties in the political opposition. When

18. In 1996–97 there was some concern in Danish governmental circles that Denmark unambiguously clear the 3% deficit/60% debt level hurdles in the Maastricht treaty.

19. The daily newspaper *Politiken* noted, for example, that "the counter-attack [on the budget] launched by Mr. Schlüter and his finance minister, Mr. Henning Christophersen, has so far brought some impressive results" (October 17, 1983).

either of these elements is absent, a country with a minority government will likely have difficulties in maintaining fiscal discipline.

In Sweden, a coalition government that replaced the more common one-party minority Social Democratic governments in 1976 watched helplessly as deficits ballooned and debt burdens more than doubled under its watch. It did not establish clear spending or deficit targets that would have tightened the monitoring of the budget's deterioration. Similarly, in the late 1980s under minority Social Democratic government, the finance minister's position vis-à-vis other ministers was weak, and the government had to make last-minute deals with opposition parties to pass any budget legislation. There was an institutional failure to centralize the budgetary system at both the governmental and parliamentary stages. The reforms in the early 1990s addressed both problems. They strengthened the position of the finance minister within the government, and they made explicit the nature of the fiscal contract the government would sign with the political opposition and established detailed rules on how to enforce this contract. Sweden today provides the archetypal mixed system.

Similarly, in Denmark the focus is on the relationship between the difficulty of the governments in the late 1960s and early 1970s getting anything passed and the way budget negotiations transpired. The traditional blocs of "socialist" and "bourgeois" were unable to muster consistent majorities on fiscal issues. Moreover, the blocs themselves, when in power, had difficulty coordinating common views. This was especially true for the Social Democrats, who had difficulty balancing fiscal austerity measures with the desire of their union supporters for increased spending. There was, therefore, a failure of coordination at the budget formulation stage within the government and the budget formulation stage within parliament. This situation changed during Schlüter's government in the early 1980s. The government negotiated detailed budgetary agreements with one or more opposition parties, and it widely publicized the details of the agreement so that there would be little doubt when either the government or cooperating parties broke the agreement.

Although the focus of this chapter has been to trace the evolution of budgetary institutions in these two countries, the discussion has broader implications for the literature that considers the relationship between political economy variables and budgetary performance. Roubini and Sachs's (1989) oft-cited article argues that minority governments are, by their very nature, prone to fiscal indiscipline. Governments must constantly "buy" opposition parties to remain in power.[20] Strøm (1990), in a book that has been equally influential in political science, argues that minority governments are just as effective as majority governments. The implication of the evidence presented here is that the difference between minority and majority govern-

---

20. See also Edin and Ohlsson (1991), who confirm the empirical results for minority governments.

ments per se does not explain differences in budgetary performance. Countries with minority governments performed poorly in some periods and well in others. What *did* change was the institutional configuration. Both Sweden and Denmark reduced the size, and the variability, of their budget deficits after adopting fiscal institutions that are consistent with a mixed form of fiscal governance.

7

Italy: Change in Party System, Change in Fiscal Governance

On January 1, 1999, Italy joined ten European Union countries in the adoption of the euro. This simple statement of fact would have been unbelievable to observers only a few years earlier, and there was good reason to be skeptical. In 1992, the first year after the Treaty of Maastricht had been signed, Italy's fiscal position left it far from the Maastricht criteria. Its public debt was over 100% of GDP, and it overshot its estimated budget by L 20,000 billion (L 1660 = $1) (Felsen 1999, 7). Italy's swift departure from the Exchange Rate Mechanism in the fall of 1992 seemed to seal Italy's fate to be outside of Economic and Monetary Union.

Yet Italy managed a remarkable turnaround. In November 1996, the Italian lira rejoined the ERM. By 1997, the fiscal year the European Commission used to make its recommendation to the Council of Ministers in March 1998 on which countries should join EMU in the first wave, Italy had satisfied the Maastricht criteria to the commission's (and later the council's) satisfaction. Perhaps most surprisingly, by 1998 Italy had brought its yearly budget deficit down to Germany's level at just 2.7%. How did a European Union country with debt levels above 100% of GDP and with yearly deficit levels double the Maastricht target in 1993 manage to get its financial affairs in shape?

In this chapter I present a political economy explanation based on the theoretical framework developed in chapter 2. Italy presents an especially strong example to test the theory. It is the only EU country in the last twenty years to make a significant change to its electoral system and then to stick by that change for at least one additional election, long enough for the change to have an effect on the corresponding fiscal institutions.[1] Such a change in the

1. As chapter 4 showed, France also made a significant change in its system in 1986 when it moved from a two-stage plurality system to proportional representation, but in the next election, which was held just two years later, the country switched back to the old system. The new system did not exist long enough to have a real impact on budgetary institutions. Similarly, Greece has fiddled with its system, but in all cases the district magnitude has remained relatively low, and there was not a major shift from one type of system to another as there was in Italy.

electoral system should affect the organization of the party system. This change in election rules in 1994, combined with the collapse of the old party system, indeed led to the development of a new party system with two rival blocs vying for the allegiance of voters. Consistent with the model in chapter 2, the government soon centralized power around the treasury minister. These reforms contributed to Italy's reduction of its budget deficit. One external actor, the European Union, was important indirectly for Italy's success. It promoted a new accounting system that allowed Italian policy makers to monitor in ways not possible previously what the government was spending. Possible exclusion from EMU, which seemed likely as late as 1996, also forced parties to focus on fiscal policy issues. Yet a reorganization of the fiscal institutions of the Italian state was necessary for Italy to reach its fiscal targets.

Political Background

The Christian Democratic Party (DC) dominated the Italian political scene in the postwar period. The Christian Democrats participated in every government formed from 1945 to 1994. They held the center of the political spectrum, and a coalition without them was not possible. In Laver and Shepsle's (1996) terms, the DC was a strong party. No party could credibly threaten the Christian Democrats as long as the political system that had developed during the Cold War remained in force. It is not an exaggeration to say that Italy was the Western European democracy where the Cold War had its greatest effect on domestic politics. The Italian Communist Party (PCI) consistently won a significant number of votes, and, although it never won enough to assume power at the national level, it did control several city governments. Although the far left was the principal electoral threat to the Christian Democrats, the far right, represented in party form by the Italian Social Movement (MSI), never completely died away after Mussolini's fall. With many parliamentary seats going to the parties of the left and right—whose share of seats reached as high as 40% in the early 1970s—there were few alternative coalition possibilities (Strøm 1990, 160). The more mainstream parties did not consider either the PCI or the MSI to be *hoffähig*. This had important implications for the structure of governments in Italy. Not only could the DC not be pushed out of government because of its position at the center of the political spectrum, the DC itself had limited potential coalition partners. This meant that it was difficult for the DC to threaten the other parties in the coalition.[2] The one exception was in the

2. This is not to say that parties did not threaten each other and dissolve governments; indeed, the opposite was the case. The issue, however, is whether one party could exclude another in future coalitions as punishment for a given act. The reality for many years was that there were reshuffles in the Italian cabinet of individuals but not of parties, and even the individuals had a tendency to reappear again and again, simply in different positions.

mid-1970s, when the DC was able to maintain a one-party minority government. This arrangement worked so long as the remaining parties believed that the DC had really formed a national unity government in practice to combat the left. But once the threat of a leftist electoral victory receded, the minority government proved to be unstable, and during the 1980s, there were in its place a series of coalition governments composed of five parties (the *pentapartito*).

One reason why coalition governments were necessary was that the electoral system made it difficult for any one party to win a majority of seats in parliament. Before the electoral reform in 1994, the country had maintained a traditional system based on two-tier proportional representation. Seats were awarded in fairly large constituencies, and a second allocation of seats was done to smooth out any great discrepancies from the first round. The allocation of seats was therefore generally proportional to the proportion of votes cast for parties. An important feature of the system was that voters could express their preferences for specific candidates on the party lists. This "open list" system encouraged parliamentarians to take policy positions that sometimes conflicted with the positions of their parties.[3]

Based on this electoral system and the party system that emerged from it, one might expect that a commitment form of governance would be the institutional solution to the common pool resource problem in Italy. These contracts were sometimes present in a loose form, but, as Verzichelli and Cotta (2000, 457) note, "There has generally been no official written agreement of the coalition parties on a common policy platform." Spending ministers enjoyed a remarkable level of independence and autonomy.

In 1994, the new electoral law introduced a mixed system based both on plurality for 75% of the seats and on proportional representation for 25%. This change made the system similar to the German electoral system, and the expectation is that the fiscal institutions would come to resemble those in Germany as well, that is, that delegation to a strong finance minister in the presence of two clear electoral blocs would be the likely solution to the common pool resource problem.

Budget Policy and Budgetary Actors, 1973–98

Italy entered the first oil crisis in rough financial shape. Its cyclically adjusted budget balance was at –6.5% of GDP in 1973. After some recovery in 1976–77, the trend reversed and the balance slipped downward to a low of almost –12% in 1981, and, with the exception of 1983, it remained below –10% of GDP

---

3. Golden (2003) argues that the open list system encouraged widespread corruption in Italy.

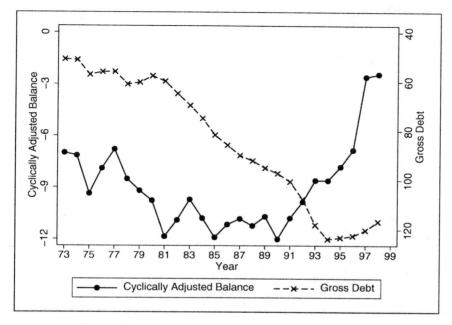

Fig. 7.1. Cyclically adjusted budget balance and gross debt level in Italy, 1973–98. Source: European Commission 1999a.

for the rest of the 1980s (fig. 7.1). The effects of this deficit spending on the overall debt burden were clear—the burden more than doubled from approximately 60% of GDP in 1981 to almost 124% in 1994. Interest payments on this debt grew apace as well, from an already high level of 6.2% of GDP in 1980 to a peak of 12% in 1993 (European Commission 1999a). To put these figures in some perspective, this meant that one out of every eight lire generated in the Italian economy was spent on interest payments for public debt.

In terms of yearly budget balances, the turnaround began somewhat earlier. The trend is clearly reversed in 1992 and, after a pause in 1994–95, continues upward with a sharp increase in the budget balance for 1997 and 1998. The first time the Italian budget balance was higher than the Maastricht level of –3% of GDP (in both real and cyclically adjusted terms) was in 1997, the year that the commission and council decided which member states would participate in Stage Three of EMU.

What political actors were responsible for the course of budget policy during this period? Through the early 1990s, three ministries (Treasury, Budget, and Finance) participated in the budget formulation stage. Consequently, although there were some negotiations between the treasury minister and the individual spending ministers, the negotiations were not very regulated.[4] Similarly, the prime minister was weak in the budget process as well—constitutionally he had little control over individual ministers, and in practice he neither selected nor appointed the spending ministers (Pitruzzello 1997).

In the remaining European countries, parliament passes the budget but is not (as a rule) a separate actor in its own right as long as there is a majority government.[5] Within parliament itself, however, Italian committees were unusually strong relative to other European legislatures; indeed, Mattson and Strøm (1995) argue that the committees were the strongest in Europe. Committees could even pass legislation without a formal vote in the full chamber, although this power did not extend to finance bills. These committees also had a tendency to decide by consensus and to include something for everyone, including the PCI.[6] In the analysis presented here, increasing the number of groups that had to be satisfied above the number in the government, without any centralization that forced the parties to consider the total tax burden, probably exacerbated the spending problem. Felsen (1999) contends that the "vast amounts of micro-amendments" that parliamentary groups could attach to the budget through the finance law made the situation worse, and indeed, "the finance law was generally approved in parliament in a form much different to how it was presented by government" (5), while others saw these committees as the device whereby clientelistic interests could pass legislation (Della Sala 1993).[7] The organization of the budget law, which forced legislators to vote on over five thousand items at once, also made it relatively easy for legislators to hide new spending in the bill. Formally, parliament was not supposed to have the right to make changes to the government's budget in ways that affected the budget balance. Article 81 of the Italian Constitution dictates that all amendments must be off-setting. Yet, as a then member of the Italian lower house put it to me, "Before 1992, this article was interpreted quite loosely" (author interview, December 2000). The relative strength of the legislature, therefore, reinforced the problems of centralizing the budget process that were endemic at the governmental level.

A final actor that lent moral authority more than anything else was the Bank of Italy. The bank had the best-trained economists in the public sector in Italy. Its governor during the years 1979 to 1993, Carlo Azeglio Ciampi, was particularly critical of government policy and in particular of the conduct of fiscal policy (see, for example, *Corriere della Sera,* May 15, 1991). The respect he earned as governor was an important reason why he was a

4. Alesina, Mare, and Perotti 1995, as cited in De Haan, Moessen, and Volkerink 1999, 294.
5. The important case of minority governments was seen in chapter 6. Even in this case, opposition parties, rather than individual parliamentarians, are the crucial actors.
6. Furlong 1994, 140, as cited in Sbragia 2001.
7. For a different interpretation of these committees see Kreppel 1997. She contends that the committees were important to break log jams caused by the many people with veto power in the system.

credible minister of the Treasury in the mid-1990s. The bank's "divorce" from the government in 1981 meant that the bank no longer had an obligation to finance the government's debts.

Fiscal Institutions and Fiscal Performance, 1973–92

The oil crisis hit Italy harder than most Western European countries. First, 75% of its total energy needs came from oil in 1973, and Italy did not have access to domestic oil fields (Ginsborg 1990, 352). Second, the budget was already in a precarious position even before the economic downturn connected with the oil crisis. The budget deficit was already at 6.5% of GDP in 1973, while the gross debt burden was already at 50% of GDP. This weak position contrasted with that of fellow Community members such as France and Germany, which each had budget surpluses the same year; and it existed despite real economic growth that year of almost 6.6%. Once the economy worsened as a result of the rapid increase in oil prices in fall 1973, the budget situation worsened as well, with the deficit hitting 10.5% of GDP in 1975 (European Commission 1999a). As was the case in the United Kingdom, the government in Italy was forced to approach the International Monetary Fund in 1977 for a small loan. The IMF's grant of the loan was seen as a "good conduct award" for Prime Minister Giulio Andreotti's government, which the IMF judged was beginning to succeed in reducing the budget deficit (*New York Times,* November 27, 1977). Indeed, the budget deficit dropped almost a full percentage point in 1977 to 7.1% of GDP.

Yet the improvement was temporary. The second oil crisis hit an economy that had not completely recovered from the first crisis. Inflation reached 20% by 1981, while public spending increased over 5 percentage points of GDP in two short years from 1979 to 1981, from 41.6% to 46.9%.

The decision-making process at the cabinet level could not slow the additional spending. During the 1980s there were a series of coalition governments composed of five parties, which included the Italian Socialist Party, the Italian Social Democratic Party, the Italian Republican Party, the Christian Democratic Party, and the Liberal Party. These five "veto players" were required to approve the budget, and with so many veto players, delegation of fiscal powers to a finance minister was clearly infeasible. It was unlikely that the four parties that did not receive the finance minister's portfolio would trust the one party that did to monitor and enforce the budget fairly. Indicating the problems of the decentralized political system, in 1981 the Christian Democratic treasury minister, Nino Andreatta, clashed with his Republican fellow minister at the Ministry of Budget and Planning, Ugo La Malfa. Andreatta wanted a cut in public spending, but La Malfa disagreed, preferring simply a shift in the overall deficit burden from current spending to capital spending. The splurge on additional investment, which benefited sectors as diverse as energy, transport, housing, and the export sector, was popular with his cabinet colleagues, and there was little the treasury minister could do (*Economist,* May 23, 1981).

The government also had problems passing any austerity legislation through parliament even when it seemed to have the votes on paper. Some details about the rise and fall of the Giovanni Goria government are illustrative. By 1987, the inflation rate had fallen consistently below 5% for the first time since 1969 and had become stable. Economic growth was also positive and almost a full point above trend GDP at around 3.1%. It would have seemed a reasonable time to consolidate the budget, which had a deficit of almost 11% of GDP in structurally adjusted terms. Indeed, Goria attempted just this after President Francesco Cossiga asked him to form a new government. The appointment was controversial because the Christian Democrats had not forwarded his name to the president as a possible candidate (Sechi 1987). In September, the government announced a finance bill for 1988 that provided for an increase in VAT, an annual levy on cars, and a cut in expenditures of up to eight thousand billion lire. In November, however, the small Liberal Party withdrew from the government coalition due to the disagreement with Goria over the new draft of the finance bill, and the government fell. President Cossiga then asked Goria to return. At the turn of the following year, Goria insisted on some cuts in health spending, and in February he lost the vote on the bill. This was the seventeenth time in less than six months his government had lost a vote, and this was in a chamber where he had won confirmation as prime minister, 371–237. Goria again resigned. Perhaps as an indication of the seriousness of the budget situation, the Bank of Italy announced that the national deficit for 1987 for the state sector was L 113,500 billion, L 13,500 billion more than originally forecast (Bank of Italy 1988).

Before moving on, one should note that Italy did begin two crucial reforms. First, it reworked the financing of local governments during this period. Before the 1990s, the central government financed localities almost exclusively through grants. Politicians in these localities had no incentives to save the government any money because they had no control over the raising of taxes that financed them. Moreover, the central government's willingness to bail out insolvent municipalities was a common, and repeated, practice. In budgetary terms, these bailouts affected the gross debt levels only and not the yearly deficits. The reforms hardened the budget constraint through increases in the localities' financial autonomy as well as through the introduction of cash controls on local expenditure (Vandelli 1992; Bordignon 1999).

Second, the Clean Hands campaign was in full swing in spring 1992, with judges investigating government corruption and jailing high-level government officials. Given this background, the Giuliano Amato government that formed in June that year was unique. Although it still included the old parties, seventeen of twenty-four ministers were fresh faces who had never served in government before (Hellman 1993). The shock of Italy falling out of the European Monetary System in September 1992 had short-term effects on the budget situation. Shortly thereafter, the government enacted its fiscal plan and cut health-care spending, blocked salary raises and further hiring in the public sector, and introduced a minimum quota that all taxpayers had to contribute. The government also asked the European Community for a L 20,000 billion loan. The loan would be disbursed in four tranches subject to satisfactory performance by the Italian government in tackling budgetary reform (*Il sole 24 ore,* October 2, 1992). As one prominent commentator and then member of the Italian Senate noted, despite some success at reducing spending, the government's ability to make changes to the budget was the result of domestic scandal and international pressure. This constellation was probably unrepeatable (Pasquino 1992).

These reforms by themselves did not solve Italy's problems, and one can exaggerate their importance. The mere fact that the local government debt forgiveness did not enter into yearly debt calculations means that the reform cannot explain why Italy got its deficit below 3% of GDP. Moreover, Amato's government lasted less than year. Instead, it took a fundamental reorganization of budgetary institutions at the national level to meet the Maastricht targets.

Fiscal Institutions and Fiscal Performance, 1993–98

Italy used a new electoral system for the first time in the 1994 elections. It represented a move away from proportional representation toward a plurality system. In both the Chamber of Deputies and the Senate three-fourths of the members were elected through plurality and one-fourth through proportional representation. In the vote for the Chamber of Deputies, the preference vote for candidates was abolished; parties had complete autonomy over their national lists; and individuals voted twice—once for an individual and once for a party. The vote in the Senate differed because individuals voted just once for a given candidate, and the party affiliation of the individual was used to determine the proportion of seats on a regional, instead of national, level (Katz 1996).

One would expect these changes to lead to bipolarity in electoral alliances, and the existence of such alliances should have important consequences for the type of fiscal institutions possible at the governmental stage in Italy. Examples come from France and Germany, discussed in chapter 4. In France, the UDF allies almost exclusively with the RPR, while the Socialist Party works equally as often with the French Communist Party. In Germany during most of the last two decades the FDP and the CDU/CSU confronted the SPD and the Greens. In both cases, delegation to a strong finance minister is feasible because the political parties in the coalition consider the electoral success of their coalition partners important for their own continued occupation of government. The existence of two opposing blocs should have made delegation to a strong finance minister, rather than fiscal contracts, the solution to the common pool resource problem.

Indeed, Italy moved in exactly this direction institutionally, albeit not as directly as many observers would have liked. One problem that arose was that a clean bipolar system did not develop as quickly or as thoroughly as in France and Germany. During the 1994 electoral campaign, the allies of Silvio Berlusconi's party, Forza Italia, varied; its supposed national partner, the National Alliance (AN), ran against the Polo della Liberta coalition (of which Forza Italia was a member) in some regions (Katz 1996). Not surprisingly, the Berlusconi government that brought these parties and others together was unstable and lasted a short seven months before falling in December 1994. It also was unable to provide a delegation form of fiscal governance that would have led to centralization of the budget process around one minister. Without a clear electoral bloc, it was unlikely that such a "strong" finance minister could exist. It was simply too uncertain which parties would run together in future elections for them to delegate fiscal authority to one individual. Although the government took on the unions on pension reform, it did little to combat the deficit.

The caretaker Lamberto Dini government that followed was unique because all the ministers in the government were unelected (Sbragia 1999). The incentive to provide particularistic goods to ministry constituencies, which is largely an electoral one, had been severed. Indeed, the Dini government took measures that stabilized the gross debt level (see fig. 7.1). Yet there was no reason to believe that these "technicians" could rule for any great length of time. The technicians were also able only to stabilize the debt level, not to make any significant cuts.

Italy therefore entered 1996 with most observers convinced that the country would not participate in EMU's first wave. As Chiorazzo and Spaventa (1999, 2–3) note, at this time "the probabilities assigned to Italy's admission—even late admission—were slim when judged by markets, nil in the eyes of our European partners, as well as of economists and opinion makers." Italy's general government balance was still –7.7% of GDP, over double the Maastricht reference value.

New elections were called in 1996, and this time the electoral system had a clear effect on the electoral alliances in Italy and more generally on the composition of Italy's budgetary institutions. The political parties began to jell into two opposing blocs, one left-center and one center-right. The parties that composed the center-left bloc, known as the Olive Tree, agreed before the elections that they would centralize the budget process around

Ciampi (author interview with parliamentarian from this bloc, Rome, December 2000). The Olive Tree polled better than the center-right, but it did not receive enough votes to establish a clear majority government. The government that formed behind Prime Minister Romano Prodi needed the votes of the Refounded Communist Party (Rifondazione Comunista) in the Chamber of Deputies because its majority was limited just to the Senate. The reformed Communists did not join the government, but they could block bills in the Chamber of Deputies by siding with the right-leaning opposition.

Soon after the Prodi government came to power in 1996, the state initiated an important reform of the budget process within both the government and the legislature. On the governmental side, a legislative decree "increase[d] the autonomy of spending ministers and their flexibility in budget management and control" (Felsen 1999, 13). This move represented a strengthening of the executive in its dealings with the legislature. All else being equal, however, this change alone could potentially have had little effect if the common pool resource problem remained significant within the cabinet. Giving spending ministers greater autonomy is only useful if the ministers do not use it to carry out the same sorts of policies the legislature would have initiated on its own.

Indeed, the most important reform followed the predictions of chapter 2, namely a significant strengthening of the Ministry of the Treasury. The reform incorporated the budget ministry into the Treasury, creating a so-called superministry. It also rationalized the structure of the ministry through several administrative changes that made the bureaucracy more responsible to its leadership (Felsen 1999). These reforms "further centralise[d] control over public expenditure in the hands of the executive counterbalancing the increased autonomy of spending ministries . . . by more effective 'guardian' control over total expenditure" (Felsen 1999, 15). This reform represented delegation of significant powers to the treasury minister. The Treasury can use these powers to reduce the common pool resource problem within the cabinet. The only outstanding and independent "fiscal" ministry remained the Ministry of Finance.[8]

The treasury minister used these powers to monitor spending that was passed, and he had the right to withhold spending if departments did not follow correct procedures in order to turn authorized spending into actual spending. This was a noticeable change from the standard operating procedures of the past in which the Treasury did not have this power (von Hagen 1992). Indeed, there are estimates that 70 trillion lire of authorized spending was not spent in 1996, and this amount more than doubled to 180 trillion in 1997; and one of the principal reasons was Ciampi's close scrutiny of,

---

8. The Ministry of Finance remained responsible for monitoring taxation policy until its merger with Treasury in 2001.

and refusal to authorize, suspect spending (*Frankfurter Allgemeine Zeitung,* October 27, 1997).

A second significant change occurred within the legislature. As noted above, the relative power of the body vis-à-vis the government declined. The budget process within the parliament was also refined. Instead of a vote on the over five thousand items found in the budget bill, the budget was reorganized according to "functional targets" and "base units" (De Haan, Moessen, and Volkerink 1999). This measure streamlined the budget and made it more difficult for committees and individual legislators to hide additional spending within the budget.

These changes had the desired fiscal policy outcome. Italy qualified for EMU with a final yearly deficit for 1998 of 2.7% of GDP. In the year before qualification, the country reduced its general government deficit 4 percentage points, which represented "one of the largest annual retrenchments recorded in the OECD area" (OECD 1998).

The Role of Europe and Explanations of Fiscal Reform in Italy

The Treaty of Maastricht laid out the procedures for the measures European Union states would need to take to qualify for participation in EMU. It also detailed the formal role of EU institutions. The European Union provided the important stick (usually missing in Italian finance) to coalition partners who regularly ignored the broader budgetary effects of their decisions. The Union also monitored the progress of the states toward greater fiscal discipline.

In fiscal policy there were two important reference values—yearly deficits no larger than 3% of GDP and total gross debt no larger than 60% of GDP. Moreover, these figures were for general government, not just the central government; all levels of government—city, regional, and central—were included. Although central governments were expected to coordinate the effort to reach these targets, they were not allowed simply to transfer their debts to another level of government. There was some debate in the years leading up to the decision on who would participate on the "absoluteness" of these reference values. The treaty itself notes in Article 104c that if a ratio has "declined substantially and continuously" it would be enough to qualify a country for EMU, but in practice this looser definition was used only for the gross debt levels. Italy had no hope of reaching the 60% debt level, but the 3% deficit level was attainable and, as we saw in chapter 3, it was this level that proved crucial in determining who would be invited to participate in the common currency. The European Union therefore had set externally predefined budgetary targets as well as a clear deadline for meeting them.

As one official at Directorate General II of the European Commission put it, "The setting of a specific deadline concentrated people's minds" (interview at DG II, Brussels, July 30, 1999).

The European Commission also played a role in monitoring the convergence programs that member states submitted to it. As I have indicated in chapter 3, these plans were to detail how the given state intended to qualify for EMU. The commission then offered private opinions to both the council and the country on the feasibility of the plans. Yet the effectiveness of this procedure was limited. Countries were not obliged to submit such programs, and at first there were no guidelines for what they should contain. The first Irish program, for example, which was meant to explain how Ireland would qualify for EMU several years down the road, had only three numbers in the entire text and was so vague that it was difficult to understand what steps the country would take (author interview at Directorate General II, European Commission, July 14, 1999). The commission eventually did set guidelines for the programs in 1994, and it encouraged states to prepare yearly programs for evaluation. But in practice only the states that were doing well bothered to submit updated versions.[9]

In sum, the commission was able to judge whether a country had hit the target levels, but it had virtually no impact on how the states were to reach those levels. Domestic institutional changes in Italy would play the key role in assuring that the European Union's stick of exclusion from EMU was not used against them. The European Union's definition of debt also directed attention to the regions, states, and localities in the member states.

One way that the European Union level did help Italy directly was in its accounting. Italy reclassified its budget according to Eurostat standards in 1996. This made it easier to understand what was being spent where and what to cut (interview, Italian Treasury, December 2000).

The explanation that focuses on external pressure is potentially more useful, and it requires a careful consideration of the role of markets for each country and the role of the European Union. It seems clear that Italy would have paid higher interest rate premia outside of EMU. In Italy, for example, by the second half of 1995, "interest rate spreads came to depend on the probabilities assigned by the markets to the prospect of joining the single currency at the outset" (Chiorazzo and Spaventa 1999, 12). The markets therefore punished Italy with higher interest payments on its large outstanding debt as long as the markets believed that Italy would not get its act together.

Yet how much of the change in interest rates was due to economic fundamentals and how much to the anticipated inclusion of the country in EMU is unclear. Favero et al. (1999) calculate that, of the improvement of a 214

---

9. This was changed under the Stability and Growth Pact. All states are now required to submit their programs, either in the form of stability programs (states taking part in EMU) or in the form of convergence programs. See chapter 3.

basis point reduction between German and Italian forward rates from 1996 to 1997, only 65 basis points can be attributed to changing perceptions of Italy's likelihood of EMU participation. Their research suggests that the interest rate premium Italy paid on EMU exclusion was less than 1%. Although this amount was certainly an increased cost for the country, it can hardly be the sole reason why Italy reduced its deficit so dramatically.

Even if one believes that Favero et al. (1999) understate the importance of the markets, the narrative here demonstrates that the turnaround in the national budget, which incidentally also lowered interest rates and made qualification for EMU that much easier through an improvement in Italy's economic fundamentals, happened only for the year 1997 during and after the government had passed crucial reforms to the budgetary process. It is likely that the strengthening of the Treasury under Carlo Ciampi increased his, and his government's, credibility with markets. Even a story that includes a role for markets must therefore take into account changes in Italy's budgetary institutions.

The European Union also played a role as an external actor. For Italy, certainly regular reminders from ECOFIN and the European Council that Italy was unlikely to get in focused the efforts of the Italian leadership. Reminders about Maastricht also entered the electoral campaign. The Olive Tree coalition promised in its electoral manifesto in 1996, for example, to reduce the budget below 3% "in order to reach the Maastricht requirements." Yet the European Commission's pressure did not in any sense make Italy's inclusion in EMU inevitable. Indeed, the commission itself anticipated that Italy would not make it. As late as April 1997, press reports indicated that the commission was privately telling Italy to prepare for life outside of EMU in the first wave.[10]

In sum, each of these arguments has a contribution to make to the explanation of Italy's fiscal volte-face, and indeed they explain some of the dynamics of the model. The markets affected the costs of not imposing fiscal discipline. Interest rate payments on outstanding debt, which were considerable, would certainly have been higher without EMU participation. Likewise, the European Union assured that there would be higher political costs, and it provided some monitoring of the budget situation. Yet by themselves these facts do not explain the changes in fiscal policy we observe.

Conclusion

The EU country with the second worst deficit and debt problems in 1991 after Belgium still managed to join the first wave of EMU. Adequate institutions to

10. See "Italy out in EMU Cold," *European,* April 10, 1997, and "Rome's Euro Prospects Sinking," *Guardian,* April 17, 1997.

reduce the common pool resource problems within the cabinet were lacking. Significant institutional reform was necessary to break the log jam. In the Italian case, after the first elections under the new electoral system, a delegation form of fiscal governance became possible, and it was put in place under Superminister Ciampi.

The reason why the new budgetary institutions stuck, however, is related to Maastricht—it was important enough for politicians to join EMU that they agreed to new fiscal institutions. This change, in turn, was related to the new competitiveness of the Italian party system. Unlike in the previous period, a party could expect to be excluded from power if voters became dissatisfied with it. No party wanted to be blamed as the party that had relegated Italy to the second division of EU member states.

There is a fundamental question about how long Italy can continue the centralization of its budget policies. Indeed, Fabbrini (2000, 191) notes pessimistically that "the reduction of the public debt . . . was made possible by the contingent suspension of ordinary parliamentary activity, not by a permanent empowerment of the executive." And he adds that "as soon as Italy entered the EMU, the contingent suspension of parliamentary activity was lifted and traditional party government resumed." Whether "traditional party government" will have any effect depends on the permanence of the new fiscal institutions. After the 2001 parliamentary elections, the remaining two ministries that regulated the budget, the Ministry of the Treasury and the Ministry of Finance, merged into one Ministry of the Economy under Giulio Tremonti. Contrary to Fabbrini's expectation, the centralizing of the budget process under a strong finance minister continued.

8

Party System Instability and Incomplete Forms of Fiscal Governance

This chapter considers fiscal governance in countries that have had one or more periods of party system instability. According to the theory presented in chapter 2, forms of fiscal governance will not develop if the party system changes frequently such that another form of fiscal governance would be more appropriate.

Here I will focus primarily on two opposite cases, Ireland and Portugal. In Ireland, there was a regular see-sawing between one-party minority or majority governments and two-party coalition governments with parties that were not that close to one another ideologically. The theory suggests that the former situations would be appropriate for centralization around a strong finance minister in the form of delegation, while the latter situations would be better for negotiated fiscal contracts in the form of commitment. Although there were some attempts in Ireland to institutionalize one or the other form of fiscal governance, they ended when the type of government changed. This lack of institutionalization of one of the forms of fiscal governance had a tangible impact on fiscal performance. Budget deficits spiraled, and the debt burden was over 100% of GDP by the mid-1980s. After 1989, however, multiparty coalition governments became the rule. Moreover, there was more competition among parties to join governments, and parties had exit options if they thought that one party was violating the coalition. Commitment then became the form of fiscal governance that was institutionalized. Ireland easily qualified for Economic and Monetary Union based on its economic numbers in 1997.

Portugal would seem to be similar to Ireland, yet it is not. It, too, had a regular turnover of different types of governments because of the instability of the party system. In 1987, a landslide victory led to a one-party majority government. The government took some measures that strengthened the role of the finance minister. In 1995, however, a minority government replaced the majority government. The change in power led to a reduction in the power and influence of the finance minister. Portugal managed to qualify for EMU only after a series of mostly short-term measures. The weakness of Portugal's fiscal institutions contributed to the country's failure to maintain fiscal discipline, and it became the first country to breach the Stability and Growth Pact's limit of a 3% of GDP deficit.

In addition to Ireland and Portugal, in this chapter I also discuss, more briefly, Spain and Austria. Spain was similar to Ireland, although instead of institutionalizing a commitment form of fiscal governance it built a mixed form. Its strengthening of its finance minister in 1997 served it well when the country switched to a one-party majority government in 2000. Austria is, if anything, the reverse of the other countries in this chapter. It experienced regular one-party governments in the 1970s and grand coalitions from the 1980s through the mid-1990s. The rise of the Freedom Party, however, changed the party system in ways that made the grand coalitions increasingly unstable. The form of fiscal governance has recently been unstable in Austria as a result, and the country had some unexpected difficulty qualifying for EMU.

Ireland

When considering fiscal policy, there are grounds to consider Ireland as the biggest success story in the European Union. The country was a seeming basket case through the mid-1980s. Deficits were high, and the gross debt burden reached a peak of 114% of GDP in 1987. Just ten years later, its budget was in surplus and its gross debt burden was at almost exactly 60% of GDP. An explanation of why Ireland improved so dramatically may be instructive for other countries with similar fiscal difficulties.

There are two principal reasons for the consolidation of Irish finances. The first is the high real growth rates that the country experienced over the course of a decade that earned it the nickname "Celtic Tiger." While this is obvious to many scholars, the second reason is probably less so. Ireland also made some concrete changes to its budget process that moved it toward a commitment form of fiscal governance.

Ireland is a country with cleavage structures that are difficult to define. According to Lijphart (1999, 80–81), there are only two cleavages—the standard left-right cleavage and a less dominant foreign policy cleavage. Even under pure proportional representation, one would expect no more than three political parties in this system. Yet the placement of parties on a left-right continuum is not as easy as one would think. The main governmental party in the postwar period has been Fianna Fáil (FF). It is, arguably, a party of the center. It dominated the Bretton Woods period, holding office in all but six years from 1944 to 1973. Its main opposition is Fine Gael (FG), which is just to the right of Fianna Fáil. This party traditionally does not receive enough votes to maintain a government without a coalition partner. To complicate matters, in the 1980s its main coalition partner was the small Labour Party. Labour was to the left of both FF and FG. Another small party, the Progressive Democratic Party, is to the right of Fine Gael. To complicate matters yet further, the only party with which it has entered a coalition is FF. Finally, because of the single transferable vote electoral system, there are usually a handful of independent members of parliament.

There are two clear patterns of government formation since 1973. The first period, which extends from 1973 through 1989, was marked by alternations between one-party Fianna Fáil governments and two-party coalition governments composed of FG and Labour. Fianna Fáil won enough seats to rule as a one-party majority government from 1977 to 1981, but when it lacked a majority in this period it refused to enter into a coalition agreement and ruled alone as a minority government. Fine Gael and Labour's only possibility to govern at the time was to govern together.

This cycle was broken in 1989. After a two-year stint controlling a minority government, Fianna Fáil formed a coalition with the Progressive Democrats. The coalition that formed four years later brought together Fianna Fáil and Labour. For the first time, there was a sense of real choice in a potential coalition partner. This pattern of regular coalition governments has continued through 2003.

The two periods of government have clear implications for the form of fiscal governance the country would be expected to adopt. Under one-party minority governments, one would expect some centralization of the budget process under the finance minister. Conversely, the prediction of the appropriate form of fiscal governance under coalition government depends on the ideological distance among them as well as the potential exit threat. Parties that are distant from one another are unlikely to support a delegation approach. At the same time, as chapter 5 demonstrates, commitment functions well only when there are possible alternative parties to keep the current parties in government honest. The Fine Gael–Labour coalitions had neither of these attributes. The ideal spending preferences of the parties were generally not close to one another. Moreover, threats to leave the coalition were not credible because there were no alternative coalition partners. The flip-flop from minority government to coalition government, moreover, made it difficult to institutionalize a set of fiscal rules consistent with one or the other approach. After 1989, however, the change in the party system has made a true commitment form of fiscal governance possible.

Fiscal Policy and Fiscal Actors

Ireland's cyclically adjusted budget balance was consistently below –6% from 1974 until 1988, with the lowest point in 1982 at –13.7% (fig. 8.1). As a result,

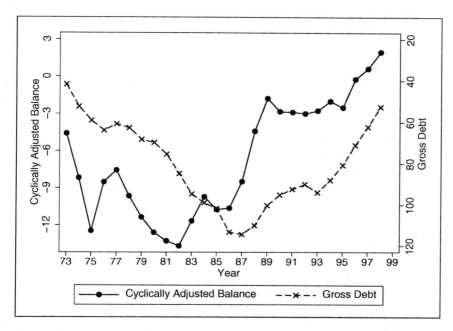

Fig. 8.1. Cyclically adjusted budget balance and gross debt level in Ireland, 1973–98.
Source: European Commission 1998a and 1999a.

the debt burden slid precipitously, doubling from around 50% in 1974 to over 100% in 1984. Because deficits remained staunchly negative, the bottom for the debt burden came only in 1988. The improvement in the cyclically adjusted balance is then dramatic, moving to –1.7% and remaining above –3% through 1998.

The main actor in the budget process is the cabinet. The finance minister's job is to coordinate the budget process. Only in 1987 and 1988, however, at the height of the budget crisis, was the finance minister a dominant figure in the budget process. The central bank does some monitoring of fiscal outcomes, but it is not a direct participant in the budget process. Similarly, the president of Ireland has no role in the budget process. The parliament, or Dáil, is technically a weak institution in the budget process. Under the many minority governments, however, the government needed to pick up votes in the chamber, and the positions of independent legislators became important.

Two Contrasting Styles of Fiscal Governance

For a commitment form of fiscal governance to function effectively, the coalition partners need detailed rules in their coalition document; a way to ensure that their coalition partners are not cheating on them; and the capacity to punish their partners if they do not honor the coalition agreement. Conversely, under a system with one-party minority governments, one would expect a strengthening of the finance minister. Until the early 1990s, steps were taken toward one of these forms of fiscal governance, but a particular form of fiscal governance was not institutionalized.

Ireland entered the oil crisis with a Fine Gael–Labour coalition. The coalition agreement was not detailed, amounting to no more than twelve hundred words (Mitchell 2000, 141). There was, however, a new system that would allow coalition partners to check on each other and that would become important later. For the first time, coalition parties had what were known as "program managers" who monitored developments in a given ministry for the party that did not control the ministry. They were not particularly widespread, however, and they lasted only as long as the coalition. Although it served out its full term, it lost the 1977 elections, with Fianna Fáil picking up enough seats to form the only one-party majority government of the period with Jack Lynch as *taoiseach* (prime minister).

Charles Haughey succeeded Jack Lynch at the end of 1979. As the deficit worsened to more than 11% of GDP during the beginning of the second oil crisis, he received advice from his finance ministry that deep budget cuts were needed. In January 1980, he appeared on national television to announce a fiscal consolidation: "We have been borrowing an enormous amount of money, borrowing at a rate that just cannot continue. We will have to reorganize government spending so that we can undertake only those things we can afford" (Collins 2001, 139). Yet, although the government set deficit and spending targets, it took few measures to meet them. Public sector pay in particular pushed up spending, with an increase in the wage bill of 34% alone in 1980, the year the government had promised to reduce spending.

The role of the finance minister under this government and the one that followed characterized the problems in enforcing fiscal discipline. In practice, the different departments sent spending proposals to the government each year at the beginning of the budget process. The finance minister then reconciled these proposals. There would usually be a crunch time where the ministries said that they could accept no more cuts. The finance minister would then put together a long list of proposed cuts for full cabinet discussion. This list became known as the "*Asgard* list," and the fate of the list was symptomatic of government inaction. The *Asgard* is a yacht that was used in 1913 to run arms to nationalist volunteers. It became an open museum, and the government maintained the yacht for public viewing. To the finance ministry, the yacht represented something that could easily be sold off. Yet the total savings to the state budget would be small, and, more important, the yacht was too symbolic for the state to sell it to a private owner. Government ministers would not agree to cut it. The list was alphabetical, so the

Asgard inevitably appeared year after year at the top of the list. It would not be cut, and other items below it were also unlikely to be cut. The *Asgard* therefore assumed a new symbolism in Irish politics for the futility of the finance minister's attempts to rein in spending (interview with former government advisor, Dublin, January 2003).

Deficits continued to increase, from 12.6% of GDP in 1980 to 13.3% in 1981. After elections in which Fianna Fáil lost its majority, Fine Gael and Labour formed a short-lived minority coalition government. The coalition depended crucially on independent deputies for its majority, and, only eight months after the coalition was formed, independents balked at the government's proposal to eliminate the budget deficit in four years, and to do it through cuts in many subsidies as well as tax increases on items such as children's shoes (Marsh and Mitchell 1999, 45). A minority Fianna Fáil then replaced the coalition, but it was plagued with a series of scandals under Charles Haughey's second stint as prime minister, and it fell only eight months into its term.

The 1982 election gave Fine Gael and Labour a majority, and they immediately formed another coalition under Prime Minister Garret FitzGerald. While their first budget included more welfare spending, the coalition did introduce real spending cuts, and overall public spending decreased from 54% of GDP in 1982 to 52.4% by 1984. The budget deficit as a percent of GDP also dropped from almost 14% to below 10% (European Commission 1999a). Yet this strategy caused increasing concern, especially within the Labour Party. The government consistently cut social programs vital to its constituency after the immediate postelection increase in funds in 1983, and the party's standing in the polls dropped precipitously. Labour parliamentarians became increasingly dissatisfied with the compromises their ministers were making in the cabinet. Labour ministers became increasingly restless in government, and the coalition had difficulty producing a common budget.

In 1987, with an election approaching, Labour pulled out of the coalition after refusing to back further spending cuts in social programs. There was a clear sense among politicians, and among the population, that Ireland was approaching an economic crisis. Economic growth was at a standstill, and continued high unemployment was leading to more people leaving the country. The public debt burden had reached 113% of GDP in 1986, and there were rumors that the government would have to approach the IMF for help. Fianna Fáil won the election, although it fell three seats short of an absolute majority. In what became known as the Tallaght Strategy (after the city where a Fine Gael leader gave a speech detailing the party's position) Fine Gael pledged to support the government on budget votes so long as the government followed a sound economic program (Marsh and Mitchell 1999, 51).

The next two years witnessed the only period in which Ireland approached a delegation form of governance. Finance Minister Ray MacSharry had held the same position before under the brief minority government in 1982, but on his return to office the combination of one-party government, public frustration with the state of the economy, and almost unconditional opposition support in parliament allowed him to impose real austerity. As one European Commission observer in Brussels put it, "He was the first finance minister to say 'no' " (interview, Brussels, July 1999). Importantly, MacSharry had the clear backing of his prime minister, Charles Haughey. Also, to support him institutionally, the government set up a temporary committee composed of two civil servants and an economist that became known within the government as the An Bord Snip. With a role similar to Britain's EDX Committee, its job was to evaluate ministry spending proposals and to make suggestions about what to cut from each ministry (interview, Dublin, January 2003). MacSharry's budget measures included a public service pay and hiring freeze. He was able to make an agreement with unions that they would moderate wage demands in exchange for tax cuts later when the budget situation improved. He also pushed through a series of expenditure cuts in education, health, and capital spending. He followed this budget with a second tough one for 1989 that included additional spending cuts as well as tax increases on gasoline and cigarettes (*Financial Times*, April 1, 1987, and January 28, 1988).

By 1989, the economic situation had improved dramatically. Real economic growth was above 4% in 1987 and 1988, and it would hit 6.5% in 1989. The budget deficit dropped to just 1.8% under MacSharry's last budget in 1989, and the debt to GDP ratio fell almost 10 percentage points in one year. The short-term delegation worked to end the economic crisis, but it could continue only if the government would continue to support it, and if the opposition would continue to support the minority government.

Sensing an opportunity to gain an absolute majority, Haughey called an election in 1989. Contrary to expectations, however, his party lost four seats. Unable to find secure backing among enough deputies for a minority government, he formed a coalition government with the Progressive Democrats, the first coalition government in the postwar period for Fianna Fáil. This government lasted only through 1992. Increasing dissension within Fianna Fáil caused increasing problems for the government. There was a financial scandal in 1991 involving allegations of insider trading and property speculation in state companies, and the finance minister, Albert Reynolds, challenged Haughey's leadership position of the party. Reynolds lost this challenge and resigned from government. Another scandal soon developed, however, when it became clear that Haughey had known about an illegal wiretap while he was prime minister in the early 1980s. He soon resigned, and Reynolds returned to government as prime minister. The Progressive Democrats nevertheless withdrew from the coalition later in the year.

In the 1993 elections, the clear winner was the Labour Party. Before the elections it had 15 of 166 seats in the Dáil, and it had never had more than

19 since 1973. The 1993 elections boosted its representation to 33. Instead of forming a coalition with its usual partner, it joined a coalition with Fianna Fáil. The form of the coalition agreement, as well as the supporting institutions to monitor the agreement's execution, was important. The coalition agreement was the most detailed in Irish history, running to 23,500 words. Policies for every ministry for the life of the coalition appeared in the document (Mitchell 2000, 142, 145–46). To monitor the agreement, the coalition revived the program managers that had been used in the mid-1970s. In this case, however, every ministry received a program manager. Moreover, the program managers met as a committee to smooth out any differences. Disputes were not to reach the full cabinet. This system brought Ireland under a commitment form of fiscal governance. It negotiated detailed fiscal contracts, and the program manager system allowed governmental parties to monitor one another.

This coalition lasted only a little more than a year, but its collapse was different from the collapse of previous governments. Rather than move to new elections, the Labour Party switched partners midstream to enter a coalition with Fine Gael and the small Democratic Left Party, which had entered parliament for the first time in 1993, after another scandal brought down a Fianna Fáil prime minister. The new coalition agreement was shorter than the previous one because of the shortness of time, but the system of program managers remained in place, and, if anything, became more critical to the coalition. They have since become a part of the Irish political system. The Fianna Fáil–Progressive Democrat coalition that entered power after the 1997 elections also appointed its share of program managers (author interviews, Dublin, January 2003).

These changes, combined with rapid growth of the Irish economy, contributed to the first sustained period of fiscal discipline in Ireland since 1973. The debt burden dropped to approximately 60% by 1997, and Ireland maintained consistent budget surpluses in the late 1990s.

Evaluation of Ireland's Fiscal Turnaround

Stable party systems are important. The change to regular coalition governments in 1989 changed the type of fiscal governance that was most appropriate for Ireland. The commitment form of fiscal governance, which required detailed fiscal targets, became possible. The system of program managers allowed the parties to monitor one another, and greater electoral competition, combined with the willingness of most parties to form coalitions with one another under the appropriate terms, made it possible for a party to punish another if it violated the terms of the coalition agreement by withdrawing from the coalition and forming another one with other parties in the Dáil.

What effect did the Maastricht treaty and market pressure have on Ireland's consolidating its budget position? The timing of the reforms suggests that Maastricht had little to do with Ireland's success. The austerity program under Finance Minister MacSharry in the late 1980s predated Maastricht, and the change to commitment had more to do with the internal political situation in the country. The European Commission, moreover, had indicated already in 1994 that Ireland did not have an excessive deficit. Ireland could, and did, qualify with no change in policy from what it was already doing prior to Maastricht.

Market pressure is a somewhat more persuasive explanation for the change. The Irish government essentially borrowed as much as it could in the 1980s from capital markets. Interest rates were high, and there was a fear in the government that capital might someday refuse to finance the government's deficit. Yet finance ministers were, if anything, surprised at how much capital markets would give to the government (interview with former government advisor, Dublin, 2003). The capital constraint began to bite only when the debt burden was well above 100% of GDP and there was concern that the government would not be able to repay the loans.

The most compelling explanation, however, remains a combination of electoral pressure and party system stability. The electorate made it clear in the 1987 election that it wanted real change. The developments in the party system, which allowed a commitment form of fiscal governance to solidify, made that change sustainable.

Portugal

Portugal returned to democracy after more than four decades of dictatorship with the parliamentary elections of 1975. Initially, two factors constrained the civilian government. First, the elected president had some powers concerning both the formation of government and its dissolution. Second, the Movement of the Armed Forces, which had overthrown the dictatorship, had a right to supervise the government through the Council of the Revolution. In 1982, however, the government lost these constraints. A constitutional revision reduced the powers of the president and eliminated the Council of the Revolution (Magone 2000, 530).

The country uses a proportional representation system, which implies that the number of parties should be proportional to the number of political cleavages. There is a highly salient left-right cleavage, and there are also less dominant religious, regime support, and foreign policy cleavages (Lijphart 1999). One would expect multiple political parties. Indeed, four principal parties have won seats in parliament through 2002. The names of the two largest parties are confusing. The Social Democrats (PSD) represent the main party of the political right, while the Socialist Party (PS) is the main party of the left. A small populist party, the Party of the Democratic Social Center, also competes regularly in elections and wins a smaller number of parliamentary seats. It has shades of Christian democracy mixed with a pronounced anti-Maastricht euro-pessimism. Finally, there is the small, orthodox Portuguese Communist Party. As in Italy in the 1980s, there was a general understanding that the other parties would not enter a formal coalition government with the Communists.

The position of the parties in ideological space, combined with their varying political strengths, has led to no consistency in the type of government that is formed. There was a one-party minority Socialist government from 1976 until its collapse through a vote of no confidence in 1978. The Socialists then formed a brief coalition with the Christian Democrats (or Democratic Social Center). In the early 1980s, there were coalition governments among the Social Democratic Party, the Christian Democratic Party, and a third small party that received seats only in 1979 and 1980, the Monarchic People's Party. From 1983 to 1985, a central bloc, or, in German and Austrian terms, a grand coalition, brought together the two largest parties. This coalition, too, fell apart, leaving a single-party minority government under the PSD. Through 1987, in fact, there had been sixteen different cabinets over almost thirteen years. There was then some stability, as the PSD won decisively in the 1987 elections, and it formed one-party majority governments through 1995 (Magone 2000). A one-party Socialist minority government then replaced the Social Democrats and remained in office until it lost the 2002 elections and was replaced with a one-party Social Democratic minority government. No one party usually receives a majority of the seats in parliament.

This catalog of types of government is important because it shows the instability of the government's structure. In chapter 2 I predicted that different forms of fiscal governance are appropriate for different types of governments. The prediction would be for some type of commitment in the early period, followed by delegation in the middle period and a mixed form of fiscal governance since 1995. Yet, each of these forms of fiscal governance implies different combinations of fiscal rules. The brief narrative below will indicate that there have been attempts to introduce reforms consistent with the predictions of the theory but that these reforms have often been incomplete and have not held.

Fiscal Policy and Fiscal Actors

Portugal had persistent problems maintaining fiscal discipline as its fiscal policy evolved during the period from 1976 to 1998 (fig. 8.2). Bad cyclically adjusted budget balances in the late 1970s worsened to a low of –15.6% of

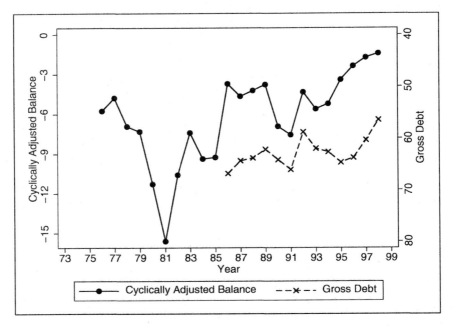

Fig. 8.2. Cyclically adjusted budget balance (1976–98) and gross debt level (1986–98) in Portugal. Source: European Commission 1998a and 1999a.

GDP in 1981. They then improved to near –3% of GDP in the mid-1980s only to fall again in the early 1990s to a low of –7.6% in 1991. There was a clear fiscal consolidation in 1992, and Portugal succeeded in getting its cyclically adjusted balance, as well as the true balance that was used to determine EMU membership, above –3% of GDP by 1997. The debt burden naturally follows a similar pattern. The country began the period with little debt, but the debt burden increased every year from 1976 to 1986, from 28% to 68% of GDP. It then flattened out, and the fiscal consolidation in 1992 led to a decrease in the debt burden as well. Portugal had a gross debt burden at about the Maastricht limit of 60% of GDP in 1997.

The principal actor in the budget process is the cabinet, which is named the Council of Ministers in the Portuguese system. In principle, the finance minister has the most power over budgetary matters. She prepares the budget and oversees the finances of other ministries. She also appoints the governor of the Bank of Portugal and, prior to the bank's independence because of Maastricht treaty requirements, she could replace him before the end of his term (Joaquim 1983). Yet, in practice, the finance minister's ability to control spending within the council has varied. It was weak in the 1980s, strong in the early 1990s, then weaker again until the finance minister became a key actor in the budget process again in 2002. Traditionally, when the finance minister was weak, the full council made decisions on the composition of the budget. One common way to get around the finance minister was to approve supplementary budgets. Spending ministers would routinely spend all of their money by the early fall and argue that there would be drastic consequences for the budget if a supplementary budget authorizing more spending was not passed.

Other actors do not play a prominent role. The president's ability to influence the government declined after 1982, and at no time did the president have direct authority over the budget. The Bank of Portugal monitors fiscal policy developments and makes occasional public statements.

The Development of Fiscal Policy

Portugal experienced real budget problems in the mid-1970s. While several other European countries initiated fiscal consolidations during this period after the end of the first oil crisis, Portugal continued to have chronic problems. In 1978, the IMF sent a mission to deal with the problem. This led to a collapse of the minority Socialist government. Matters only worsened, however, as the succeeding coalition of mostly parties on the right at the beginning of the 1980s could not control the deterioration of the budget balance. The finance minister, Anibal Cavaco e Silva, froze ministerial budgets in 1980. There were expectations that increased enforcement of tax laws would lead to a 31% rise in tax revenue (*Economist*, April 12, 1980). In nominal terms, real revenue increases fulfilled expectations for 1981. Yet the freeze on government spending was not respected. From 1980 to 1981, overall expenditure increased 7 percentage points of GDP to exactly 50% of the economy (European Commission 1999a). The sector that was most difficult for the government to cut was nationalized industry. There had been a wave of nationalizations in 1975, and the losses these firms incurred worsened during the recession at the beginning of the 1980s. Government subsidies increased 2 percentage points of GDP, from 7.1 to 9.1% of GDP. Management of these firms also ignored government restrictions on wage increases, which led to higher salaries and larger government deficits (*Financial Times*, February 7, 1983).

Soon after the central bloc came to power in 1983, the bleak budget situation forced Portugal to approach the IMF for another loan. The IMF agreed to a four-part loan so long as the country would agree to a number of conditions, including reducing its budget deficit to 8.5% of GDP. The IMF agreement reinforced the coalition agreement between the two parties, which promised an austerity program to reduce the deficit (Magone 2000, 547). The combination of the domestic fiscal contract and the IMF agreement was effective for one year only. While Portugal did manage to bring down its deficit in 1983, deficits stuck stubbornly at 12% of GDP in 1984 and 1985. The central bloc dissolved and, after elections, was replaced with a minority government led by the former finance minister Cavaco e Silva.

For Portugal, 1986 was an auspicious year for several reasons. Most important, it was the year that Portugal joined the European Community. Portugal quickly became a net recipient of EU aid, and this aid was crucial especially for infrastructure projects. Second, the minority government came clean about the extent of the fiscal problems it faced. Public companies in particular were to blame, with operating losses over the period 1979–84 equivalent to 7% of GDP in 1984.[1] As the *Financial Times* commented in 1986, "A decade of constantly changing governments with attendant shifts in management, hasty investment with little thought for its profitability, over manning and constant labour problems have left many of the public companies in difficult straights." The prime minister, who had also served as the head of the Bank of Portugal's research department in addition to his service as finance minister, instituted a "growth through austerity" program.

The program proved both popular and successful. In the 1987 elections after a censure vote brought down the minority government, the PSD increased its share of the vote from 29.9% in 1985 to 50.2%. Voters clearly backed the prime minister's efforts to prune the public sector and reform the economy. Several foreign observers, including the *New York Times* and the *Economist,* hailed Cavaco e Silva's victory as representing the maturation of democracy in Portugal. The economy was also doing well, with real growth rates between 5% and 7% in the late 1980s. By the beginning of the 1990s, Portugal passed Greece in per capita income, and there were fears the economy would overheat. One of the prime minister's principal tasks became the privatization of many of the firms that had been so problematic to the health of the government's budget. The escudo also joined the EMS in 1989. Cavaco e Silva's majority government easily won reelection in 1991.

The election may not have been that helpful to public finances. Fiscal policy was lax in the electoral year of 1991, with the cyclically adjusted budget balance almost doubling to –7% of GDP. In a policy change that would affect budgets over the longer term, the government promised an additional month in wages to public employees. As is common in other European countries, employees had traditionally received an additional month of salary in December, so that one's yearly salary was equivalent to thirteen monthly checks. The government promised, and then instituted after its election, an increase in pay equivalent to fourteen monthly checks (interview, Bank of Portugal, December 2000). To compound these weights on public finances, the economy then slowed significantly, with real negative growth in 1993.

The initial reaction of the government was again to keep spending at roughly the same level of GDP while increasing taxes. The finance minister, Jorge Braga de Macedo, introduced a value-added tax on basic foodstuffs, and government receipts that year increased 3 percentage points of

1. Percentage calculated from data in *Financial Times,* February 25, 1986, and European Commission 1999a.

GDP over the previous year. In explaining the need for the tax increases, Braga de Macedo emphasized that they were part of a "Common Market budget" that would prepare Portugal for participation in the single European currency after 1997 (*Financial Times,* January 21, 1992). Lower tax receipts, combined with higher social security spending than expected, nevertheless led to a doubling of the budget deficit in 1993 to 6.1% of GDP. Portugal also had problems on the currency front. While it did not fall out of the ERM, the bands on the Portuguese escudo were widened to 15% in summer 1993.

A turning point in public finances was coming, but not before it hurt the government's standing with the public. Acknowledging falling popularity, Cavaco e Silva reshuffled his cabinet in fall 1993. He replaced Braga de Macedo with Eduardo Almeida Catroga. One of the last measures that Braga de Macedo took before he left, however, was a reform of social security. Civil servant contributions to the fund increased, the retirement age for women was set to increase from sixty-two to sixty-five over six years, and self-employed persons were required to pay more into the system. Once Almeida Catroga was in office, the prime minister gave him almost unconditional backing to maintain spending limits within the government. This made it difficult for the spending ministers to bypass the finance minister through supplementary budgets (interview, Bank of Portugal, December 2000). Spending as a percent of GDP dropped 0.5% of GDP in 1994.

The Socialists replaced the PSD after the 1995 elections, and Antonio Guterres became prime minister, although the party fell four seats short of an absolute majority. This change in government also led to a change in the influence of the finance ministry under Antonio de Sousa Franco. The finance minister did not have the same influence in the council. Instead of making the decisions with the prime minister's backing, Guterres often pressured his finance minister to make some sort of compromise. One example is a public fight he had with Minister of the Economy Augusto Mateus over bailouts of insolvent firms in 1996. The list of possible beneficiaries for government support was fairly long, and it included some financially unstable football clubs. Although the finance minister protested openly, his prime minister did not at first step into the fray with full backing for de Sousa Franco (*Independiente,* February 8, 1996).

Most significantly from a structural perspective, the finance ministry lost control over personnel decisions. The office of the prime minister, instead, made hiring decisions. This change meant that the finance minister could not object once decisions had been made by the prime minister's staff. Unions, for example, had input on hiring practices before the finance minister did. The public wage bill increased more than 8% a year from 1996 to 1999, while the government hired fifty thousand new employees (interview, Bank of Portugal, December 2000; *Economist,* December 2, 2000).

Despite these structural problems in the budget process, the government did prepare Portugal to qualify for Economic and Monetary Union in 1997 with a balance of –2.0%, and it did so for several reasons. First, interest charges on the national debt dropped because of privatization revenues, which amounted to 4.8% of GDP in 1997. Although accounting rules did not allow this money to count directly against the budget deficit, they did indirectly help by reducing the total debt burden and, with it, interest payments. The total interest charge dropped 0.5% of GDP from 1996 to 1997 (IMF 1998). Second, following the French example of transferring pension responsibilities from France Telecom to the government in exchange for a onetime cash payment (see chapter 4), the government transferred pension responsibilities from the private Banco Nacional Ultramarino to the government. This generated 0.3% of GDP in revenue. The final important change was in the social security account. Although it had a balance of –0.4% of GDP in 1995, the balance was 1.2% of GDP in 1997 (OECD 1998).

In the October 1999 elections, with EMU membership, a booming economy, and dropping unemployment, the Socialist Party returned to the government with exactly half the 230 seats in parliament. This meant that in order to pass legislation or budgets all Socialist parliamentarians would need to attend important votes and that at least one person from the opposition would need to vote with the government. The budget vote in 2000 illustrated the increasing difficulty the minority government faced in passing its budget. The opposition parties promised to unite against the budget and to force the government to resign. It passed, however, when one Popular Party member of parliament abstained in exchange for government support for a cheese factory, a fishing port, and a health care center in his home town. With the one abstention, the budget passed 115–114.

The new council also seemingly centralized the control of public spending. As had been the case in Greece since 1996 (chapter 4), the same person became minister of both Economy and Finance (in this case, Joaquim Pina Moura). Yet this experiment lasted less than a year. As economy minister, Pina Moura was expected to uphold his party's pledge to subsidize fuel prices, while as finance minister he was to hold down spending. Fuel costs increased significantly in 2000, and, with the exception of one price increase, the government decided to stick with its election pledge. The merging of the two responsibilities in the form of one person was generally considered ineffective, and Pina Moura kept only the finance ministry until his resignation in June 2001. The fiscal situation deteriorated further, however, and the government was in disarray. The president called new elections in March 2002, and the PSD won the most seats, although not enough to form a one-party majority government.

The new Durão Barroso minority government in April 2002 faced a budget deficit clearly above 3% of GDP. Although the prime minister had discussed tax reductions in the electoral campaign, he announced immediately after his election the need for an austerity package. He appointed as finance minister Manuela Ferreira Leite, who already had a reputation as a *dama de ferro* (iron lady). The intent was to strengthen the role of the finance minister. One month later, she raised the value-added tax, forbade municipalities from incurring new debts, and closed or merged several government institutes. She also tried to tackle a pervasive source of increased spending, the public employment bill. She froze public service recruitment. She also announced that the budget deficit in the previous year under the Socialist government had been well above 3% at 4.1% of GDP (*Frankfurter Allgemeine Zeitung,* April 7, 2002; *Financial Times,* May 8 and July 28, 2002).

These measures did not come in time to prevent the European Union from initiating an excessive deficit procedure against Portugal in fall 2002. The stakes are high for the Portuguese. The continuation of the excessive deficit procedure would mean an end to the allocation of cohesion funds, which remain an important part of infrastructure spending in the country.

Explanation for the Course of Fiscal Policy

Through 1987, coalition and one-party minority governments in Portugal dissolved almost yearly. Fiscal discipline was lax during this period, with the deficit once reaching nearly 15% of GDP. The period 1987–95 seemed to bring some stability to the government, and to public finances. Indeed, while the recession in the early 1990s affected public finances, one can observe an attempt to strengthen the finance minister and to move the country toward delegation. Yet the move back to a minority government, combined with a change in power, weakened the drive to centralize the budget process around the finance minister.

Given this background, the question then is how and why Portugal qualified for EMU. It is clear that joining the common currency was popular. Both major parties supported Maastricht, and the PSD finance minister expressed the need to consolidate public finances only a month after his government had signed the Maastricht treaty. Moreover, there was a clear sense among the parties that EMU membership would be an election issue. The Socialists replaced a PSD government that had trouble with the economy, and, while it expected to win an absolute majority in the 1999 elections, it considered qualification for EMU a major accomplishment.

Yet it is also the case that Portugal was one of the countries that needed to make a series of short-term adjustments in 1997 to be sure it could qualify. Portugal already had a budget deficit above 3% of GDP in 2001.

Spain

This section reviews briefly the development of the party system and fiscal forms of governance in Spain. The country experienced a large increase in the public sector's share of the economy, jumping from less than 25% of GDP in 1975 to 44% by 1990 (European Commission 1999a). Much, if not most, of this increase was desirable, and, with a debt burden of just 12% in 1975, there was general willingness to fund some of the increase in spending with debt issues. The Spanish population wanted to establish a European welfare state after the end of Franco's dictatorship. The question, therefore, concerns not whether there were increases in public spending but whether the government maintained some measure of fiscal discipline during this increase.

The most important institution in the budget process is traditionally the Ministry of the Economy and Budget. On paper, this ministry controls all aspects of the budget process, from budget proposal through budget execution. As Nieto (1996, 126) notes, "In the Spanish administration, not even a leaf moves legally without the consent of this ministry." Yet in practice the power of this ministry over the budget has not always matched its formal power.

Parliament has few powers on the budget, and it has been a relevant actor only under Spain's minority governments from 1989 through 2000. Similarly, the Bank of Spain had no effective role prior to its independence in 1994. Since this date, the bank has developed a greater capacity to monitor government fiscal policy.

Finally, the regional level is important in current budget discussions. The 1978 constitution, which structured Spain's return to democracy, allowed the creation of regional governments. In 1981 these governments were small in fiscal terms, representing only 3% of total general government spending. By 1999, however, they accounted for roughly one-third of general government spending. The exact relationship between the center and the regions, however, has been the source of regular negotiations between them. A new accord that became law in January 2002 gave the regions increased ability to tax. A second law that passed at the same time required regional governments to run balanced budgets (Gordo and Hernandez de Cos 2000; Hernandez de Cos 2002). The regional balances had a negligible effect on general government balances over the period discussed here, so the regional level is not discussed further, but it is becoming increasingly relevant.

I focus here on the period 1982–2000. From 1982 to 1993, Spain had four Socialist one-party majority governments. The government then lost its majority but continued as a minority until 1996 with tacit support from Jordi Pujol's Catalan party, the Covergencia i Unio (CiU), and from the smaller Basque Nationalist Party. The Popular Party then replaced the Socialists, but it, too, did not have enough seats in parliament to form a majority party, and it also cut deals with Pujol's Catalan party and the Basque Nationalist Party.

One would expect an attempt at a delegation form of fiscal governance during the first period. Boix (1998, 108–9) argues that Socialist Prime Minister Felipe Gonzalez did not want to repeat the mistakes of the French Socialists in the early 1980s or the British Labour Party in the late 1970s, and he made macroeconomic discipline a government priority. Yet the government's success through 1990 was a decidedly mixed success. The Socialist government did initiate fiscal consolidations in 1986, 1987, and 1989 that reduced the budget deficit from 6.4% of GDP in 1985 to 3.7% in 1989. Yet these gains were short-lived. The deficit increased to 7% of GDP by 1993, or 6% of GDP in cyclically adjusted terms.

One reason for these developments was certainly the generally weak position of the Spanish minister of the Economy and Budget. Despite formal powers mentioned before, the minister in practice had little power in the budget process in 1991. Von Hagen's (1992) interviews of Spanish policy makers indicated that the full council, rather than bilateral negotiations common in delegation states, set the budget. There was also a clear lapse in fiscal discipline in 1992 for three reasons. The first was the general economic slowdown affecting all European economies. The second was the many cost overruns associated with two events Spain hosted that year, the Olympics in Barcelona and the World Expo in Seville (interview with journalist, Madrid, December 2000). The third was the upcoming election, which made the government skittish about alienating any of its constituencies. The government took no action to respond to growing expenditure overruns.

In the last years that Gonzalez was in power under a minority government, the Socialists changed tack and made meeting the Maastricht criteria a priority. The minister of the Economy and Budget, Pedro Solbes, received more support from his prime minister, and the government initiated some cuts on the expenditure side. Moreover, Pujol's Catalan party pledged opposition support for the minority government, and the Socialists negotiated with the Basque and the Catalan nationalist parties a form of fiscal contract one would expect under a mixed form of fiscal governance. This arrangement ended in July 1995, however, when Pujol announced that he would no longer reach an agreement with the Socialists. The following October, the Catalan party voted against the government's budget, forcing early elections.

It was not until after the 1996 elections, however, that the Ministry of the Economy and Budget received an institutional strengthening. Moreover, the new Popular Party prime minister, José María Aznar, backed his minister, Rodrigo Rato Figaredo. He appointed Rato as a vice–prime minister to increase his power within the government. He negotiated bilaterally with spending ministers, and it was difficult for the council to overrule him (Hallerberg, Strauch, and von Hagen 2001). The government also received more or less unconditional support from the Catalan party on the budget. This would have been unthinkable politically without the carrot of EMU membership. The Catalans remained bitter about their treatment under Franco's regime, and few rank-and-file members of the party wanted anything to do with the conservative Popular Party. The Catalan leader, Jordi Pujol, explained to his membership that cooperation with Aznar was necessary to ensure EMU membership. On a more practical political level, Pujol also ran a minority government in Catalonia that depended on Popular Party support to pass its own budget.

The austerity course the government took under Rato's leadership was a success. Spain just managed to get its budget deficit below 3% of GDP for 1997. Its burden, admittedly, was around 66% of GDP, but the EU chose not to enforce strictly the 60% cutoff.

Events after the 2000 election, however, show that a finance minister can be too successful. The Popular Party won an absolute majority of the seats, ending the need for cooperation in parliament with Pujol's Catalans. Fearful that Rato was gaining too much power, Aznar split the Ministry of Economy and Budget in two and gave Rato only the Budget ministry. This had rather perverse effects on the country's formulation of its stability program. While the Ministry of Budget continues to write the budget, the Ministry of the Economy writes the Spanish Stability Programme.[2]

Changes in the form of fiscal governance in Spain are at least consistent with the argument in this book. When the government wanted to enforce greater discipline to bring the country into EMU, it strengthened the role of its equivalent of the finance minister, as would be expected.

Austria

Austria defies the expectation that countries with proportional representation systems must, by necessity, have many political parties. The main cleavage in society is a left-right cleavage, with a less dominant religious cleavage also playing a role. The lack of many cleavages in society contributed to essentially a two-party system through the middle 1980s. The Social Democrats (SPÖ) represented the center-left while the People's Party (ÖVP) represented the center-right. The Social Democrats had one-party majority governments in place from 1971 through 1983. The finance minister played a centralizing role in the budget process, and budget outcomes were generally good. It had budget deficits above 3% of GDP only in 1976 and 1982–83. The Social Democrats then fell short of an absolute majority and formed a coalition with the Freedom Party (FPÖ) that lasted through 1987. Up until 1986, the Freedom Party had been a traditional liberal party, but in 1986,

2. A civil servant in the Ministry of the Budget said wistfully that he hoped that the staff in the Ministry of the Economy would call him when they formulated their next stability program (author interview, Madrid, December 2000).

with the election of Jörg Haider as its leader, it moved to the populist right, and the Social Democrats immediately ended their coalition with it.

The grand coalition government that followed in 1987 at first adopted almost a classic form of commitment. The parties reached agreement on a true fiscal contract that included detailed spending figures. The finance minister's power was shared. The Social Democrats received the position of minister, while a People's Party representative was appointed as his junior minister (state secretary). In addition, junior ministers from the party not controlling the relevant ministry were appointed throughout the government (Müller 2000). This arrangement allowed the parties to check the ministers' behavior and to verify whether the respective ministry was acting in accordance with the coalition agreement.

The first coalition between these parties functioned well. This cooperation also had a positive effect on the budget, especially in the first two years of the government, with the deficit remaining at, or below, 3% of GDP. Voters, however, regarded the coalition partners differently. While the SPÖ won essentially the same percentage of seats in the 1990 elections, the ÖVP lost over 9 percentage points to the FPÖ. The SPÖ and the ÖVP agreed that they could not form a coalition with Haider's party, and they again entered a coalition. The coalition agreement was even more detailed than under the first coalition (Müller 2000, 102). Public finances at first held, but 1993 and 1994 were bad years, with deficits climbing to almost 5% of GDP by 1994. The economic recession combined with an upcoming election in October 1994 to loosen the purse strings. In this election, both major parties did poorly, with the SPÖ losing votes to a young Green Party.

After the elections, it was clear that more needed to be done to reduce the budget deficit. In January 1995, the same month that Austria joined the European Union, the two coalition partners agreed to limit the growth in public sector pay to 2%. Unions were outraged, however, and Chancellor Franz Vranitzky backed down and proposed a "solidarity contribution" from the wealthy. The People's Party opposed this measure, however, and there was a stalemate. The frustrated Social Democratic finance minister, Ferdinand Lacina, demanded cuts in the budget. He threatened to resign if the budget deficit was projected to be S 100 billion, and, without any action, the deficit was expected to be at least S 100 billion (S 11.80 = $1) (Agence France Presse, February 1, 1995). A compromise a month later seemed to avoid a collapse of the coalition government. The gasoline tax would increase, while there would also be some higher taxes on companies. Yet the dispute continued during the formulation of the 1996 budget. The Social Democrats wanted higher taxes, while the People's Party demanded cuts in spending on welfare programs. In October the coalition collapsed, and new elections were held two months later. The Social Democrats won 3% more seats, but mostly at the expense of the small Green Party, as the vote for the People's Party remained the same.

The FPÖ remained an ostracized party with which neither of the major parties wanted to enter into a coalition, and the large parties again had no choice but to form a grand coalition government. The budget figures that would be used to decide euro membership would be the ones for the following year, and the coalition this time agreed on an austerity program that would cut S 110 billion over two years. The finance minister, Victor Klima, tied the need for fiscal discipline directly to EMU (AFE News, March 20, 1996). The coalition did succeed in bringing the budget deficit down from 3.8% in 1996 to 1.9% in 1997. Relations between the two parties, however, remained frayed. When the FPÖ won as many seats as, and slightly more votes than, the ÖVP in 1999, the ÖVP demanded that it receive the Ministry of Finance in any renewal of the grand coalition. The Social Democrats refused, and the first coalition government with the Free Democrats since Jörg Haider became party leader was formed.

Clearly, in the Austrian case Maastricht mattered in the short-term to keep the parties working together. Once euro membership passed, however, there was little incentive to maintain the same coalition.

Conclusion

In looking at the evolution of fiscal rules in four countries that did not have stable party systems during the entire period, it is clear that a given form of fiscal governance to centralize the budget process does not become institutionalized if the party system leads to frequent changes in the form of government. Ireland is the classic case of a country with an unstable party system moving to one where regular coalition governments are the predictable outcome. Moreover, the fact that several parties could form coalitions with one another meant that parties could punish a partner who violated the coalition agreement. A commitment form of fiscal governance then arose in this country.

Austria in some sense has been the reverse. It began the period with a stable party system, but the introduction of new parties, as well as the rise of an ostracized party (the Freedom Party), undermined the use of commitment in this country. The two large parties each wanted out of the coalition, but they had no alternative party with which to partner. EMU was an important reason why the political parties stayed together.

Spain represents a case where instability in the party system led to fiscal difficulties, especially under the first minority government. The country adjusted, however, when it centralized the budget process further under its minister of the Economy and Finance. The requirements of delegation and mixed systems at the governmental level were similar, and Spain had an effective ministry through the 2000 elections.

Finally, Portugal illustrates the problems of a country that has had only rare periods of party system stability. Unlike its neighbor, Spain, it has not been successful in strengthening the role of the finance minister. The new government in 2002 promised to take exactly this step. A stronger finance minister would be the desired reform at the governmental stage of the budget process in Portugal. If minority governments are likely for the foreseeable future, however, the examples of Denmark and Sweden indicate that some form of fiscal contracts negotiated with one or more opposition parties would also increase fiscal discipline.

9

Conclusion: Applications of the Fiscal Governance Approach in Europe and Beyond

Why did member states put their budget houses in order prior to the creation of the euro? To answer this question, one needs to understand the budget process. One also needs to know how budgets were made prior to Maastricht, as well as after, in order to assess how Maastricht may have mattered.

I have presented a theoretical model that can be used to assess packages of fiscal rules—what I refer to as forms of fiscal governance—in parliamentary democracies. All governments confront a common pool resource problem that plagues budgeting. This problem arises when decision makers do not consider the full tax implications of their spending decisions. In Western Europe, where most budget decisions are made at the cabinet level, ministers tend to focus on the spending and tax implications of their budget decisions for their ministry only. The decision-making process then determines whether the common pool resource leads to suboptimal budgets. A decentralized budget system allows ministers to receive the amount of money they request. This represents a fiefdom form of fiscal governance. Because ministers do not consider the full tax burden when they make their budget requests, aggregate spending levels and budget deficits will be higher than the ministers themselves want. Belgium and Italy in the 1980s are cases of fiefdom governance.

Centralization of the budget process reduces the problem, and in practice there are two ideal ways to achieve this centralization. One involves delegation to a finance minister. This form of fiscal governance relies on the discretionary ability of a finance minister to maintain fiscal discipline. The finance minister generally is the most important actor in the cabinet after the prime minister in such countries. She also has particular powers in the budget process, such as the right to propose the initial budget, to negotiate bilaterally with spending ministers, and to impose cash limits. Politically, this form of fiscal governance is possible when there are few ideological differences among cabinet ministers. This in turn requires party systems that generate either regular one-party majority governments or governments with coalition partners that are close politically to one another. The United Kingdom is the ideal case.

The second solution involves detailed fiscal rules in the form of a commitment to a fiscal contract. Coalition partners negotiate what amount to fiscal contracts with one another. They set spending for every ministry for the expected life of the coalition. They also develop institutions to monitor one another and rules to deal with unexpected situations, such as a recession or strong economic growth. The Netherlands is the ideal case.

I also have tried to explain why countries employ the form of fiscal governance that they do. Countries with stable, competitive party systems that yield regular one-party majority governments are ideal settings for delegation. Governments with coalitions of parties that are quite close to one another can also employ this form of governance. As the ideal preferences of political parties diverge, they are increasingly unwilling to delegate budgetary powers to one central minister such as the finance minister. Commitment functions well under majority governments when coalition partners are not close to one another. Minority governments add a new wrinkle to the argument. Centralization of the budget process within the cabinet does not solve the problem by itself, because the budget must still pass through parliament. A mixed form of fiscal governance, which combines a strong finance minister at the governmental stage and fiscal contracts with one or more opposition parties at the parliamentary stage, can effectively centralize the budget process. Sweden since the mid-1990s best typifies a mixed system.

There are two factors that have a bearing on the effectiveness of these forms of fiscal governance. First, party systems must be stable. Stability exists when parties can anticipate the type of government that will be in place from election to election. Regular one-party majority governments, for example, allow a country to institutionalize and to develop a delegation form of fiscal governance. Second, the party system must be competitive. Parties that do not expect electoral sanction if they mismanage the budget will not want to centralize the budget system. Ministers will decide the budget for their ministries more or less unimpeded, and a fiefdom form of fiscal governance will be the rule.

With this theoretical framework in place, one can evaluate the development of forms of fiscal governance in the fifteen states that comprise the European Union. I began this study with the year 1973, which coincides with the end of the Bretton Woods system as well as the beginning of the first oil shock. I concluded about the year 2000, with the first years under Economic and Monetary Union. The evidence suggests that one can place the countries in three groups based on the timing of their introduction of a given type of fiscal governance. The first group, composed of France, the United

Kingdom, Germany, and Austria, entered the period with a centralized form of fiscal governance already in place. They made some adjustments to their fiscal institutions, but the adjustments were incremental rather than radical changes. A second group made reforms in the early 1980s, during and after the second oil shock. Denmark, the Netherlands, and (in 1987) Ireland belong to this group. A final group of countries made reforms in the mid-1990s. As the case studies demonstrate, the form of fiscal governance adopted in a given country depended on the underlying party system. In countries with unstable party systems, such as Austria and Portugal, the reforms have not taken hold.

Maastricht was therefore a catalyst for change in two ways. At a superficial level, a few countries, such as France and Germany, introduced a series of measures so that their deficits would fall below 3% in 1997. At a deeper level, Maastricht changed the nature of the party system in a few countries. In Greece, qualification for EMU became a political issue, and it appears to have increased competition among political parties. Yet the Swedish case should remind the reader not to associate all change in the 1990s with Maastricht. The Swedes did not intend to introduce the euro even if they met the economic criteria to do so. Other states, including Finland, wanted to participate in EMU, but they had no intention of linking EMU membership with domestic reforms.

So, to the extent that there is a punch line to this analysis, it is that there was a limited "Maastricht effect." One nevertheless needs to understand the shape and competitiveness of the party system in order to predict what types of fiscal reform are desirable and whether reforms that have been made will be effective and take hold.

Relevance for Research on the European Union

There is a growing literature that examines the interplay between European Union decisions and policies and domestic politics (e.g., Rometch and Wessels 1996; Cowles, Caporaso, and Risse 2001). Economic and Monetary Union has clear domestic economic policy consequences. After the start of Stage Three of Economic and Monetary Union, governments lost two tools to influence the course of their economies: monetary policy and exchange rate policy. The main policy area that remains in their hands is fiscal policy. Yet no study to date traces the development of fiscal policy in the member states. An understanding of the making of fiscal policy to date would further our comprehension of the functioning of the European Union's fiscal framework today.

The effect of the European-level framework on domestic politics remains asymmetric. The framework may reinforce the domestic institutions in commitment states, but it has little, if any, effect in delegation states. The requirement to submit yearly stability or convergence programs, the increased monitoring of those programs, and the greater transparency of the budget process prescribed in the Stability and Growth Pact all likely benefit commitment states. The rules-based framework is familiar. Probably more important, there are additional institutions at the national level that reinforce the EU–level rules. Commitment is about more than just setting targets. A country such as the Netherlands has a set of rules written into coalition agreements that dictate what to do when the country experiences unexpected events. It also has parliamentary committees that match the competence of a given ministry and monitor the developments in that ministry, and that provide an early warning if a ministry is straying from its target.

In contrast, the EMU rules are unlikely to benefit delegation states. Some discretion on the part of the finance minister is useful for responding to fiscal shocks (both good and bad) in delegation states, and rigid rules from Brussels can undermine the finance minister's position. Moreover, there are simply not the rules and institutions at the national level to translate EU–level requirements into policy as there are in the commitment states. One argument I have heard in a commitment state is that European Union pressure should be beneficial even in delegation states because it provides additional support for the finance minister's position. One can imagine occasions in which the finance minister returns home from an ECOFIN meeting and tells her colleagues that other ministers lectured her about the domestic budget. Pressure from the European Union level may, therefore, be beneficial even in delegation states. Although there may be a minor effect, I doubt that such discussions make much difference. If the finance minister is weak to begin with, lectures in Brussels will probably not be enough to change domestic policy. If she is strong domestically, she probably does not need to refer to ECOFIN's opinion to strengthen her position. The real question is, Under what conditions is the finance minister weak and under what conditions is she strong? More generally, it should be no surprise to observers that states that in 2003 are undergoing an excessive deficit procedure either made few reforms after Maastricht (Portugal and, to a lesser extent, Germany) or are delegation states where adherence to rigid rules is alien to them (France, Germany).

The implication of these conclusions is that it may not be possible to design an effective fiscal framework at the European Union level. As I have argued before (Clark and Hallerberg 2000), the source of fiscal discipline is at the domestic level. *Domestic Budgets* suggests that one should pay attention to the design of party systems in particular.

Comparative Political Economy

Lijphart (1999) and Powell (2000) indicate how packages of political institutions reinforce one another. A Westminster, or "majoritarian" (Powell's term), system has a plurality electoral system, one-party government, two parties in the party system, and few or no institutional checks and balances on the operation of the government. A consensual, or proportional, system, in contrast, has a proportional representation system, multiple parties in the party system, coalition governments, and several institutional checks and balances.

I argue that political institutions arise out of the relevant political systems. Delegation arises in countries that Lijphart (1999) and Powell (2000) would usually consider as majoritarian. The one exception, Germany, is also the country where delegation works least well. In contrast, commitment arises in countries that these scholars would consider to be either consensual or proportional. An additional wrinkle is the importance of party competition. In uncompetitive systems, the majoritarian/proportional dichotomy is useful to suggest what type of *potential* form of fiscal governance could centralize the budget process.

I also suggest another way that the veto-player literature is relevant. Tsebelis (2002) shows that one should expect greater policy stability the greater the increase in the ideological distance between, or among, relevant participants in the policy process that can veto a change from the status quo. In practice in parliamentary democracies, these actors are political parties. In chapter 2 I demonstrated that increases in ideological distance can have a direct effect on how governments make budgets. Governments with small, or no, ideological distance among coalition partners can centralize the budget process under a strong finance minister in a delegation form of fiscal governance. Conversely, governments where the ideological distance among coalition partners is large can adopt a commitment form of fiscal governance.

There are also clear implications for what is often referred to as "fragmented government." There is general agreement that fragmented government leads to less fiscal discipline. Fragmentation of the budget process leads to an increased common pool resource problem, and some sort of centralization of the budget process is needed to eliminate the fragmentation. Conceptually, however, some scholars measure "fragmentation" as simply an increase in the number of parties in government or in parliament (Roubini and Sachs 1989; Skilling 2001; Volkerink and de Haan 2001). "War of attrition" models, in particular, regard coalition governments as a danger to the economy that should be avoided (Alesina and Drazen 1991; Padovano and Venturi 2001). In chapters 2 and 5 I made clear, however, that countries with many parties in coalition, such as Finland and the Netherlands, can have better fiscal performance than one-party majority governments in countries such as Greece. The key question is whether the budget-making process is centralized, not whether the government is centralized. In institutional design terms, this is good news indeed. Both Lijphart (1999) and Powell (2000) insist that consensual/proportional systems can be as, or more, representative than majoritarian systems. When this theory is combined with the "war of attrition" work, one would expect to find a tradeoff between representation and economic performance. This tradeoff is a false one. Combined with the proper form of fiscal governance, consensual/proportional systems can yield good fiscal performance in addition to better representation.

Next Steps

There are several potentially fruitful avenues of future research based on the framework I have set out here. Scholars should take their theories on the road and test them in alternative political and institutional settings. The more the theory holds up in different settings, the more useful it is. Can this framework be applied outside Europe?

There are at least two factors that one should consider when applying this work to other countries. First, party discipline is a variable that is more or less constant in Europe. Party discipline is high, especially when compared with the parties in the United States. In the American system, a cabinet secretary can attempt to get spending added back into the budget in a congressional committee. A secretary of agriculture may be successful in reinserting spending that was not in the president's proposal into legislation when an agriculture committee considers the bill. In Europe, deals made at the cabinet level are done deals by the time they reach the legislature. The most glaring exception to this general rule in Europe, Italy, indicates that the legislature becomes another important arena even under majority governments if party discipline is not high. More attention needs to be paid to executive-legislative relations in such cases.

Second, politics are different in presidential systems, and the cases in this book are all parliamentary democracies. The power to dissolve the government, to form new coalitions, and, where necessary, to call elections is important to the functioning of commitment. This is absent in presidential countries that, as a rule, have fixed terms of office and no dissolution power. In the American case, for example, Gramm-Rudman-Hollings set fiscal targets that, in broad terms, resemble the types of targets that commitment governments make. In parliamentary systems, there is a clear "punishment" in the form of the collapse of the government if one of the parties reneges on the deal. In presidential systems, in contrast, the government cannot fall. Other, more informal, sanctions are likely present when writing a fiscal contract that dictates the shape of the budget.

Another avenue of future research should consider additional levels of government in greater detail. I have mostly focused on central government behavior. The exceptions are cases where the subnational level had clear implications for the general government debt and deficit that were relevant for achieving the Maastricht criteria. In chapter 4 I discussed the German

Länder, in chapter 5 the Belgian regions, in chapter 7 the Italian regions, and in chapter 8 the Spanish regions. Yet the study of this level of government, and intergovernmental relations more generally, was neither systematic nor particularly detailed. Recent work by a group of young scholars indicates that the structure of these relations affects the level of fiscal discipline (Tommasi, Saiegh, and Sanguinetti 2001; Rodden 2002; Rodden and Wibbels 2002; Wibbels 2003). A future project on forms of fiscal governance should link this work explicitly with the excellent work being done on intergovernmental fiscal relations.

Coalition theory is another relevant literature for future research. In the most distinguished book of this past decade on coalition theory, *Making and Breaking Governments* (1996), Laver and Shepsle assume that parties care about the distribution of ministerial portfolios because they can set policy autonomously in a given ministry once they capture it. This model parallels the behavior of fiefdom forms of fiscal governance, and, as I demonstrated in chapter 2, it leads to poor fiscal performance for the government. The behavior of ministers under either delegation or commitment differs in the making of budgets. Does the form of fiscal governance have an effect on the type of coalitions that parties are willing to form in the first place?

There is also a more historical question that should be explored. How did forms of fiscal governance function in the Bretton Woods period? I have suggested that delegation states such as France, Germany, and the United Kingdom needed to get their budgets in order in a previous period. We know that the small countries that have multiparty coalition governments also had little effective political competition in the Bretton Woods period. Belgium, the Netherlands, Finland, and (a noncommitment state) Sweden all had long periods with the same party in power. Did the Bretton Woods system impose fiscal discipline on these states that was lost when the system collapsed?

Finally, there is a more general theoretical point worthy of consideration. I have presented a model of budgeting that focuses especially on the consequences of common pool resource problems. There are, however, other theoretical perspectives on budgeting. Some scholars, for example, worry especially about how principal-agent problems can lead to bureaucrats receiving higher budgets than governments—and the populations they represent—want (Niskanen 1971; Banks 1989). An explicit test of common pool resource problem theory with competitors such as principal-agent theory would advance our state of knowledge in the field.

The European Union's fiscal framework will not remain the same. Looking to the immediate future, the enlargement of the Union will provide a real challenge. Ten countries have joined in 2004. In the next decade, the euro-zone will spread eastward, and possibly southward, to include some or all of these countries. A larger euro-zone composed of countries that have less developed economies than those of current euro-zone members will lead to new challenges for the European Central Bank, in particular, to manage monetary policy. On the fiscal front, the convergence criteria will largely remain the same. Whether there will be more European Union pressure for domestic fiscal reforms in these countries is an open question. There are sound economic arguments for these countries to wait until their economies develop further before they join EMU. In *Domestic Budgets* I provide a possible road map for the types of reforms these countries should make. Given the prevalence of multicoalition governments, a commitment form of fiscal governance would seem to be most appropriate for most countries. Detailed fiscal contracts that political parties sign when the government is first formed may enhance fiscal discipline. The European Union–level framework, which already requires future member states to submit economic Pre-Accession Programs to the Economic Commission, will serve a useful function if it can reinforce domestic-level agreements among political parties.

The spread of commitment in Eastern Europe will only succeed, however, in developed, competitive party systems. The examples of Belgium and Italy in the 1980s indicate that fiscal contracts can fail repeatedly if party systems are uncompetitive. Similarly, unstable party systems make it difficult for parties and voters alike to hold a "defecting" party accountable for its actions if it chooses to violate a fiscal contract. The strengthening of democratic institutions is critical if properly designed fiscal institutions are to have their intended effects.

Bibliography

Alesina, Alberto, and Allan Drazen. 1991. "Why Are Stabilizations Delayed?" *American Economic Review* 81: 1170–88.

Alesina, Alberto, M. Mare, and Roberto Perotti. 1995. "The Italian Budget Procedures: Analysis and Proposals." Columbia University Working Paper no. 755.

Alesina, Alberto, and Roberto Perotti. 1995. "Fiscal Expansions and Adjustments in OECD Countries." *Economic Policy* 10: 207–48.

Alesina, Alberto, Nouriel Roubini, with Gerald Cohen. 1997. *Political Cycles and the Macroeconomy.* Cambridge: MIT Press.

Alesina, Alberto, and Guido Tabellini. 1990. "A Positive Theory of Fiscal Deficits and Government Debt." *Review of Economic Studies* 57: 403–14.

Alivizatos, Nikos. 1990. "The Difficulties of 'Rationalization' in a Polarized Political System: The Greek Chamber of Deputies." In *Parliament and Democratic Consolidation in Southern Europe: Greece, Italy, Portugal, Spain, and Turkey,* edited by Ulrike Liebert and Maurizio Cotta, 131–53. London: Frances Pinter.

AMECO (Annual Macroeconomic Database, European Commission). 1999. Luxembourg: Eurostat.

Apel, Hans. 1991. *Der Abstieg.* Munich: Knaur.

Arter, David. 1987. *Politics and Policy-Making in Finland.* New York: St. Martin's.

———. 1999. "From Class Party to Catchall Party? The Adaptation of the Finnish Agrarian-Center Party." *Scandinavian Political Studies* 22: 157–80.

Bank of Finland. Various Years. *Annual Report.* Helsinki: Bank of Finland.

Bank of Greece. 1999. *Annual Report 1998.* Athens: Bank of Greece.

Bank of Italy. 1988. *Economic Bulletin.* Rome: Bank of Italy.

Banks, Jeffrey S. 1989. "Agency Budgeting, Cost Information, and Auditing." *American Journal of Political Science* 33: 670–99.

Baron, David P. 1991. "Majoritarian Incentives, Pork Barrel Programs, and Procedural Control." *American Journal of Political Science* 35: 57–90.

Baron, David P., and John A. Ferejohn. 1989. "Bargaining in Legislatures." *American Political Science Review* 83: 1181–1206.

Beck, Neal. 2001. "Time-Series-Cross-Section Data: What Have We Learned in the Last Few Years?" *Annual Review of Political Science* 4: 271–93.

Beck, Neal, and Jonathan Katz. 1995. "What to Do (and Not to Do) with Time-Series-Cross-Section Data in Comparative Politics." *American Political Science Review* 89: 634–47.

Bell, Edmund. 1991. *A Hard Pounding: Politics and Economic Crisis, 1974–1976.* Oxford: Oxford University Press.

Benner, Mats, and Torben Bundgaard Vad. 2000. "Sweden and Denmark: Defending the Welfare State." In *Welfare and Work in the Open Economy,* vol. 2: *Diverse Responses to*

227

Common Challenges, edited by Fritz W. Scharpf and Vivien E. Schmidt, 399–466. Oxford: Oxford University Press.

Bergman, Torbjörn. 2000. "Sweden: When Minority Cabinets Are the Rule and Majority Coalitions the Exception." In Müller and Strøm 2000, 192–230.

Bernhard, William. 1998. "A Political Explanation of Variations in Central Bank Independence." *American Political Science Review* 92 (2): 311–27.

——. 2002. *Banking on Reform: Political Parties and Central Bank Independence in Industrialized Democracies*. Ann Arbor: University of Michigan Press.

Blom-Hansen, Jens. 2000. "Budget Procedures and the Size of the Budget: Evidence from Danish Local Government." Paper delivered at American Political Science Association meeting, Washington, D.C., August 31–September 3, 2000.

——. 2001. "Organized Interests and the State: A Disintegrating Relationship? Evidence from Denmark." *European Journal of Political Research* 39: 391–416.

Bogaert, Henri, and Thérèse Père. 2000. "Consolidation of Public Finances in Belgium: An Example of Application of European Norms in a State with a Federal Structure." Manuscript, Belgian Federal Planning Bureau.

Boix, Carles. 1998. *Political Parties, Growth and Inequality.* Cambridge: Cambridge University Press.

——. 2000. "Partisan Government, the International Economy, and Macroeconomic Policies in Advanced Nations, 1960–1993." *World Politics* 53: 38–73.

——. 2001. "Democracy, Development, and the Public Sector." *American Journal of Political Science* 45: 1–17.

Bordignon, Massimo. 1999. "Problems of Soft Budget Constraints in Intergovernmental Relationships: The Case of Italy." Manuscript, Catholic University of Milan.

Bräuninger, Thomas, and Mark Hallerberg. 2003. "Cabinet Decision-Making and Policy Outcomes in Parliamentary Democracies." Paper presented to the 2003 Midwestern Political Science Association meeting, Chicago, Illinois.

Bruno, Michael, and Jeffrey Sachs. 1982. "Energy and Resource Allocation: A Dynamic Model of the 'Dutch Disease.'" *Review of Economic Studies* 49: 845–59.

Bundesbank. Various Years. *Monthly Report of the Deutsche Bundesbank.* Frankfurt: Bundesbank.

Bundesministerium der Finanzen. 2003. *Monatsbericht des BMF February 2003.* Berlin: Bundesministerium der Finanzen.

Burk, Kathleen, and Alec Cairncross. 1992. *"Goodbye, Great Britain": The 1976 IMF Crisis.* New Haven: Yale University Press.

Buti, Marco. 2000. "Comment." In *Fiscal Sustainability*, edited by Banca d'Italia, 725–46. Rome: Banca d'Italia.

Buti, Marco, D. Franco, and H. Ongena. 1998. "Fiscal Discipline and Flexibility in EMU: The Implementation of the Stability and Growth Pact." *Oxford Review of Economic Policy* 14: 81–97.

Callaghan, James. 1987. *Time and Chance.* London: Collins.

Cameron, David R. 1978. "The Expansion of the Public Economy: A Comparative Analysis." *American Political Science Review* 72: 1243–61.

——. 1997. "Economic and Monetary Union: Transitional Issues and Third-Stage Dilemmas." University of Pittsburgh Center for West European Studies Policy Paper no. 4, May.

Castles, Francis G., and Peter Mair. 1984. "Left-Right Political Scales: Some 'Expert' Judgments." *European Journal of Political Research* 12: 73–88.

Chapman, Richard A. 1997. *The Treasury in Public Policy-Making.* New York: Routledge.

Chiorazzo, Vincenzo, and Luigi Spaventa. 1999. "The Prodigal Son or a Confidence Trickster? How Italy Got into EMU." In *From EMS to EMU: 1979 to 1999 and Beyond*, edited by David Cobham and George Zis, 129–56. New York: St. Martin's.

Christensen, Jørgen Grønnegård. 1985. "In Search of Unity: Cabinet Committees in Denmark." In *Unlocking the Cabinet: Cabinet Structures in Comparative Perspective*, edited by Thomas T. Mackie and Brian W. Hogwood, 114–37. London: Sage.

Clark, William Roberts. 2003. *Structuring Strategies: Capital Mobility, Central Bank Independence, and the Political Control of the Economy*. Ann Arbor: University of Michigan Press.

Clark, William Roberts, and Mark Hallerberg. 2000. "Strategic Interaction between Monetary and Fiscal Actors under Full Capital Mobility." *American Political Science Review* 94, no. 2: 323–46.

Clark, William Roberts, Mark Hallerberg, and Taeko Hiroi. 2003. "Monetary and Fiscal Cycles in Latin American Countries." Manuscript, University of Pittsburgh.

Collins, Stephen. 2001. *The Power Game: Ireland under Fianna Fáil*. Dublin: O'Brien Press.

Conseil Superieur des Finances. 1999. *Rapport Annuel 1999*. Brussels. June.

Couttenier, Ivan. 1987. "Belgian Politics in 1986." *Res Publica* 29: 359–82.

Cowles, Maria Green, James Caporaso, and Thomas Risse, eds. 2001. *Transforming Europe: Europeanization and Domestic Change*. Ithaca: Cornell University Press.

Cukierman, Alex. 1992. *Central Bank Strategy, Credibility, and Independence*. Cambridge: MIT Press.

Dafflon, Bernard, and Sergio Rossi. 1999. "Public Accounting Fudges towards EMU: A First Empirical Survey and Some Public Choice Considerations." *Public Choice* 101: 59–84.

Damgaard, Erik. 2000. "Denmark: The Life and Death of Government Coalitions." In Müller and Strøm 2000, 231–63.

Deakin, Nicolas, and Richard Parry. 2000. *The Treasury and Social Policy: The Contest for Control of Social Policy*. Houndsmills, Basingstoke, Hampshire: Palgrave Macmillan.

De Grauwe, Paul. 2000. *The Economics of Monetary Integration*. Oxford: Oxford University Press.

De Haan, Jakob, Wim Moessen, and Björn Volkerink. 1999. "Budgetary Procedures—Aspects and Changes: New Evidence for Some European Countries." In Poterba and von Hagen 1999, 265–99.

De Haan, Jakob, and Jan-Egbert Sturm. 1994. "Political and Institutional Determinants of Fiscal Policy in the European Community." *Public Choice* 80: 157–72.

———. 1997. "Political and Economic Determinants of OECD Budget Deficits and Government Expenditures: A Reinvestigation." *European Journal of Political Economy* 13: 739–50.

Dell, Edmund. 1991. *A Hard Pounding: Politics and Economic Crisis, 1974–76*. Oxford: Oxford University Press.

Della Sala, Vincent. 1993. "Committees in the Italian Parliament: Parliament at Work." *Legislative Studies Quarterly* 18: 157–84.

De Winter, Lieven, and Patrick Dumont. 2004. "Belgium: Delegation and Accountability under Partitocratic Rule." In *Delegation and Accountability in Parliamentary Democracies*, edited by Kaare Strøm, Wolfgang C. Müller, and Torbjörn Bergman, 253–80. Oxford: Oxford University Press.

Donovan, Mark. 1995. "The Politics of Electoral Reform in Italy." *International Political Science Review* 16: 47–64.

Duverger, Maurice. 1954. *Political Parties: Their Organization and Activity in the Modern State*. New York: Wiley.

———. 1980. "A New Political System Model: Semi-Presidential Government." *European Journal of Political Research* 8: 165–87.

Dyson, Kenneth H. F., and Kevin Featherstone. 1999. *The Road to Maastricht: Negotiating Economic and Monetary Union*. Oxford: Oxford University Press.

Edin, Per-Anders, and Henry Ohlsson. 1991. "Political Determinants of Budget Deficits: Coalition Effects versus Minority Effects." *European Economic Review* 35: 1597–1603.

Eichengreen, Barry, and Charles Wyplosz. 1998. "The Stability Pact: More Than a Minor Nuisance?" *Economic Policy*. 13, 26: 65–113.

Eijffinger, Sylvester C. W., and Jakob de Haan. 2000. *European Monetary and Fiscal Policy*. Oxford: Oxford University Press.

Elklit, Jørgen. 1999. "Party Behavior and the Formation of Minority Coalition Governments: Danish Experiences from the 1970s and 1980s." *Policy, Office, or Votes? How Political Parties in Western Europe Make Hard Decisions*, edited by Wolfgang C. Müller and Kaare Strøm, 63–88. Cambridge: Cambridge University Press.

Emmerson, Carl, and Chris Frayne. 2002. "The Government's Fiscal Rules." *Institute for Fiscal Studies Briefing Note* no. 16.

Esping-Andersen, Gøsta. 1985. *Politics against Markets*. Princeton: Princeton University Press.

——. 1990. "Single-Party Dominance in Sweden: The Saga of Social Democracy." In *Uncommon Democracies: The One-Party Dominant Regimes*, edited by T. J. Pempel, 33–57. Ithaca: Cornell University Press, 1990.

European Central Bank. 2000. *Convergence Report 2000*. Frankfurt: European Central Bank.

European Commission. 1998a. *Statistical Annex of European Economy*. Luxembourg: Office for Official Publications of the European Communities.

——. 1998b. "The Economic and Financial Situation in Finland: Coping with EMU." *European Economy*. Luxembourg: Office for Official Publications of the European Communities.

——. 1999a. *Statistical Annex of European Economy*. Luxembourg: Office for Official Publications of the European Communities.

——. 1999b. *European Economy Supplement: Economic Trends*. No. 3, March.

——. 2002. "Co-ordination of Economic Politics in the EU: A Presentation of Key Features of the Main Policies." *Euro Papers* 45, July.

——. 2003. *Statistical Annex of European Economy*. Luxembourg: Office for Official Publications of the European Communities.

Fabbrini, Sergio. 2000. "Political Change without Institutional Transformation: What Can We Learn from the Italian Crisis of the 1990s?" *International Political Science Review* 21, no. 2: 173–96.

Favero, Carlo A., Francesco Giavazzi, Fabrizio Iacone, and Guido Tabellini. 2000. "Extracting Information from Asset Prices: The Methodology of EMU Calculators." *European Economic Review* 44: 1607–32.

Feldt, Kjell-Olof. 1991. *Alla dessa dagar . . . I regeringen, 1982–1990*. Stockholm: Norstedts.

Felsen, David. 1999. "Changes to the Italian Budgetary Regime: The Reforms of Law n. 94/1997." *The Return of Politics—Italian Politics: A Review*, edited by David Hine and Salvatore Vassallo. New York: Berghahn Books.

Finansdepartementet. 2000. *Utvärdering och vidareutveckling av budgetprocessen*. Stockholm: Finansdepartementet.

Finansministeriet. 1999. *Budget Preparation in Denmark*. Copenhagen: Finansministeriet.

Fleming, J. Marcus. 1962. "Domestic Financial Policies under Fixed and Floating Exchange Rates." *IMF Staff Papers* 9: 369–80.

Franzese, Robert John. 2002. *Macroeconomic Policies of Developed Democracies*. Ann Arbor: University of Michigan Press.

Frieden, Jeffry. 2002. "Real Sources of European Currency Policy: Sectoral Interests and European Monetary Integration." *International Organization* 56: 831–860.

Furlong, Paul. 1994. *Modern Italy: Representation and Reform*. London: Routledge.

Garrett, Geoffrey. 1998. *Partisan Politics in the Global Economy*. Cambridge: Cambridge University Press.

——. 2000. "Capital Mobility, Exchange Rates, and Fiscal Policy in the Global Economy." *Review of International Political Economy* 7: 153–70.

——. 2001. "The Politics of Maastricht." In *The Political Economy of European Monetary Unification*, edited by Barry Eichengreen and Jeffry Frieden, 111–30. Boulder: Westview.

Garrett, Geoffrey, and Peter Lange. 1991. "Political Responses to Interdependence: What's 'Left' for the Left?" *International Organization* 45: 539–64.

Ginsborg, Paul. 1990. *A History of Contemporary Italy: Society and Politics, 1943–1988.* London: Penguin.

Golden, Miriam A. 2003. "Electoral Connections: The Effects of the Personal Vote on Political Patronage, Bureaucracy, and Legislation in Postwar Italy." *British Journal of Political Science* 33: 189–212.

Goodman, John B. 1992. *Monetary Sovereignty: The Politics of Central Banking in Western Europe.* Ithaca: Cornell University Press.

Gordo, Luis, and Pablo Hernandez de Cos. 2000. "The Financing Arrangements for the Regional (Autonomous) Governments for the Period 1997–2001." Banco de España Documento de Trabajo no. 0003.

Goudswaard, K. P. 1990. "Budgetary Policies in the Netherlands: 1982–1990." *Finanzarchiv* 48: 271–84.

Green-Pedersen, Christopher. 2001. "Minority Governments and Party Politics: The Political and Institutional Background to the 'Danish Miracle.' " Max Planck Institute for Societies, Cologne, Discussion Paper 01/1, March.

Grilli, Vittorio, Donato Masciandaro, and Guido Tabellini. 1991. "Political and Monetary Institutions and Public Financial Policies in the Industrial Democracies." *Economic Policy* 6: 341–92.

Gros, Daniel, and Niels Thygesen. 1998. *European Monetary Integration.* London: Longman.

Hahm, Sung Deuk, Mark S. Kamlet, and David C. Mowery. 1996. "The Political Economy of Deficit Spending in Nine Industrialized Parliamentary Democracies: The Role of Fiscal Institutions." *Comparative Political Studies* 29: 52–77.

Hall, Peter. 1985. "Socialism in One Country: Mitterrand and the Struggle to Define a New Economic Policy for France." In *Socialism, the State, and Public Policy in France*, edited by Philip Cerny and Martin Schain, 81–107. London: Frances Pinter.

——. 1986. *Governing the Economy: The Politics of State Intervention in Britain and France.* Oxford: Oxford University Press.

Hallerberg, Mark. 2000. "The Role of Parliamentary Committees in the Budgetary Process within Europe." In Strauch and von Hagen 2000, 87–106.

——. 2004. "Electoral Laws, Government, and Parliament." In *Patterns of Parliamentary Behavior*, edited by Herbert Döring and Mark Hallerberg, 11–34. Aldershot: Ashgate.

Hallerberg, Mark, and Patrik Marier. 2004. "Executive Authority, the Personal Vote, and Budget Discipline in Latin American and Caribbean Countries." *American Journal of Political Science.*

Hallerberg, Mark, Rolf Strauch, and Jürgen von Hagen. 2001. *The Use and Effectiveness of Budgetary Rules and Norms in EU Member States.* Report prepared for the Dutch Ministry of Finance.

Hallerberg, Mark, Lucio Vinhas de Souza, and William Roberts Clark. 2002. "Political Business Cycles in EU Accession Countries." *European Union Politics* 3: 231–50.

Hallerberg, Mark, and Jürgen von Hagen. 1998. "Electoral Institutions and the Budget Process." In *Democracy, Decentralisation, and Deficits in Latin America*, edited by Kiichiro Fukasaku and Ricardo Hausmann, 65–94. Paris: Organisation for Economic Cooperation and Development.

——. 1999. "Electoral Institutions, Cabinet Negotiations, and Budget Deficits within the European Union." In Poterba and von Hagen 1999, 209–32.

Hardin, Russell. 1982. *Collective Action*. Baltimore: John Hopkins University Press.

Harmon, Mark. 1997. *The British Labour Government and the 1976 IMF Crisis*. London: Macmillan.

Heclo, Hugh, and Aaron Wildavsky. 1974. *The Private Government of Public Money*. Berkeley: University of California Press.

Hellman, Stephen. 1993. "Politics Almost as Usual: The Formation of the Amato Government." In *The End of Postwar Politics in Italy: The Landmark 1992 Elections*, edited by Gianfranco Pasquino and Patrick McCarthy, 143–59. Boulder: Westview.

Henning, C. Randall. 1998. "Systemic Conflict and Monetary Integration in Europe." *International Organization* 52: 537–74.

Hernández de Cos, Pablo. 2002. "The New Framework for the Spanish Regional (Autonomous) Governments." *Bank of Spain Economic Bulletin* (July 2002): 67–74.

Hibbs, Douglas A. 1977. "Political Parties and Macroeconomic Policy." *American Political Science Review* 71: 1467–87.

HM Treasury. 2002a. *Government Deficit and Debt under the Maastricht Treaty*. August 30, 2002.

———. 2002b. *Reforming Britain's Economic and Financial Policy: Towards Greater Economic Stability*. New York: Palgrave.

———. 2003. *Public Finances Databank*. Downloaded at http://www.hm-treasury.gov.uk/economic_data_and_tools/pubfinance/data_pubfinance_databank.cfm on February 1, 2003.

Honkapohja, Seppo, and Erkki Koskela. 1999. "Finland's Depression: A Tale of Bad Luck and Bad Policies." *Economic Policy* 14, 29: 399–436.

Hooghe, Liesbet. 1991. "A Leap in the Dark: Nationalist Conflict and Federal Reform in Belgium." Western Societies Program Occasional Paper no. 27, Cornell University.

Horst, Patrick. 1995. *Haushaltspolitik und Regierungspraxis in den USA und der Bundesrepublick Deutschland*. Frankfurt am Main: Peter Lang.

House of Commons Treasury Committee. 2003. *The 2002 Pre-Budget Report: Second Report of the Session 2002–03*. HC 159.

Howe, Geoffrey. 1995. *Conflict of Loyalty*. London: Pan Books.

Huber, Evelyne, and John D. Stephens. 2001. *Development and the Crisis of the Welfare State: Parties and Policies in Global Markets*. Chicago: University of Chicago Press.

Huber, John D. 1996. *Rationalizing Parliament: Legislative Institutions and Party Politics in France*. Cambridge: Cambridge University Press.

Inter-American Development Bank. 1997. *Latin America after a Decade of Reforms*. Baltimore: Johns Hopkins University Press.

International Monetary Fund. 1997. "IMF Concludes Article IV Consultation with Finland." IMF press release, July 23, 1997.

———. 1998. *Sweden—Selected Issues*. IMF Staff Report no. 98/124.

———. 1999. *Portugal—Selected Issues*. IMF Staff Report no. 99/135.

Irwin, Galen A. 1999. "The Dutch Parliamentary Election of 1998." *Electoral Studies* 18: 271–76.

Iversen, Torben. 1999. *Contested Economic Institutions: The Politics of Macroeconomics and Wage Bargaining in Advanced Democracies*. Cambridge: Cambridge University Press.

Joaquim, Aguian. 1983. *A ilusão do poder: Analíse do sistema partidário portugues, 1976–1982*. Lisbon: Dom Quixote.

Jenkins, Roy. 1998. *The Chancellors*. London: Macmillan.

Jensen, Kirsten Østergaard. 2000. "The Budget Process under Minority Coalition Government." Master's thesis, Victoria University of Wellington, New Zealand.

Jones, Erik, 1995. "Economic Adjustment and the Political Formula: Strategy and Change in Belgium and the Netherlands." Ph.D. diss., Johns Hopkins University.

——. 1998. "Belgium: Keeping Up with the Pack?" In *Joining Europe's Monetary Club: The Challenges for Smaller Member States*, edited by Erik Jones, Jeffry Frieden, and Francisco Torres, 43–60. New York: St. Martin's.

Kaelberer, Matthias. 2001. *Money and Power in Europe: The Political Economy of European Monetary Cooperation*. Albany: State University of New York Press.

Katz, Richard S. 1980. *A Theory of Parties and Electoral Systems*. Baltimore: Johns Hopkins University Press.

——. 1996. "Electoral Reform and the Transformation of Electoral Politics in Italy." *Party Politics* 2: 31–53.

Katzenstein, Peter. 1985. *Small States in World Markets*. Ithaca: Cornell University Press.

Kenen, Peter B. 1995. *Economic and Monetary Union in Europe: Moving beyond Maastricht*. Cambridge: Cambridge University Press.

Knapp, Andrew, and Vincent Wright. 2001. *The Government and Politics of France*. 4th ed. London: Routledge.

König, Thomas, and Vera Tröger. 2001. "Haushaltspolitik und Vetospieler." Manuscript, University of Constance, May.

Kontopoulos, Yianos, and Roberto Perotti. 1999. "Government Fragmentation and Fiscal Policy Outcomes: Evidence from OECD Countries." In Poterba and von Hagen 1999, 81–102.

Kreber, Markus C. 2002. *Der verdrängte Finanznotstand*. Berlin: Springer.

Krehbiel, Keith. 1991. *Information and Legislative Organization*. Ann Arbor: University of Michigan Press.

Kreppel, Amie. 1997. "The Impact of Parties in Government on Legislative Output in Italy." *European Journal of Political Research* 31: 327–50.

Lamont, Norman. 2000. *In Office*. London: Warner Books.

Lancaster, Thomas D. 1986. "Electoral Structures and Pork Barrel Politics." *International Political Science Review* 7: 67–81.

Larsson, Torbjörn. 1993. "The Role and Position of Ministers of Finance." In *Governing Together: The Extent and Limits of Joint Decision-Making in Western European Cabinets*, edited by Jean Blondel and Ferdinand Müller-Rommel, 207–22. London: St. Martin's.

Laver, Michael, and W. Ben Hunt. 1992. *Policy and Party Competition*. New York: Routledge, Chapman, and Hall.

Laver, Michael, and Kenneth A. Shepsle. 1994. "Cabinet Ministers and Government Formation in Parliamentary Democracies." In *Cabinet Ministers and Parliamentary Government*, edited by Michael Laver and Kenneth A. Shepsle, 3–14. Cambridge: Cambridge University Press.

——. 1996. *Making and Breaking Governments: Cabinets and Legislatures in Parliamentary Democracies*. New York: Cambridge University Press.

Lawson, Nigel. 1993. *The View from No. 11: Britain's Longest-Serving Cabinet Member Recalls the Triumphs and Disappointments of the Thatcher Era*. New York: Doubleday.

Leeftink, Berthold. 2000. "Rules versus Flexibility—Does the Stability Pact Limit Budgetary Stabilizers?" In *Fiscal Sustainability*, edited by Banca d'Italia, 653–80. Rome: Banca d'Italia.

Lehmbruch, Gerhard, and Philippe C. Schmitter. 1982. *Corporatism and Policy-Making in Contemporary Western Europe*. London: Sage.

Lijphart, Arend. 1975. *The Politics of Accommodation: Pluralism and Democracy in the Netherlands*. 2nd ed. Berkeley: University of California Press.

——. 1984. *Democracies: Patterns of Majoritarian and Consensus Government in Twenty-one Countries*. New Haven: Yale University Press.

——. 1994. *Electoral Systems and Party Systems: A Study of Twenty-Seven Democracies, 1945–1990*. Oxford: Oxford University Press.

———. 1999. *Patterns of Democracy: Government Forms and Performance in Thirty-Six Countries.* New Haven: Yale University Press.

Lupia, Arthur, and Mathew D. McCubbins. 1994. "Who Controls? Information and the Structure of Legislative Decision Making." *Legislative Studies Quarterly* 19: 361–84.

Magone, Jose. 2000. "Portugal: The Rationale of Democratic Regime Building." In Müller and Strøm 2000, 529–58.

Marsh, Michael, and Paul Mitchell. 1999. "Office, Votes, and Then Policy: Hard Choices for Political Parties in the Republic of Ireland, 1981–1992." In *Policy, Office, or Votes? How Political Parties in Western Europe Make Hard Decisions,* edited by Wolfgang C. Müller and Kaare Strøm, 36–62. Cambridge: Cambridge University Press.

Mattson, Ingvar. 1996. *Förhandlingsparlamentarism—en jämförande studie av riksdagen och folketinget.* Lund, Sweden: Lund University Press.

Mattson, Ingvar, and Kaare Strøm. 1995. "Parliamentary Committees." In *Parliaments and Majority Rule in Western Europe,* edited by Herbert Döring, 249–307. New York: St. Martin's.

McNamara, Kathleen. 1998. *The Currency of Ideas.* Ithaca: Cornell University Press.

Meklin, Pentti, Juha Liinavuori, and Jukka Nummikoski. 2000. "Expenditure Inflexibility in the State Budget: The Fiscal Policy Latitude of the Council of State in Finland." *Public Administration* 78, no. 1: 193–207.

Melloan, G. 1997. "How Do You Qualify for the Euro Club? By Cheating." *Wall Street Journal Europe,* January 28.

Messing, F. 1988. "Het economisch leven in Nederland 1945–1980." In *Geschiedenis van het Moderne Nederland: Politieke, economische, en sociale ontwikkelingen,* edited by J. C. Boogman. Houten: De Haan.

Minderman, Gozewijn Diederik. 2000. *Tweede Kamer en Rijksfinanciën. Ein Studie naar parlentaire Sturing van Rijksfinanciën in Nederland.* Den Haag: Boom Juridische Uitgevers.

Ministry of the Economy, Finance, and Industry (France). 2001. "Towards New Public Management." *Newsletter on the Public Finance Reform* no. 1, September.

Ministry of Finance (Sweden). 1996. *The Swedish Budget 1997: Budget Statement and Summary.* Stockholm: Ministry of Finance.

———. 2001. *Budget Statement and Summery [sic]: From the Spring Budget Bill of 2001.* Stockholm: Ministry of Finance.

Mitchell, Paul. 2000. "Ireland: From Single Party to Coalition Rule." In Müller and Strøm 2000, 126–57.

Molander, Per. 1992. *Statsskulden och Budgetprocessen: Repport till expertgruppen för studier I offentlig ekonomi.* Stockholm: Finansdepartementet.

———. 2000. "Reforming Budgetary Institutions: Swedish Experiences." In Strauch and von Hagen 2000, 191–214.

———. 2001. "Budgeting Procedures and Democratic Ideals: An Evaluation of Swedish Reforms." *Journal of Public Policy* 21: 23–52.

Moravcsik, Andrew. 1998. *The Choice for Europe.* Ithaca: Cornell University Press.

Morgan, Kenneth O. 1997. *Callaghan: A Life.* Oxford: Oxford University Press.

Mosley, Layna. 2000. "Room to Move: International Financial Markets and National Welfare States." *International Organization* 54: 737–73.

Muet, Pierre-Alain, and Alain Fonteneau. 1990. *Reflation and Austerity: Economic Policy under Mitterrand.* New York: Berg.

Müller, Wolfgang C. 2000. "Austria: Tight Coalitions and Stable Government." In Müller and Strøm 2000, 86–125.

Müller, Wolfgang C., and Kaare Strøm, eds. 2000. *Coalition Governments in Western Europe.* Oxford: Oxford University Press.

Mundell, Robert A. 1963. "Capital Mobility and Stabilization Policy under Fixed and Flexible Exchange Rates." *Canadian Journal of Economics and Political Science* 29: 475–85.

National Audit Office. 2001. *Measuring the Performance of Government Departments*. Report by the comptroller and auditor general, United Kingdom.

Naughtie, James. 2002. *The Rivals: The Intimate Story of a Political Marriage*. London: Fourth Estate.

Neto, Octavio Amorim, and Gary W. Cox. 1997. "Electoral Institutions, Cleavage Structures, and the Number of Parties." *American Journal of Political Science* 41: 149–74.

Nieto, Alejandro. 1996. *La "nueva" organizacion del desgobierno*. Barcelona: Ariel.

Niskanen, William A. 1971. *Bureaucracy and Representative Government*. Chicago: Aldine Atherton.

Nousiainen, Jaako. 2000. "Finland: The Consolidation of Parliamentary Governance." In Müller and Strøm 2000, 264–99.

———. 2001. "From Semi-Presidentialism to Parliamentary Government: Political and Constitutional Developments in Finland." *Scandinavian Political Studies* 24, no. 2: 95–109.

Oatley, Thomas. 1997. *Monetary Politics: Exchange Rate Cooperation in the European Union*. Ann Arbor: University of Michigan Press.

———. 1999. "How Constraining Is Mobile Capital? The Partisan Hypothesis in an Open Economy." *American Journal of Political Science* 43: 1002–27.

OECD. 1987. *The Control and Management of Government Expenditure*. Paris: Organisation for Economic Cooperation and Development.

———. 1992. *Public Management: Profiles 1992*. Paris: Organisation for Economic Cooperation and Development.

———. 1998a. *Economic Survey of Italy, December 1998*. Paris: Organisation for Economic Cooperation and Development.

———. 1998b. *OECD Economic Survey, Portugal, 1997–1998*. Paris: Organisation for Economic Cooperation and Development.

———. 1999. *OECD Economic Surveys 1998–99: Belgium/Luxembourg*. Paris: Organisation for Economic Cooperation and Development.

———. 2001. *OECD Statistical Compendium*. Paris: Organisation for Economic Cooperation and Development.

———. 2002. *Database of National Economic Indicators*. Data downloaded from http://www.sourceoecd.org in June 2002.

Olson, Mancur. 1965. *The Logic of Collective Action*. Cambridge: Harvard University Press.

Ostrom, Elinor. 1990. *Governing the Commons*. Cambridge: Cambridge University Press.

Ostrom, Elinor, Roy Gardner, and James Walker. 1994. *Rules, Games, and Common Pool Resources*. Ann Arbor: University of Michigan Press.

Padovano, Fabio, and Larissa Venturi. 2001. "War of Attrition in Italian Government Coalitions and Fiscal Performance: 1948–1994." *Public Choice* 109: 15–54.

Pasquino, Gianfranco. 1992. "Il traghetto del governo Amato." *La Rivista dei Libri* (December): 32–36.

Persson, Göran. 1997. *Den som är satt i skuld är icke fri*. Stockholm: Atlas.

Persson, Torsten, and Guido Tabellini. 2003. *Economic Effects of Constitutions*. Cambridge: MIT Press.

Peters, Guy. 2000. "Reforming the Finnish Government." European Union Center and Center for West European Studies Newsletter, University of Pittsburgh, October.

Pitruzzello, Salvatore. 1997. "Social Policy and the Implementation of the Maastricht Fiscal Convergence Criteria: The Italian and French Attempts at Welfare and Pension Reforms." *Social Research* 64, no. 4: 1589–1642.

Poterba, James, and Jürgen von Hagen, eds. 1999. *Fiscal Institutions and Fiscal Performance*. Chicago: University of Chicago Press.

Powell, G. Bingham. 2000. *Elections as Instruments of Democracy: Majoritarian and Proportional Visions*. New Haven: Yale University Press.

Rodden, Jonathan. 2000. "Breaking the Golden Rule: Fiscal Behavior with Rational Bailout Expectations in the German States." Prepared for the workshop European Fiscal Federalism in Comparative Perspective, Center for European Studies, Harvard University.

———. 2001. "And the Last Shall Be First: The Political Economy of Federalism and Deficits in Germany." Manuscript, MIT, October 2.

———. 2002. "The Dilemma of Fiscal Federalism: Grants and Fiscal Performance around the World." *American Journal of Political Science* 46: 670–87.

Rodden, Jonathan, and Erik Wibbels. 2002. "Beyond the Fiction of Federalism: Macroeconomic Management in Multitiered Systems." *World Politics* 43, no. 4: 494–531.

Rometsch, Dietrich, and Wolfgang Wessels, eds. 1996. *The European Union and the Member States: Towards Institutional Fusion?* New York: Manchester University Press.

Ross, George. 1995. *Jacques Delors and European Integration.* New York: Oxford University Press.

Roubini, Nouriel, and Jeffrey D. Sachs. 1989. "Political and Economic Determinants of Budget Deficits in the Industrial Democracies." *European Economic Review* 33: 903–33.

Sandholtz, Wayne. 1993. "Choosing Union: Monetary Politics and Maastricht." *International Organization* 47: 1–39.

Sbragia, Alberta. 2001. "Italy Pays for Europe: Political Leadership, Political Choice, and Institutional Adaptation." In Cowles, Caporaso, and Risse 2001, 79–96.

Scharpf, Fritz. 1991. *Crisis and Choice in European Social Democracy.* Ithaca: Cornell University Press.

Schick, Allen. 1986. "Macro-Budgetary Adaptations to Fiscal Stress in Industrialized Democracies." *Public Administration Review* 46: 124–34.

———. 1993. "Government versus Budget Deficits." In *Do Institutions Matter?* edited by Bert R. Rockman and Bert A. Weaver, 187–236. Washington, D.C.: Brookings Institution.

Schmitter, Philippe C. 1977. *Corporatism and Policy-Making in Contemporary Western Europe.* London: Sage.

Sechi, Salvatore. 1987. "Giocarsi la dote: L'Incognita PSI nelle riforme istituzionali." *Il Mulino* 36, no. 6: 963–78.

Seitz, Helmut. 1999. "Subnational Government Bailouts in Germany." Center for European Integration Studies (ZEI) Working Paper B 20 1999, Bonn, Germany.

Shepsle, Kenneth A., and Barry R. Weingast. 1994. "Positive Theories of Congressional Institutions." *Legislative Studies Quarterly* 29: 149–79.

Simmons, Beth. 1999. "The Internationalization of Capital." In *Continuity and Change in Contemporary Capitalism,* edited by Herbert Kitschelt, Peter Lange, Gary Marks, and John Stephens, 36–69. Cambridge: Cambridge University Press.

Skilling, David. 2001. "Policy Coordination, Political Structure, and Public Debt: The Political Economy of Public Debt Accumulation in OECD Countries since 1960." Ph.D. diss., Harvard University.

Smits, Jozef. 1983. "Belgian Politics in 1982." *Res Publica* 25: 181–217.

———. 1985. "Belgian Politics in 1984." *Res Publica* 27: 229–68.

———. 1986. "Belgian Politics in 1985." *Res Publica* 28: 441–74.

Snels, Bart. 1999. *Politics in the Dutch Economy: The Economics of Institutional Interaction.* Brookfield, Vt.: Ashgate Publishing.

Stienlet, Georges. 2000. "Institutional Reforms and Belgian Fiscal Policy in the 1990s." In Strauch and von Hagen 2000, 215–34.

Strauch, Rolf, and Jürgen von Hagen. 1999. "Tumbling Giant: Germany's Experience with the Maastricht Fiscal Criteria." Center for European Integration Studies (ZEI) Working Paper B 5 1999, Bonn, Germany.

——. 2001. "German Public Finance: Recent Experiences and Future Challenges." Center for European Integration Studies (ZEI) Working Paper B 13 2001, Bonn, Germany.

Strauch, Rolf, and Jürgen von Hagen, eds. 2000. *Institutions, Politics, and Fiscal Policy.* Boston: Kluwer.

Strøm, Kaare. 1990. *Minority Governments and Majority Rule.* Cambridge: Cambridge University Press.

Study Group on the Budget Margin. 1988. *Towards Sound Public Finance.* Eighth report of the Study Group on the Budget Margin.

Sturm, Roland. 1994. "The Chancellor and the Executive." In *From Adenauer to Kohl: The Development of the German Chancellorship,* edited by Stephen Padgett, 78–105. Washington, D.C.: Georgetown University Press.

——. 1998. "Die Wende im Stolperschritt—eine finanzpolitische Bilanz." In *Bilanz der Ära Kohl: Christlich-liberale Politik in Deutschland, 1982–1998,* edited by Göttrik Wewer, 183–200. Opladen, Germany: Leske and Budrich.

Swedish Riksdag. 1999. "The Riksdag and the Central Government Budget." *The Swedish Riksdag Factsheets* no. 7.

Taagapera, Rein, and Bernard Grofman. 1985. "Rethinking Duverger's Law: Predicting the Effective Number of Political Parties in Plurality and PR Systems—Parties Minus Issues Equals One." *European Journal of Political Research* 13, no. 4: 341–52.

Tanzi, Vito, and Ludger Schnuknecht. 2000. *Public Spending in the Twentieth Century: A Global Perspective.* Cambridge: Cambridge University Press.

Thain, Colin, and Maurice Wright. 1995. *The Treasury and Whitehall: The Planning and Control of Public Expenditure, 1976–1993.* Oxford: Clarendon.

Thomson, Robert. 2001. "The Programme to Policy Linkage: The Fulfillment of Election Pledges on Socio-Economic Policy in the Netherlands, 1986–1998." *European Journal of Political Research* 20: 171–97.

Timmermans, Arco, and Rudy B. Andeweg. 2000. "The Netherlands: Still the Politics of Accommodation?" In Müller and Strøm 2000, 356–98.

Tommasi, Mariano, Sebastian Saiegh, and Pablo Sanguinetti. 2001. "Fiscal Federalism in Argentina: Policies, Politics, and Institutional Reform." *Economia* 1: 157–200.

Treisman, Daniel. 2000. "Centralization and Inflation: Commitment, Collective Action, or Continuity?" *American Political Science Review* 94: 837–57.

Tschentscher, Axel, ed. 2002. *The Basic Law (Grundgesetz).* Würzburg: Jurisprudentia Verlag.

Tsebelis, George. 1995. "Decision Making in Political Systems: Veto Players in Presidentialism, Parliamentarism, Multicameralism, and Multipartyism." *British Journal of Political Science* 25: 289–325.

——. 1999. "Veto Players and Law Production in Parliamentary Democracies: An Empirical Analysis." *American Political Science Review* 93: 591–608.

——. 2002. *Veto Players: How Political Institutions Work and Why.* Princeton: Princeton University Press.

Tsebelis, George, and Jeanette Money. 1997. *Bicameralism.* Cambridge: Cambridge University Press.

Vandelli, Luciano. 1992. *Il Nuovo ordinamento delle autonomie locali: Commento alla legge 8 giugno 1990.* Rimini: Maggioli.

Velasco, Andrés. 1999. "A Model of Endogenous Fiscal Deficits and Delayed Fiscal Reforms." In Poterba and von Hagen 1999, 37–58.

——. 2000. "Debts and Deficits with Fragmented Fiscal Policymaking." *Journal of Public Economics* 76: 105–25.

Verdun, Amy. 1999. "The Role of the Delors Committee in the Creation of EMU: An Epistemic Community?" *Journal of European Public Policy* 6: 308–28.

——. 2000. "Governing by Committee: The Case of Monetary Policy." In *Committee Governance in the European Union,* edited by Thomas Christiansen and Emil Kirchner, 132–44. Manchester: Manchester University Press.

Versteeg, Coos. 2000. "Dancers of All Countries." In *Dancing Dutch: Contemporary Dance in the Netherlands,* edited by Coos Versteeg, 60–81. Amsterdam: Theater Instituut Nederland.

Verzichelli, Luca, and Maurizio Cotta. 2000. "Italy: From 'Constrained' Coalitions to Alternating Governments?" In Müller and Strøm 2000, 433–97.

Visser, Jelle, and Anton Hemerijck. 1997. *"A Dutch Miracle": Job Growth, Welfare Reform, and Corporatism in the Netherlands.* Amsterdam: Amsterdam University Press.

Volkerink, Björn, and Jakob de Haan. 2001. "Fragmented Government Effects on Fiscal Policy: New Evidence." *Public Choice* 109: 221–42.

von Hagen, Jürgen. 1991. "A Note on the Empirical Effectiveness of Formal Fiscal Restraints." *Journal of Public Economics* 44: 199–210.

——. 1992. "Budgeting Procedures and Fiscal Performance in the European Communities." *Economic Papers,* Commission of the European Communities, Directorate-General for Economic and Financial Affairs, no. 96.

von Hagen, Jürgen, and Ian Harden. 1994. "Budget Processes and Commitment to Fiscal Discipline." *European Economic Review* 39: 771–79.

von Hagen, Jürgen, Andrew Hughes-Hallett, and Rolf Strauch. 2001. *Budgetary Consolidation in EMU.* Economic Papers 148. Brussels: European Commission.

Warwick, Paul. 1994. *Government Survival in Western European Parliamentary Democracies.* New York: Cambridge University Press.

Weingast, Barry, Kenneth A. Shepsle, and Christopher Johnsen. 1981. "The Political Economy of Benefits and Costs: A Neoclassical Approach to Distributive Politics." *Journal of Political Economy* 89: 642–64.

Wibbels, Erik. 2003. "Bailouts, Budget Constraints, and Leviathans: A Comparative Federalism and Lessons from the Early U.S." *Comparative Political Studies* 36: 475–508.

Wildavsky, Aaron. 1975. *Budgeting: A Comparative Theory of Budgetary Processes.* Boston: Little, Brown.

Willett, Thomas D. 1999a. "Developments in the Political Economy of Policy Coordination." *Open Economies Review* 10: 221–53.

——. 1999b. "A Political Economy Analysis of the Maastricht and Stability Pact Fiscal Criteria." In *Fiscal Aspects of European Monetary Integration,* edited by Michael Hutchinson, Svend Jensen, and Andrew Hughes Hallett, 37–66. Cambridge: Cambridge University Press.

——. 2001. "The Political Economy of External Discipline: Constraint versus Incentive Effects of Capital Mobility and Exchange Rate Pegs." Paper presented at the 2001 annual meeting of the American Political Science Association, San Francisco, August 30–September 2.

Woldendorp, Jaap, Hans Keman, and Ian Budge. 1998. "Party Government in 20 Democracies: An Update (1990–1995)." *European Journal of Political Research* 33: 125–64.

Zohlnhöfer, Reimut. 2001. "Die Bundesrepublik Deutschland: finanzpolitischen Zielkonflikt zwischen Wiedervereinigung und europäischer Integration." *Zeitschrift für Politikwissenschaft* 11 (4): 1547–71.

Index

ABM Amro Bank, 7
accounting tricks argument, 2, 4–5, 8
agenda setter, 29
Agrarian Party, 138
Aho, Esko, 141
Ahold, 117
Ahtisaari, Martti, 139 n
Almeida Catroga, Eduardo, 209
Alsace-Lorraine, 103
Amato, Giuliano, 188–89
Amsterdam, Treaty of, 45, 51, 53–59
Andreatta, Nino, 187
Andreotti, Giulio, 187
Andriessen, Frans, 122
Annually Managed Expenditure (AME), 80
Antwerp, 131
Apel, Hans, 24, 92, 100
Arthuis, Jean, 108–9
Asgard, 200–201
Asquith, H. H., 66
Aubry, Martine, 25
Austria, 10, 30, 43, 61, 197; and fiscal
    governance, 37–40, 214–16, 220; and
    party system, 11, 18, 214–15
Austrian National Bank, 16 n
Aznar, José María, 213–14

Baldwin, Stanley, 66
Balladur, Eduard, 107–8
Balls, Ed, 81
Banco Nacional Ultramarino, 210
Bank of England, 67
Bank of Finland, 145–46, 149
Bank of France, 105
Bank of Greece, 109
Bank of Italy, 186, 188
Bank of Portugal, 206–8
Bank of Spain, 212
Barcelona, and Olympics, 213
Baron, David P., 26 n
Barschel Affair, 96
Basque Nationalist Party, 212–13
Baudouin, King, 132

Bavaria, 86
beggar-thy-neighbor argument, 47–48
Belgian National Bank, 129, 134, 136
Belgium, 1, 22, 28, 32 n, 52, 117 n, 142, 179;
    and European Monetary System, 7, 127;
    and fiscal actors, 128–29; and fiscal
    governance, 38–40, 53, 115–16, 128–37;
    and Golden Hamster Rule, 34; and
    party system, 17, 43, 127–28, 224; and
    regions, 127–28, 132–33, 136–37; and
    similarity with Italy, 131, 194, 218, 225;
    and Treaty of Maastricht, 135–37
BEPG (Broad Economic Policy Guidelines),
    50, 56–57, 60–61
Bérégovoy, Pierre, 107, 109
Berlusconi, Silvio, 190
Biaudet, Eva, 141
Biffen, John, 74
Blair, Tony, 64–65, 67 n, 79
Blüm, Norbert, 25
Bonn, Economic Summit of, 44, 93
Braga de Macedo, Jorge, 208–9
Brandt, Willy, 87, 90, 92
Bremen, 50
Bretton Woods, 1, 3, 44, 103, 128, 154, 197,
    219, 224
Britain. *See* United Kingdom
Brittan, Leon, 74
Broad Economic Policy Guidelines (BEPG),
    50, 56–57, 60–61
Brown, Gordon, 64, 67, 79, 81, 84 n
Budgetary Committee, 49
Bundesbank, 84–85, 88–89, 91, 94, 95 n,
    97–98, 100, 102, 105, 119; and Dutch
    central bank, 120 n
Bundesrat, 85, 90–94, 97–101
Bundestag, 24, 86–87, 92–93, 95, 97, 100;
    and Reconciliation Committee
    (Vermittlungsausschuss), 92
Bureau for Economic Policy Analysis
    (CPB), 119

Callaghan, James, 65, 67, 69–71

Calvinism, 117
capital controls, 149, 160
capital mobility argument, 6–7, 83 n
Cardiff, European Council of, 56 n, 59
Carlsson, Ingvar, 157
cash limits, 69, 82, 218
Catholic People's Party (Netherlands),
    118 n
Cavaco e Silva, Anibal, 207–9
Celtic Tiger. *See* Ireland
Center Party (Finland), 138, 144, 147
Center Party (Sweden), 153–54, 159, 161,
    164 n, 165
Center Union party (France), 106
Central Planning Bureau (CPB), 119
CGCB (Committee of Governors of Central
    Banks), 49–50
Chamber of Deputies (Italy), 22, 189, 191
Chamberlain, Neville, 66
Chirac, Jacques, 107–8
Christian Democratic Party (DC), 183–84,
    187–88
Christian Democrats (Belgium), 128, 131
Christian Democrats (CDA), 17, 118,
    122–25
Christian Democrats (CDU), 25, 86–87,
    90–96, 99, 189
Christian Democrats (Flanders), 132
Christian League of Finland, 138
Christian Social Union (CSU), 32, 86–87,
    90, 92–93, 95–96, 189
Christophersen, Henning, 178–79
Churchill, Winston, 66
Ciampi, Carlo Azeglio, 22, 186, 190–91,
    194–95
Civil Service Department (United
    Kingdom), 72, 82
Clarke, Kenneth, 78
Clean Hands campaign, 18, 188
closed rules, 12, 25 n
cohabitation, 104
collective action problem, 27–28, 52
commitment form of fiscal governance:
    defined, 13–14, 20
Committee of Governors of Central Banks
    (CGCB), 49–50
Committee of Permanent Representatives
    (COREPER), 49, 57
common pool resource problem, 11–12, 20,
    22–24, 83, 115, 128, 155–57, 218, 222,
    224; and budget deficits, 40–42; and
    cabinet, 12, 31, 142, 190–91, 195; and
    fiefdom governance, 27–29, 33, 132,
    139–40; and minority government, 35,
    152, 159, 170; and parliament, 162–64,
    175, 184; and party competition, 15, 21,
    187

Communist Party (Denmark), 169
Communist Party (East Germany), 87
Communist Party (Finland), 142
Communist Party (France), 13, 106–7, 189
Communist Party (Greece), 110
Communist Party (Italy), 183
Communist Party (Portugal), 205
Communist Party (Sweden), 17–18, 152–55,
    159
Conservative Party (Denmark), 168
Conservative Party (Finland), 138
Conservative Party (Sweden), 153, 156
Conservative Party (United Kingdom), 70,
    72, 75–77
constitution (European Union), 58
Constitutional Court (Germany), 85
constrained discretion, 79, 81
convergence criteria. *See* Maastricht, Treaty
    of
convergence program, 54–55, 59, 220; and
    Belgium, 134; and Italy, 193; and the
    United Kingdom, 84
COREPER (Committee of Permanent
    Representatives), 49, 57
Cossiga, Francesco, 188
Council of Economic and Finance Ministers
    (ECOFIN), 1, 45, 48–50, 54–58, 60–62,
    85, 88, 97, 101, 134, 182, 194, 221
Council of Ministers. *See* Council of the
    European Union
Council of Ministers (Portugal), 206
Council of the European Union (Council
    of Ministers), 45, 51. *See also* Council of
    Economic and Finance Ministers
    (ECOFIN); European Council
Council of the Revolution, 204
Covergencia i Unio, 212
Cresson, Edith, 107

D66 (Dutch Political Party), 117 n, 118, 122,
    125–26
Dáil, 199, 202–3
Danish Center Democratic Party, 169
Danish Liberal Party, 168
Darley, Alistair, 79
De Nederlandsche Bank, 119–20
de Sousa Franco, Antonio, 209
deficit reference point, 4
Dehaene, Jean-Luc, 132
delegation form of fiscal governance:
    defined, 13, 20
Delors, Jacques, 106, 109
Democratic Left Party (Ireland), 203
Democratic Social Center, 205
Denmark, 4 n, 8, 16–18, 36–38; and Euro
    Group, 58; and European Monetary
    System, 6; and fiscal actors, 168–71; and

fiscal governance, 36–38, 40, 71, 105–6, 116, 151–53, 165, 170–81, 220; and party system, 43, 127–28, 217; and Treaty of Maastricht, 52, 178–79

Departmental Expenditure Limit (DEL), 80

Deutsche Telekom, 98 n

Diepgen, Eberhard, 99

Dini, Lamberto, 190

dioxin scandal (Belgium), 131 n

Duisenberg, Wim, 17, 122

Dutch central bank. *See* De Nederlandsche Bank

"Dutch disease," 121 n

Duverger, Maurice, 37, 65

ECOFIN. *See* Council of Economic and Finance Ministers

Economic and Financial Committee, 54–58, 60–62

Economic and Monetary Union (EMU), 1, 3–5, 7–8, 38, 41, 43, 46, 49–56, 62, 64, 221; and accession countries, 225; and Austria, 216; and Belgium, 133–34, 136; and Denmark, 151–53; and Finland, 116, 148, and France, 106, 220; and Germany, 88, 98, 220; and Greece, 109, 112–14, 220; and Italy, 182–83, 185, 190, 192–95; and the Netherlands, 119, 126; and Portugal, 197, 206, 210–11; and Spain, 213–14; and Sweden, 167, 220; and the United Kingdom 78, 83

Economic Policy Committee, 45, 49, 56–57

ecu, 145

EDX Committee, 77–79, 82–83

Eichel, Hans, 89, 99–103

electoral blocs, 12, 21, 32, 36, 43, 63, 95, 102, 168–70, 173, 180, 183–84, 190

electoral systems: personalized proportional representation, 86; proportional representation, 9, 18, 182 n, 184, 189; proportional representation and number of parties, 10–12, 25, 37, 103, 118, 127, 151, 154, 169, 197, 204, 214, 222; plurality, 9–13, 25, 37, 65, 68, 86, 103, 182 n, 184, 189, 222; reinforced proportional representation, 110, 112; single transferable vote, 10, 198

EMI (European Monetary Institute), 45, 50

EMS. *See* European Monetary System

EMU. *See* Economic and Monetary Union

epistemic communities, 3

Eppler, Erhard, 92

Erhard, Ludwig, 82, 95

ERM. *See under* European Monetary System

escudo, 51, 208–9

euro, 7, 58, 85, 97–100, 103, 105, 115, 148, 151 n, 182, 216, 218, 220

Euro Group, 58–59

European Central Bank (ECB), 2, 45–46, 49–50, 57–59, 122, 225

European Coal and Steel Community, 102

European Commission, 2–3, 48–49, 51–52, 55, 57–59, 61–62, 135–37, 182, 194, 202

European Convention, 58

European Council, 45–46, 50, 52–56, 59, 167, 194

European Currency Unit (ecu), 145

European Monetary Institute (EMI), 45, 50

European Monetary System (EMS), 6–7, 51, 53, 126–28, 145, 179, 220; Exchange Rate Mechanism (ERM) of, 52 n; and crisis, 77–78, 84; and Italy, 182; and Portugal, 209; and United Kingdom membership, 83

European Parliament, 11, 50, 61

European System of Integrated Economic Accounts (ESA), 5, 99 n, 135

Eurostat, 15, 45, 108; and Italy, 65, 193

"evening school," 141–42

excessive deficit procedure, 45–46, 49–56, 59, 61; and Belgium, 136; and France, 221; and Germany, 85, 99, 221; and Ireland, 204; and Portugal, 211, 221

Exchange Rate Mechanism (ERM). *See under* European Monetary System (EMS)

Fabius, Laurent, 25

Falklands war, 73

Federal Planning Bureau, 128

Feldt, Kjell-Olof, 35, 156–60

Ferreira Leite, Manuela, 211

Fianna Fáil (FF), 18, 197–203

fiefdom form of government: defined, 12, 20

Finance Committee (Belgium), 141–42

Finance Committee (Denmark), 176–77

Finance Committee (Riksdag's, Sweden), 162, 165

Fine Gael (FG), 18, 197–201, 203

Finland, 16, 39 n; and fiscal actors, 138–40; and fiscal governance, 17, 32 n, 38, 43, 53, 115–16, 139–50, 156, 222; and party system, 13, 37, 40, 137–38, 224; and president, 138; and Treaty of Maastricht, 148–49, 220

fiscal governance. *See under individual country entries*

fiscal institutionalists, 11–12

fiscal policy coordination, 45–48, 59, 61

fiscal rules, 9, 14, 16, 18–19, 34, 115, 198, 205–6, 216, 218–19; and Annually Managed Expenditure (AME), 80; and

fiscal rules *(contnued)*
  Departmental Expenditure Limit
    (DEL), 80; and functional targets in
    Italy, 192; and golden rule, 80, 91, 171;
    and New Control Total, 77–78; and
    public sector borrowing requirement
    (PSBR), 68, 73, 84; and rules for budget
    discipline, 124; Sustainable Investment
    Rule, 80–81; and top-down budgeting,
    77, 82, 166
FitzGerald, Garret, 201
fixed exchange rate argument, 6–7, 41–42
Flanders, 17, 127; and fiscal policy in
    Belgium, 130–34
Folgeting, 169, 176
Ford, Gerald, 69
Forza Italia, 190
France, 1, 114; and censure motion, 105–7;
    and European Council, 50; and
    European Monetary System, 6; and
    fiscal actors, 104–5; and fiscal
    governance, 19, 25, 29, 38, 54, 61–64,
    101–10, 113, 119, 123, 138, 157 n, 187,
    219–21, 224; and party system, 17, 32,
    40, 43, 103–4, 110, 170, 182 n, 189; and
    Treaty of Maastricht, 109, 210
France Telecom, 108, 210
Free Democratic Party (FDP), 32, 40, 87,
    89–91, 93–96, 98, 189
Freedom Party (FPÖ), 61, 197, 214–16
French central bank. *See* Bank of France

G-7 industrialized nations, 44–45, 58
game theory, 173; and prisoner's dilemma,
    29; and war of attrition, 9; and zero-sum
    game, 31
Garrett, Geoffrey, 6
George, David Lloyd, 66
Germany, 4 n, 44, 127; and Basic Law,
    88–89, 91; and economic miracle, 84;
    and European Monetary System, 6, 77;
    and fiscal actors, 25, 87–91; and fiscal
    governance, 19, 24–25, 30, 38, 45, 54,
    61–64, 84–102, 104, 113–14, 182, 184,
    187, 220–22, 224; and Länder, 50, 90,
    98–101, 224; and party system, 17, 32,
    40, 43, 86–87, 189–90; and solidarity
    surcharge, 96–98; and Treaty of
    Maastricht, 100, 109; and weakness of
    finance minister after reunification, 101
Ghent, 131
Giant Supermarkets, 117
Glistrup, Mogens, 174
golden rule, 80, 91, 171
Gonzalez, Felipe, 213
Goria, Giovanni, 188
Gramm-Rudman-Hollings Act, 223

grand coalition (Austria), 197, 205, 215–16
grand coalition (Finland), 143–44
grand coalition (Germany), 86, 205
Great Britain. *See* United Kingdom
Greece, 1, 4, 5, 161; and fiscal actors,
    109–11; and fiscal governance, 22, 38,
    63–64, 109–13, 182 n; and party system,
    17, 36, 40, 43, 110, 222; and Portugal,
    208, 210; and Treaty of Maastricht, 9, 52,
    220
Green parties (Belgium), 127
Green Party (Austria), 215
Green Party (Finland), 138, 147
Green Party (France), 103
Green Party (Germany), 32, 87, 95, 99, 190
Green Party (Sweden), 36, 154, 162 n,
    165–66
Greenland, 168 n
Guterres, Antonio, 209

Haider, Jörg, 215–16
Hamburg, 24
Hartling, Poul, 172
Haughey, Charles, 200–202
Healey, Dennis, 68–70
Heath, Edward, 72
Heinesen, Knud, 173
Herfindahl index, 39
Heseltine, Michael, 76
Hesse, 91, 95, 99
High Council of Finance (HCF), 116,
    128–29, 133–35, 137, 141, 150
House of Commons, 65, 67, 74; and
    Treasury Committee, 84
Howe, Geoffrey, 71

inflation, 5, 10 n, 46, 61, 67, 69; and
    Denmark, 175; and France, 103; and
    Germany, 85; and Italy, 187–88; and the
    Netherlands, 121, 123, 125; and
    Sweden, 157, 160; and the United
    Kingdom, 72–73, 77
Inter-American Development Bank, 11, 31 n
International Monetary Fund (IMF), 108;
    and Finland, 145, 148; and Ireland, 201;
    and Italy, 187; and Portugal, 207; and
    the United Kingdom, 69–70, 84
Ireland, 51–52; and convergence program,
    193; and electoral system, 10; and fiscal
    actors, 198–99; and fiscal governance,
    37–38, 196–204, 220; and party system,
    11, 18, 40, 43, 216; reprimand of, 60–61;
    and Treaty of Maastricht, 204
Irvine of Lairg, Lord, 79
Italian Republican Party, 187
Italian Social Democratic Party, 187
Italian Social Movement, 183

Italian Socialist Party, 187
Italy, 1, 4 n, 7, 45, 52–53, 62; and deficit
    requirement after EMS, 53; and
    European Monetary System, 145, 179;
    and fiscal actors, 185–87; and fiscal
    governance, 18, 38, 161, 182–95, 218;
    and interest rate premium, 8, 194; and
    party system, 15, 28, 39–40, 43, 183–84,
    190–91, 205, 225; and regions, 188; and
    strength of parliament in budget
    process, 14 n, 186, 223; and Treaty of
    Maastricht, 9, 136, 192–93

Japan, 44, 117
Jelved, Marianne, 178
Jospin, Lionel, 107
Juppe, Alain, 107–9
Justice Party (Denmark), 168

Kekkonen, Urho, 138
Kissinger, Henry, 69
Klima, Victor, 216
Kohl, Helmut, 25, 88–90, 92, 94–96, 99,
    102
Kok, Wim, 125
kronor (Denmark), 175, 177
kronor (Sweden), 151, 157, 160
Kullberg, Rolf, 145

La Malfa, Ugo, 187
Labour Party (Ireland), 198, 201–3
Labour Party (United Kingdom), 79, 84,
    213
Lacina, Ferdinand, 215
Lafontaine, Oskar, 96, 99, 101
Lahnstein, Manfred, 94
Lambsdorff, Otto, 94
Lamont, Norman, 76–78
Lancaster, Thomas D., 25
Latin America, 7, 11, 25 n
Laws, David, 84 n
Lawson, Nigel, 74–75
Left Party (Sweden), 36, 153–54, 162 n, 165,
    166
Liberal Party (Italy), 187–88
Liberal Party (Netherlands), 17
Liberal Party (Sweden), 153
Liberal Party (United Kingdom), 65, 70
Lib-Lab pact, 70–71
Liège, 131
lira (Italy), 6, 51, 182
Lower Saxony, 93
Lubbers, Ruud, 119, 123
Lufthansa, 96, 98
Luxembourg, 5, 38, 43, 51; and Council
    Meeting, 58
Lynch, Jack, 200

Maastricht, Treaty of, 1, 3, 16, 44, 49, 51, 53,
    107, 167, 182, 192; bailout clause, 50,
    52, 59, 131; effect of (see under individual
    country entries); fiscal definitions 16, 53,
    81, 98 n
MacSharry, Ray, 201–2, 204
Madelin, Alain, 107–9
Madrid European Council, 53
Major, John, 65–66, 76–78, 79 n, 81, 83
Making and Breaking Governments (Laver and
    Shepsle), 224
mark (Germany), 94; and Dutch shadowing
    of currency, 126
markka (Finland), 145
Martens, Wilfried, 130
Marx, Karl, 3
Mateus, Augusto, 209
Matthöfer, Hans, 93–94
McCreevy, Charlie, 61
Medium-term Financial Strategy, 73
Medium-term Planning Committee, 49
Mitterrand, François, 104–6
mixed form of fiscal governance: defined,
    14, 20
Molander, Per, 161
Möller, Alex, 90
Monarchic People's Party, 205
Monetary Committee, 45, 48–49, 51, 54,
    56–57
Moody's, 144
moral hazard problems, 48–49, 52, 54, 59
Movement of the Armed Forces, 204
Mundell-Fleming model, 5, 7

National Alliance (AN), 190
National Assembly (Belgium), 128, 135
National Assembly (France), 103, 105–8
National Coalition Party, 138
NATO (North Atlantic Treaty
    Organization), 169
neocorporatism, 3
Netherlands, 7, 139, and European
    Monetary System, 126–27; and fiscal
    actors, 119–21; and fiscal governance,
    16, 32, 37–38, 53, 82, 115–27, 142, 147,
    149, 150, 156, 219–21; and
    parliamentary committee chairs, 33; and
    party system, 13, 17, 40, 43, 103, 117–19,
    169 n, 222, 224; and Wassenaar
    Agreement, 124
New Control Total, 77–78
New Democracy (Greece), 64, 110, 112
New Democracy Party (Sweden), 161
Niinistö, Sauli, 141
Normandy, 103
North Atlantic Treaty Organization
    (NATO), 169

Northern Ireland, 65
Norway, 116, 146, 164

oil crisis, 16; and Belgium, 129–30, 149; and
    Germany, 91; and Ireland, 200; and
    Italy, 184, 187; and the Netherlands,
    115, 121–22, 149; and Portugal, 207;
    and Sweden, 155; and the United
    Kingdom, 68, 75, 83
Olive Tree Coalition, 190–91, 194
Olympics, Barcelona, 213
Organization for Economic Cooperation
    and Development (OECD), 143
overhanging seat, 86 n

Palme, Olof, 156
panel-corrected standard errors, 41
Papandreou, Andreas, 64, 110–11
Papantoniou, Yannos, 111, 113
parliamentary commission to study
    constitutional reform, 146, 160–61
partisanship thesis, 5–6, 41–42
party competition, 15, 19, 40, 222
party discipline, 14, 25 n, 27 n, 223
Party of Democratic Socialism, 86–87
Party of the Democratic Social Center, 205
PASOK, 64, 109–12
pentapartito, 28, 184
People's Party (ÖVP), 61, 214–16
Performance Management Unit, 161
performance-based management, 80
Perho, Maija, 141
Persson, Göran, 163–64
peseta, 6, 51
Philips, 117
Pim Fortyn List, 118
Pina Moura, Joaquim, 210
Plaid Cymru, 65
Planning Committee (Denmark), 172–73,
    177
Plaza-Louvre, 44
Plowden Report, 73
Pohl, Karl Otto, 94
poll tax, 76
Popular Party, 210, 212–14
Portugal, 4; censure motion, 208; and fiscal
    actors, 217–19; and fiscal governance,
    18, 38, 40, 51, 207–11, 217; and party
    system, 18, 39, 43, 196, 204–5, 220; and
    president, 138; and Treaty of Maastricht,
    8, 54, 197, 211, 221; and veto players, 41
Portuguese Communist Party, 205
pound, 6, 51, 69, 77
Pre-Accession Programs, 225
principal-agent problem, 31, 224
Prodi, Romano, 48, 191
program managers, 200, 203

Progress Party, 169, 172, 174–75, 177, 179
Progressive Democratic Party, 198, 202–3
proportional representation. *See under*
    electoral systems
Provence, 103
Public Expenditure Survey, 67
public sector borrowing requirement
    (PSBR), 68, 73, 84
Public Services and Public Expenditure
    Committee (PSX), 79, 81–82
Pujol, Jordi, 212–14
Pym, Francis, 73

Radical Liberal Party, 168–70, 175, 177
Radicals (Netherlands), 117 n
Rally for the Republic (RPR), 13, 32, 103,
    107, 189
Rato Figaredo, Rodrigo, 213
Rawlinson, Sir Anthony, 71 n
Rees, Peter, 74
Refounded Communist Party, 191
Reynolds, Albert, 202
Rifkind, Malcolm, 78
Riksdag, 155, 157, 159–62, 165–68
Rocard, Michel, 104, 106–7
Roman Empire, 127
Rome, Treaty of, 48
Rotterdam, 117, 124
Royal Dutch Shell, 117
Ruding, H. Onno, 123, 125
Rural Party, 138, 142

Saarland, 50, 93
Scharpf, Fritz W., 3
Scharping, Rudolf, 89
Schiller, Karl, 90
Schleswig-Holstein, 95
Schlüter, Poul, 174–75, 179–80
Schmidt, Helmut, 24, 64, 87, 91–95, 102
Schröder, Gerhard, 89–91, 99, 102
Scottish National Party, 65
Senate (Belgium), 128
Senate (France), 116
Senate (Italy), 189, 191
Seville, and World Expo, 213
Short-term Economic Committee, 49, 57
Siimes, Suvi-Anne, 141
Simitis, Kostas, 111
Simon, William, 69
single transferable vote electoral system, 10,
    98
Skilling, David, 39 n
Skopbank, 146
Social Democratic Party (Austria) (SPÖ),
    214–15
Social Democratic Party (Denmark), 151,
    168, 174

Social Democratic Party (Finland), 138
Social Democratic Party (Portugal), 205
Social Democratic Party (Sweden), 151, 153–54, 158
Social Democratic Party of Germany, 32, 87
Social Liberals (Denmark), 175, 178
Socialist Party (France), 13, 25, 103, 107, 205
Socialist Party (Portugal), 210
Socialist Unification Party of Germany, 87
Solbes, Pedro, 213
Sorsa, Kalevi, 142
South Africa, 96
Soviet Union, 138–39, 143, 152
Spain, 5; and fiscal actors, 212–13; and fiscal governance, 38, 197, 212–17; and party system, 18, 39–40, 43; and regions, 212; and Treaty of Maastricht, 213–14
Stability and Growth Pact, 4, 15, 43, 47, 53–62, 85, 193 n, 197, 221; punishment mechanism of, 45, 50, 54, 59, 62
stagflation, 69
Star-chamber committee, 74–78, 81–82
Stich, Otto, 29
Stoltenberg, Gerhard, 90, 95–96, 100
Strang, Gunnar, 155
Strauss, Franz-Josef, 90
"strong party," 33–34, 183
Study Group on the Budget Margin (Studiegroep Begrotingsruimte), 120–21, 124–25, 150; in comparison with High Council of Finance, 128
Sustainable Investment Rule, 80–81
Sweden, 4 n, 5; and banking crisis, 146; and EU membership referendum, 116; and fiscal actors, 155–56; and fiscal governance, 16–18, 21, 36, 38, 71, 105, 151–53, 155–67, 217, 219; and party system, 37, 40, 43, 153–55, 180–81, 224; and trade with Finland, 143; and Treaty of Maastricht, 52 n, 58, 148 n, 167; and welfare state, 137
Swedish People's Party, 40, 138, 141

Tallaght Strategy, 201

Thatcher, Margaret, 67, 70–77, 83
Tietmeyer, Hans, 98
Tindemans, Leo, 130
top-down budgeting, 77, 82, 166
Treasury and Civil Service Committee, 83
Treasury and Whitehall (Thain and White), 82
Tremonti, Giulio, 195
Treuhandanstalt, 97, 101

Ulster Unionist, 65
Union for French Democracy (UDF), 13, 32, 103, 107, 189
United Kingdom 1, 4 n, 102; and Black Wednesday, 77; and European Monetary System, 6, 77, 145; and fiscal actors, 65–67; and fiscal governance, 30, 32, 38, 63, 65–85, 100, 113, 119, 123, 157 n, 224; and Germany, 86, 89; and IMF, 69–70, 187; and party system, 13, 17, 40, 43, 64–65, 103, 209; and trade with Finland, 143; and Treaty of Maastricht, 52 n, 53, 58, 84–85
United States, 22, 39 n, 93, 223

Van Agt, Andreas, 122
van der Stee, Fons, 122
veto players, 9, 39, 222; and forms of fiscal governance, 9–10, 40–42; and Italy, 187
von Hagen, Jürgen, 161
Voss, Friedrich, 90
Vranitzky, Franz, 215

Waigel, Theo, 53–54, 96–98, 100–102, 109, 133
Wallonia, 17, 127, 130–34
Werner Report, 46, 48
Whitelaw, Lord William, 74
Wigforss, Ernst, 155
Willett, Thomas D., 47, 52, 59
Wilson, Harold, 68–69, 71
World Expo, 213

Younger, George, 74

Zalm, Gerrit, 125